THEO KNELL

A Hell for Heroes

CORONET

First published in Great Britain in 2012 by Coronet
An imprint of Hodder & Stoughton
An Hachette UK company

First published in paperback in 2013

1

ISBN 978 1 444 75500 8

Printed and bound by Clays Ltd, St Ives plc

Hodder & Stoughton policy is to use papers that are natural,
renewable and recyclable products and made from wood grown
in sustainable forests. The logging and manufacturing processes
are expected to conform to the environmental regulations
of the country of origin.

Hodder & Stoughton Ltd
338 Euston Road
London NW1 3BH

www.hodder.co.uk

Dedicated to my wife, whose unconditional love carried a bright light through some of the darkest days of my life.

'True merriment comes from those who have looked into their own open graves and walked away'

– from a poem by Chas Lotter, formerly of the Rhodesian Army Medical Corps

Contents

Part IV: Joining the Brotherhood

Part V: New Challenges

Part VI: At the Pointy End of the Spear

Part VII: Contact

Part VIII: Dark Times

Part IX: Life After Death

PART I:
THE WHY AND WHERE FROM?

Introduction

My name is Theodore (Theo) Knell, and among many other things I am a writer and poet and this is my story. However, before we start I would like to make a few things clear. First, I will not be mentioning anyone in this book by their real name, although the physical descriptions I give will be those of real people – people who have either enriched or coloured my life – but I genuinely believe that it's each man's God-given right to tell his own story. Secondly, and more importantly, this book is in no way an invitation to a 'pity party'. I have never considered myself a victim. Nor do I blame anyone for the cards that life has dealt me, or for the life I've led.

This all started out as a totally selfish act. It was suggested by my wife that I might benefit from writing about my experiences and feelings as a way of clearing my head, a sort of banishing my demons thing. If only it was that easy.

However, once I started writing I did find it easier to be honest with myself about my experiences. How I had dealt with them at the time and the inevitable aftermath over the following years. The result of this exercise was a book entitled *From the Corners of a Wounded Mind*.

Corners concentrated on the effects that combat had on the mind of a soldier. How we deal with it at the time and the inevitable aftermath over the subsequent years, in some cases many years after the events themselves. It was a small book, only some 18,000 words, and a mere pamphlet compared to the massive volumes normally produced by academics when dealing with the subject of PTSD (post-traumatic stress disorder).

However, it was written in plain English and came straight from the heart, and the darkest corners of my mind. It was eventually picked up by a small independent publisher who agreed that it was something which needed to be published, and even though the subject material was way outside of what they normally published, they decided to put it out anyway, and I owe them huge thanks for giving me a chance.

That said, the book was very well received, and had some wonderful reviews. It was also very well accepted by the families of soldiers past and present, who believed it answered so many of the questions they had about the changes they'd seen in their loved ones on their return from combat. More surprisingly, it was also very well regarded by those professionals who were currently treating soldiers, police and firemen suffering from PTSD, and especially so in the USA.

The book eventually found its way into the hands of John Jeffcock, a former captain in the Coldstream Guards, who was compiling a new book of war poetry entitled *Heroes: 100 Poems from the New Generation of War Poets*. As a result I had nine of my poems published in this very powerful book. At this point, and as a direct consequence of *Corners* and a meeting with John Jeffcock, I was introduced to Roger Field, a literary agent and another ex-soldier. He loved *Corners* and took it to Mark Booth at Coronet, who fully agreed, although he wanted to see much more, and this book is the end result.

Written as a collection of short stories, in a combination of prose and verse, it covers the period from my early childhood, through my twenty-two years in the British Army, most of it spent with Special Forces, and my return to a sometimes traumatic civilian life.

Although it portrays the people and events that shaped and changed my life, I hope that any soldier who reads it will find some sort of connection with their own. For their loved ones and those of you who have not been so blessed to serve – or cursed, depending on your perspective – I hope it will provide a brief insight into the life and mind of a professional soldier. What makes us the way we are, what drives us on when lesser men would fold, what binds us together like no other brotherhood on earth, what makes us laugh and what scares us shitless.

Although I could fill half a dozen books with events from just my military career, I thought it important to include parts of my childhood, as this is where the seeds of what we are, and what we will become, are sown.

Why include poetry? I see your point; it's a strange medium for someone who has spent most of his life living in a hard, sometimes violent world. For most of us the word 'poet' conjures up images of a flamboyant, somewhat flowery individual, not a battle-hardened soldier. Yet it's often said that poetry is the natural voice of both the warrior and the oppressed. So, after reading the book, I hope you'll agree that I have it covered on both counts.

Poetry also allows me to tell a story quickly and accurately. To set the scene and describe the actual event without subjecting you, the reader, to pages of irrelevant drivel. Poems also have fewer words to carry their power, and their impact strikes more deeply, allowing the reader to experience both the power and the pain. That may also make them harder to read.

I make no apologies for my work. Love it or loath it, I feel that story-telling, especially when in the form of poetry, is not about adhering to the accepted formats of childish rhyming or winning literary prizes. It's all about the content and delivering the underlying message.

Throughout the book I have tried to share my experiences honestly, and in this spirit all of the incidents portrayed within it are true. Some were so dark and painful that I often questioned whether I wanted to remain part of this thing we call the human race. Yes, in the really dark times I even considered that.

The Why and Where From?

My Italian Grandfather and Prussian Grandmother.

I was born on a cold and foggy March morning in 1952 at the London Hospital, Whitechapel, in the heart of the East End. At the time life in the East End of London was hard. Most of the area still lay in ruins after the Blitz. Rationing was in operation, and work was hard to find even for those with a skill.

My mother was what they referred to in those days as 'mixed race'. She was the daughter of an Italian father. A talented stonemason who was a short, powerfully built, but gentle man, he would wander around the house on a Sunday morning singing opera while cooking family lunch. My mother's mother was of Prussian descent. A stern and upright woman, she ran a neat house, and was one of those people who had to have everything just right. Amazingly, neither of them was interned during the Second World War.

My father and his parents before him were, like me, all born within the sound of Bow Bells, making us genuine cockneys. My Italian–Prussian–cockney heritage is something I have always been very proud of (even a mongrel has its pride) and that mix of an explosive Latin temperament, Prussian attention to detail and cockney generosity has stood me in good stead throughout my life.

My childhood was short and extremely brutal. My dad left us when I was just five years old. I learned how to fight and could hold my own on the streets long before I started school, and it seems like I've been fighting ever since. I was abandoned to a mental institution at the tender age of six, where I stayed for the next four years. I was then sent to a state-run boarding school, where I remained until I was sixteen.

By the time I left secondary school I had developed into a strong, independent, single-minded and very angry loner. On reflection it was probably the perfect combination for a life in the military and ultimately the Special Forces.

During my time I have served with and met people from all walks of life. Everybody from world leaders to subsistence farmers. Some you wouldn't follow into a bus queue or leave in charge of an empty pram. But there were others I would have willingly died for, and nearly did on more than one occasion.

After facing down death a number of times and winning through, the one thing that life has taught me is that every new day is an adventure. A gift to be enjoyed and cherished and, no matter how bad it gets, it's always worth living and there is an upside to everything.

The Great Escape

Warm but alone in the darkness of my cell
I hear muffled voices through these thick but cushioned
walls.
I've never met a soul,
smelt a smell,
or seen my own face.
My body's supported by a liquid ensuring I'll never fall.

It's like I've been here for ever and wonder will I ever leave?
There's a bright light ahead surrounded by an icy chill.
My body's being crushed
like it's in a vice
and I'm finding it hard to breathe.

A sharp pain from behind forces me to take a breath.
My first sound is a cry and I spread my fingertips.
Tightly bound,
tired and hungry, I need to sleep
as something soft and moist is forced between my lips.

The noises are much louder now,
they start to hurt my ears.
This brave new world brings freedom
but with it many fears,
and as I drift into sleep
I hear a voice, so much softer now,

whisper

'You have a healthy son.'

Harsh Beginnings

My father left us – that's me, my mum, a little sister and my baby brother – back in 1957; I was just five years old. After he went we moved across the Thames into a three-bedroom flat on the second floor of Gower House, a red-brick tenement block in Walworth, south-east London.

There were three such blocks, one on each side of a large, flat tarmacked area. Between two of them, Grays House and Paxton House, there was a large air-raid shelter, a remnant of the Second World War. On the fourth side there was an old abandoned church. Although the church had been left virtually unscathed by the bombing, its Victorian graveyard had suffered badly at the hands of the Luftwaffe during the Blitz. As a result it now looked like it had received a number of visits from Burke and Hare – the infamous Irish grave robbers of the eighteenth century – as it was strewn with smashed headstones and Victorian tombs with their tops missing. It was a great game hiding in the tombs, then jumping out and frightening the shit out of the other kids as they walked past. Or searching for skeletons and headless bodies, but of course we never found any.

The churchyard was flanked by two bomb sites that had also been left over from the Blitz. This was what we kids called 'the square', and during those early years it was our only playground. Health & Safety and Social Services would have had a fit.

From the minute my dad left us we were up against it. Most days would start with the whole family hiding from, or lying to, the rent man or some other debt collector. The hiding was a game, the whole family crouched down behind the settee (sofa for you people who have a lounge instead of a front room), not making a sound until whoever it was had gone. Even my little brother, who was still a babe in arms, seemed to know what was required of him. The lying wasn't so much fun, though. In fact I hated it. Not because it was a bad thing to do, but because I was absolutely crap at it. I could never keep a straight face.

Life on the whole was pretty grim. We all wore secondhand clothes, even my mum. If we wore any shoes at all they would only ever be plimsolls, and there was never enough food to eat. In fact if it hadn't been for Messrs Sunblest and Heinz we would have starved on most days.

That first Christmas in Walworth was a trial. Mum did the best she could but money was always in short supply. As a result I woke up on Christmas morning to a collection of secondhand and broken toys that had been retrieved from boxes near 'the chute'. This was a wide brick chimney which ran the full height of the building. On each of the four floors, opposite the central staircase, there was a large, pull-down hatch giving access to the chute, and this is where the occupants of the flats would put their daily rubbish. The rubbish would then slide down into a big metal bin that was housed in a brick shed at the bottom, ready for collection.

Mum had retrieved most of our Christmas presents from boxes that were too big to put down the chute, and had been left at the side for the bin men. I received a big plastic truck which had a searchlight on the back, but I couldn't understand why it was missing one of its back wheels. Well, that was until the next morning, Boxing Day, when I took it down into the square to play with it. It was then that the kid who lived upstairs informed me that it used to be his.

As you can imagine, he started the name calling, and I

replied the only way I knew how: with my fists. It was as I was repeatedly banging his head against the bumper of an abandoned Austin A40 that the 'good will to all men' thing went right out of the window. I spent the rest of that day nursing a sore backside courtesy of my mum.

In an effort to escape the daily grind I would leave the house early in the morning and spend most of the day playing on my own (the loner gene was already beginning to emerge) on top of the air-raid shelters, rooting around the bomb sites and graveyard, or listening to the stories of 'Dan Dan the Tattoo Man' in East Street Market, which we called East Lane. I would then come home late in the evening just in time for my beans on toast or sugar sandwich (don't ask).

Dan Dan the Tattoo Man

His old brown overcoat,
threadbare
darned and stained,
hangs loosely over a shabby suit and a pair of battered
    brogues.
Sweat-stained collar
and cuffs that were made for links of gold
tell the same sad story.
Like the man

they've all seen better days.

A painted skin and wicked smile hide a furrowed brow,
the tell-tale signs of worried days and many sleepless nights.
Tired legs and blistered feet that have walked a thousand
    miles,
flat knuckles and a twisted nose

show this man has had to fight.

But for all his ugliness,
the dirt and bruises,
we are not afraid
as we sit quietly and listen to his stories
of seamanship,
bootlegging,
gangsters and their molls,

we bring him food stolen from the market as a way of
    being paid.

Every morning it's a new story
and as we listen,
for that short while our misery is gone.
As he talks we search his skin for pictures;
a dragon,
a heart with a name,
the naked lady that makes us laugh,

we find them all, one by one.

Like God's blotting pad,
he's covered in ink with no room for a face.
Years later
I read about the life of an old man
covered in tattoos
who had died alone
poor
without a friend

in a slum of a place.

It's then that I remembered Dan Dan the Tattoo Man
whose stories brought laughter and happiness to our
   wretched lives
and I smile
when I realise that all the stories he told,
sitting on that cold and wet market wall,

That every single word was true.

Always an Upside

My eventual appearance at the front door was normally enough to push my mum over the edge. It nearly always resulted in me getting a bloody good hiding. The beatings weren't that bad and of course, like any other five-year-old boy, no matter how much it hurt, you would never cry in front of your mum. I was also becoming even more of a loner, which would not be a bad thing in later life. It was a quality my military masters and those from other agencies (which will remain nameless) immediately recognised and then exploited for their own ends. The fact that I could function perfectly well in a hostile environment with little external support was seen as a bit of an asset.

I was going to get lots of practice as I grew up. As I became more independent I spent even less time at home and naturally the hidings got a lot more frequent. After a while my mum became lonely. This was understandable: she was only twenty-seven when my dad left us.

This was also when my life turned for the worse. The hidings I got from mum I could handle. But it was about this time that her boyfriends decided they needed to get more involved. The flat of my mum's open hand on my backside, or around the ear, soon became a clenched fist in the stomach, and eventually the face, from her boyfriends, which left me with numerous black eyes, busted lips, and in the end much, much worse.

I remember coming home late one evening and answering Mum back. Her fella at the time was a tall, thick-set white South African with a square jaw. He had long fair hair, which he wore combed back off his forehead. I suppose he thought it was time he demonstrated to my mum just how much he loved her. Following my outburst he didn't say a word. He just quietly made his way into the bathroom, where he took a soaking wet bath towel and twisted it tightly, until it resembled a girl's plaited hair.

He then trapped me in the narrow hallway between my sister's and my mum's bedrooms, and beat me so severely that I peed blood and couldn't stand up straight, or lie down, for three days. However, it did get me off school for a week. So, as I said earlier, there's always an upside to everything.

Sight of Pain

Sitting alone on a chair
bent double in pain
like a half shut knife,
half naked and unwashed,
shivering with the cold,
nobody's even bothered to comb his dirty matted hair.

He wants to move
maybe even run
but he just sits there,
his pain worsening with every move he makes.
Anyway where would he go?

The doors are all locked
and there's no sign of his mum.

Head bowed,
staring vacantly at the lino-covered floor,
his eyes begin to wander up and down his bruised and
    battered legs
and he wonders just what it was that he did wrong.

He pauses momentarily
gazing at his blood and urine stained underwear,
the sight of which brings back the pain,

so he turns away,

he can look no more.

PART II: CARING INSTITUTIONS

Holiday Camp

Bethlem Mental Hospital, part of the Maudsley.

A few days after my sixth birthday my mum told me I was going on holiday. I was over the moon. I'd never been on holiday before.

'What about my little sister?'

'No. It's just you on your own.'

That was a plus, I thought, because although she was younger than me she could be a real pain sometimes. The next day the two of us, me and my mum, caught a number fifteen bus from the end of East Lane and headed for Denmark Hill, Camberwell.

Although I didn't realise it at the time that short bus ride would be the start of a ten-year nightmare. Mum had reached the end of the road with three kids and very little money to support them, and Social Services had now decided to step in. Yes, they were at it, even way back then.

It had become very clear to the social workers that my mum

was already struggling with three of us to look after, and now there was another one on the way: a parting gift from her thug of a South African boyfriend. Even though I was still only six I had basically gone native, left the reservation and become a real handful. As a result I was about to become the family's sacrificial lamb.

Social Services had branded me as 'out of control' and I was to be abandoned to a psychiatric facility: the Maudsley Hospital at Denmark Hill.

I remember it as if it was yesterday. I was so excited to be going on holiday.

We arrived at the front door of a very large red and white brick building. Once we were inside we were shown into a smart room with polished floors, big brown leather settees and pictures on the wall.

There I sat in my ill-fitting jumper and shorts, quietly swinging my legs as I watched my mum fidget in silence. It seemed like we'd been there for ages – well, five or ten minutes is a lifetime to a six-year-old – especially one who was waiting to start his first holiday.

The large door at one end of the room opened and a tall man in a white coat entered. He had light brown skin and large, dark rings around both his eyes. He walked over to my mum, stretched out his hand and said, 'My name is Dr D*****.'

Yes. I still remember his name. I also still remember those dark-ringed eyes, and, even now, I can't see an Indian without being reminded of that day.

'I will be supervising your son's stay with us,' he said.

Bending over he picked up the brown paper carrier bag at my mum's feet.

'Are these his things?'

Alarm bells had already started to ring. This didn't sound much like a holiday camp to me – not that I knew what a holiday camp should sound like.

The man then turned to me and put out his hand in an effort to take mine, but they were gone, wrapped behind me, trapped between my back and the settee. He reached behind me, grabbed one, then started to drag me across the floor and towards the large door.

I dug my heels in and looked back at my mum, who just sat there staring at the floor. I remember asking her not to leave me there. I even promised to be good, but there was nothing, not even a glance: she just sat there in silence, staring at the floor.

Before the door slammed shut behind me I strained against the man's grip one last time and begged her to wait for me. But that was the last time I would see her, or any other member of my family, for over five years.

After what seemed like an endless journey, through a maze of long corridors with highly polished floors and through an enormous number of locked doors, we eventually stopped outside a room which was again locked. Even though we had only spent a few minutes together I think the doctor had already realised that I was a young opportunist, one who was just looking for a chance to make a run for it. At that time, though, I hadn't actually worked out how I was going to get back through all those locked doors without the keys. As a result of my continuous wriggling he now had me pinned against the wall with his knee while he tried to remove a large bunch of keys from the pocket of his white coat and unlock the door.

As the door swung open I couldn't believe my eyes. The room was a total mess, much worse than my bedroom had ever been. I remember thinking, someone's going to be in deep shit – I had learned the word from the bigger kids in the square – for this and, if the past was anything to go on, it was probably going to be me.

I was now totally confused and rooted to the spot with fear. That was until the doctor pushed me roughly into the room and sent me sprawling across the floor. As I lay there looking around me, I noticed the other kids in the room, most of them a lot bigger than me. Some of them were even grown-ups. Well, that's what a fifteen-year-old is when you're only six.

But the most frightening thing was that some of the kids had large, strange-looking heads. I know now that they were suffering from Down Syndrome. Kids nobody would listen to. Kids who desperately needed love and a cuddle, but would only ever receive isolation and punishment. To a frightened six-year-old this was the stuff of nightmares.

As I lay there on the floor I spotted an empty corner. So, without getting up, I quickly crawled into it on my hands and knees. I sat in that corner on my own for the rest of that first afternoon.

That evening, as soon as tea (dinner) was over, I was put into a bath with three other kids and told to stand still while a large lady in a blue rubber apron scrubbed us clean. After being dressed in a pair of rough pyjamas I was put to bed on a ward with twenty others. Ten minutes later the lights were turned off and the doors were locked.

I spent that first night, and many subsequent nights, wide awake. I would sit upright in bed with my knees and blankets pulled up to my chest as plastic cups of water and even metal chamber pots – some of them full – were bounced off the walls. Each and every night the darkness would be filled with the sound of scared and confused children either screaming with frustration or crying out for their mums.

However, the really frightening thing was that nobody ever came to see what was going on. Some of the kids would have fits, their bodies shaking uncontrollably as they lay in their beds or on the hard polished floor, knocking their heads against the wall or the metal bed legs, but still nobody ever came to help them.

The next morning, when the doors were unlocked, we were dressed and then herded like sheep into a large room containing tables and chairs. Here we were given breakfast and then left to our own devices until dinner (lunch) time. That very first morning, when nobody was looking, I found an empty cupboard at the far end of the room and crawled inside. I then quietly pulled the door closed and eventually cried myself to sleep. I would have done anything for a cuddle from my mum, but I honestly think the next cuddle I received was some ten years later, when I started taking an interest in girls. But, of course, by that time a cuddle meant something completely different.

This was to be my daily routine for the next six months. Awake all night and then hide in my cupboard and cry myself to sleep during the day. That was until the day I finally realised that I was totally alone and that nobody was going to come for me. It was then that I decided that enough was enough and I promised myself I would never, ever cry again. The worm was turning. I was now six and a half years old – watch out, world.

I spent the next four years at that so-called hospital. During this time I was treated like an animal. Don't get me wrong. I didn't get it harder than any other kid who was there: we were all treated the same. We were regularly fed a cocktail of experimental drugs and subjected to ECT (electro-convulsive therapy). This 'treatment' did exactly what it said on the tin. You would be strapped down to a bed, wires would then be attached to your head, and you would receive a series of powerful electric shocks which would make your body convulse violently. My only sin, for which I was now about to be severely punished – I was unruly. These days the authorities would have bought me an iPod and a brand-new pair of designer trainers and really sent me on holiday.

Most of the kids on the unit were a lot bigger than me. Some were fifteen or sixteen and most could become extremely violent if they didn't get their own way. Initially I just gave in and let them have what they wanted. Then I learned how to dodge the fists and missiles. Eventually, as I got bigger – well, I was nearly seven – I learned how to fight for what was mine. First, I learned that there was no point in arguing with some people. If it had reached the shouting and screaming stage, it would normally progress to violence in the end. So why waste time arguing? Why not just go straight to violence?

Secondly, I learned that when it came to size a chair was a great leveller. Hit a bigger kid hard across the hips or knees with a metal chair and it would take him a while to get back up. I also learned that if it looked like it was going to kick off I had to be the first to attack and that that attack had to be completely devastating. Because, if they got up, I was going to be in big trouble. Whether it was a precious book or my breakfast, if you wanted what was mine you were going to have to take it from me, and it wasn't going to be easy. Life hasn't changed much over the years.

During my time at the Maudsley I received no formal schooling. So I honed my basic reading and counting skills, those I had learned during my first year at my primary school in Walworth, using everyday events and objects. I used to spend hours on my own staring out of the windows as I watched the so-called doctors and nurses walk around the grounds. And, while I was sitting there, I would amuse myself by counting the birds and flowers.

With the help of some of the more sympathetic staff I also improved my reading using the comic books and magazines which had been discarded by staff and visitors.

I left the Maudsley Hospital at ten and a half years old and was sent to a state-run boarding school for troublesome boys. The official council description was 'a school for maladjusted children, providing care for delinquents'. The school was in Peckham, south-east London, and, like the Maudsley, it's still there, although these days it probably functions under a completely different set of rules.

Here the abuse continued, but in a slightly different form. You still had the bullies to deal with, but now it wasn't just the bigger kids you had to avoid: some of the staff would join in as well. Physical and sexual abuse of boys by staff members of both sexes was commonplace. Even in those days it was drummed into youngsters: 'You mustn't talk to strangers. If you feel you're in danger, go and find a woman.' As a result, most children saw women as some sort of safe haven, someone you could run to when you were scared or in trouble. In the majority of cases this was true, but there were some women at the school who were nothing more than vicious sexual predators.

Luckily I never joined this sad band of brothers. The closest I came was one night in an upstairs corridor when I was pinned to the wall by the housemaster. As his hands roamed all over my body, pulling at my shirt and trousers, I tried to push him off but it was useless as I was only ten and he was a grown man, just too big and strong. Finally he let go of me when I bit into his chest so hard that I drew blood. I was never bothered again, but I did miss classes for the next two weeks while my balls returned to their normal size and the black eyes and cracked ribs healed.

The Loner

After less than a year of regular classes at boarding school somebody noticed that I was brighter than most of the other kids. As a result I was offered a place at an outside day school, an all-boy comprehensive school in East Dulwich. This was an opportunity I was deeply grateful for because, as well as stimulating my mind, it also provided me with a real escape. It meant that I left boarding school just after breakfast and was alone in the outside world until I returned just before the evening meal.

But I was still a loner. I don't think I had one real friend in the five years I attended the school. I also can't remember ever owning a toy or playing the normal games kids play after I left home aged six, although I must have done so at some stage. I spent lots of time on my own. But I also improved my fighting skills through constant daily conflict with the playground bullies and I learned how to manipulate a situation in order to remove a threat. For instance, playing two bullies off against each other, then standing back and watching them fight it out.

Learning how to manage a threat was a necessity if you were going to make it through the day in one piece. There were over 1500 boys at the school and it must be said that most were OK, willing to go about their daily business without bothering anyone else. But, as you can imagine, in a school with such a large population we had our fair share of bullies. One boy in particular – we'll call him 'IT' (those actually are his initials) – was a really nasty piece of work. I had managed to avoid him during my first year at the school. The first-years' playground was off limits to boys from the other years and, as he was a year above me, we never actually came into contact. But like every other kid in the school I knew all about him.

However, in our second year we shared a playground with the year above. That meant things were going to be different from now on. IT and his cronies would regularly cruise the playground like tiger sharks, targeting the weaker kids, demanding that they hand over their pocket money and lunch tickets. These were the coupons that we would exchange for our lunch each day in the school canteen. Once they had relieved these unfortunate souls of the lunch tickets, they would sell them on cheaply to other kids, whether they wanted them or not, so making a substantial profit.

Those kids who did decide to stand up to IT and his goons would normally end up getting a good hiding, either then and there in the playground or at the bus stop or train station after school.

I knew it was only a matter of time before they got around to me, and eventually that day came. However, giving into them and handing over what they wanted was never really an option for me. I'd already seen the knock-on effects of the submissive approach. Next it would be your bus or train pass, then all of your money. And it wouldn't stop there. They would just keep coming back, day after day, week after week, making your life hell.

One day they cornered me on the stairs of the main teaching block – the ones that led from our classrooms to the two-storey block housing the dining rooms – and demanded everything I had on me.

My answer was a very definite 'no'. This was followed by a swift head-butt to IT's face, which immediately broke his nose. As his hands came up and clutched his face, the blood started to ooze through his fingers.

I knew it wasn't enough, though. I lifted him over the heavy wooden stair rail and dropped him onto the concrete stairs some ten feet below. However, before he had even stopped falling, I was already on the move, pushing past his cronies and down the stairs after him. He was just beginning to get up as I reached him but, with neither hesitation nor remorse, I immediately laid into him with both my hands and feet.

He spent the following week in hospital.

I was only just turned twelve, but that day I came close to taking my first life.

In retrospect, I felt slightly ashamed of what I'd done, but not that guilty. I had not gone looking for trouble but, once it had found me, my aggressive response had had the desired effect and I was never bothered again.

Looking back, it seems strange that I never used this drive to take part in sport at school, especially since I later represented the army and my country at four different sports, boxed as a professional for three years, and managed a Winter Olympics team.

By the time I finished school I had become a total loner and a very angry young man. I remained that way for over twenty years. Even today I have very few real friends. My best friend is my wife and, although I know lots of people to say hello to and have a coffee with, I rarely trust anyone.

Music was, and still is, a large part of my life. Even now I can hear a piece of music and recall exactly where I was and what was happening at the time. A track like 'Telstar' by the Tornados will always bring back the nightmares of the Maudsley, as it was played continually. Billy Joel's 'Breaking Glass' will take me straight back to Rhodesia and all that went with it. When I was at school it was all Motown and blues. To the likes of Percy Sledge, Otis Redding, Joe Cocker and Marvin Gaye, I've now added Dire Straits, Sting, Seal and Anita Baker.

Although I left school with five good grades at GCE O Level, I found it hard to settle or hold down a job. The problem was that I never knew when to keep my mouth shut. Well, that, a rock-hard forehead and a very fast pair of hands which would automatically take over the minute I started to run out of words.

First Conflict

Pausing at the school gates
he's resigned to the day that lies before him,
another day of conflict,
keeping himself to himself,
playing and eating alone,
What price education for the loner?

Most in his position would simply bunk off,
skip classes,
spend their dinner money on drink and fags,
but he will stick it out,
spend his day avoiding the bullies.

Like a bad smell they are everywhere,
the toilets,
the playground,
even in the classroom.
They are even there after school
at the bus stop
and train station
where once again he will be pushed and shoved.

But the time has come to make a stand (the first of many).
It's time to cut one out,
like a cheetah selecting its prey from the herd.
But unlike the cheetah
my prey will not be the weakest

No, he must be the biggest,
the strongest,
the leader of the pack,
the one they all admire and look up to.
If I am to succeed it must be him
and he must suffer like he has never suffered before.

He approaches confidently,
maybe too confident,
our noses almost touching,
his spit splashing my face as he shouts his threats.
Being that close could be his big mistake.

A flick of the head,
a blur of fists and feet and he is down,
blood flowing freely from his nose and mouth

and as I deliver the *coup de grâce*

the look on his face is one of total shock.

As for his subordinates
there is nothing.
Not a single one moves forward to help him.
not a word of support is spoken for their downed leader,

cowards every one.

It's done now,
I'm free,
back in control

but I promise I will not become him.
I will not surround myself with jackals

to pray on the weak,
the vulnerable,
the unsure.

I promise that all my victims will be fit and strong,
well armed,
and at the very worst it will be one-on-one.

No one will ever call me bully.

Trapped in a Never-ending Circle

I left school as soon as I'd finished my last O Level exam. I didn't even wait for the end of the day: I just collected my things and walked straight to the bus stop. I had kept my part of the bargain. I'd worked hard and never missed a single day in over five years, but now I was done. It was June 1968 and I was sixteen. Time for me to leave boarding school and return home. Although I'd been allowed to go back for the odd weekend during the past year, I hadn't actually been home for any longer than that since before Easter.

I didn't really have a lot to show for nearly ten years away from home. In fact all my possessions fitted into a single blue duffle bag. Even though I hated, with a passion, boarding school and all it stood for, it was still the only home I had known for close on six years. I wouldn't miss the members of staff, and I knew I wouldn't really miss any of the boys either. As I walked to the bus stop, wearing the only clothes I owned, and with just enough money in my pocket for my fare back to Walworth, I felt totally alone.

When I stepped through those gates that afternoon it was the first time that nobody had told me what time I had to be back in that night. Now I was free to do exactly what I wanted. On the downside, though, it was as though nobody cared any more. I also no longer had a bed to go back to, or any way to get my three square meals a day.

The other thing was I no longer had an imposed structure to build my daily life around and so whatever happened to me from now on was totally down to me. Although I wasn't sorry to see the back of the school, for the first time in years I was totally unsure of what lay ahead of me.

At the end of the road I caught the first of two buses that night. The first took me to the King's Arms pub, which stood on the corner of Peckham Rye Park opposite the Lido, a large open-air swimming pool. I had been changing buses here twice a day for the past five years on my way to and from school, but tonight I was going to catch one that would take me back to the Elephant and Castle. As I sat there on the top deck looking out of the window, watching people scurry around like ants below me, I had no idea what type of reception awaited me. I had no idea how I would handle it if it turned into 'a long-lost child' type of welcome. In fact the very thought of such hypocrisy just made me angry, so I thought about something else. I got off the bus at the top of East Lane just after five o'clock that evening, and then made my way through the maze of market stalls and traders who by now were clearing up. Halfway down East Lane Market I turned into King and Queen Street and then on towards 'the square'.

I had only been back there a few times during my ten years away, but walking through the square now, it seemed a lot smaller than I remembered it. As I climbed the central staircase towards the second-floor balcony of Gower House I met the half-caste kid that lived below us. His mum was white and his dad was black, a West Indian. They were really good people. They always had a kind word and a smile, but their son was a total arsehole. When I lived there as a child he had always bullied the smaller kids, taking their toys and any sweets they had managed to get hold of. He was the first to speak, and he hadn't changed. 'What are you doing around here?'

'I've come to see my mum.'

'I think you're going to be disappointed.'

I just looked at him. I could still see the arrogance in his eyes, but I'd changed. The age gap between us was the same as it had been all those years before, but physically we were now on a more equal footing, and I smiled. 'I should give a fuck what you think.'

My answer was purposely hostile. It was meant to wind him up. Shit, I was already looking for trouble and I'd only been back five minutes. He was right, though. I was going to be disappointed. Instead of taking the bait and giving me what I really wanted, a scrap, he backed down and walked off down the stairs without saying another word.

I rounded the top of the stairs and walked along the narrow balcony. Our door was the first one along. I knocked the knocker and waited. I was just about to knock again when the door suddenly opened. An attractive young woman – I'd started to notice things like that now – stood in front of me. There was a young boy dressed in only a vest, and naked from the waist down, swinging on her skirt. Nothing ever changes, I thought to myself. The young woman spoke first. 'Can I help you?'

'Yeah, who are you, and is my mum in?'

'Not unless she's living here in secret. Are you sure you have the right flat? What's her name?'

'Knell, Mary Knell.'

'Oh, they don't live here any more. They moved out about three months ago.'

'Do you know where they live now?'

'No, I'm sorry, I don't. Are you a family friend, or relative?'

I half smiled at her, then said, 'I have no idea what I am any more.'

So this was how it was going to be. They'd moved house and not even bothered to tell me where they were going. Talk about feeling wanted. But what do I do now? I couldn't go back to boarding school: I'd burned my bridges when I'd left that afternoon. As I'd walked out of the front door I'd told the staff exactly what I thought of them and their precious school.

Even if I could go back I had no money for the bus, and although I'd done it before it was a bloody long walk back to the top of Peckham Rye. So I walked back down the stairs, and as I started to make my way back across the square a woman passed me carrying two shopping bags. 'Theo?'

I turned.

The woman had stopped and put down her bags. She was now peering at me with an enquiring look on her face.

'Yeah?' I said.

She smiled. 'Theo. It's me, Mollie from number fifteen. I haven't seen you for . . .' She hesitated, like she was trying to remember the last time she'd seen me.

I smiled sarcastically. 'Years?'

She smiled back at me, but I could see she wasn't comfortable. The last time I'd seen her she was a pretty young mum with a little boy and girl, but the years hadn't been kind to her. She now looked tired and washed out. 'Are you looking for your mum?'

'Yeah. She forgot to tell me they were moving. Do you know where they are?'

'I have the address in my flat. Come up and I'll get it for you.'

We went up to her flat on the third floor. She made me a cup of tea, and eventually found the address in a sideboard drawer. They had moved only about a mile away, just the other side of the Walworth Road, to a street behind the police station.

I thanked her for the tea, then walked back through the market and over to the address Mollie had given me. She had said it was a ground-floor flat. It looked to be a relatively modern block, and I knocked on the door. It was answered by my little brother. He was a handsome little lad of about ten. He was still a babe in arms when I had been put in the Maudsley, but he actually looked quite pleased to see me. It made me feel warm and I smiled before asking, 'Hello, mate. Is Mum in?'

He smiled back at me and then, without letting go of the door, he moved back against the wall, allowing me to come into the flat. I walked down the short corridor and into the front room. My mum and younger sister were watching telly. The look on my sister's face when she saw me would have turned milk. But this was no surprise, as we had never got on.

My mum just looked up and smiled. 'You found us, then?'

'Eventually. I bumped into Mollie at number fifteen. She told me where you lived.'

'Oh, OK. How long are you thinking of staying?'

I thought to myself, great response, Mum. Now I was really feeling the warmth. 'I've left school now.'

My sister didn't even take a breath. 'Well, you can't stay here, there's no room.'

My little brother, in an effort to defuse what was rapidly becoming a hostile atmosphere, offered to make me a cup of tea.

'Yeah. Let's go and make a brew, mate.'

I spent that weekend sleeping on the settee while living on tea and toast. On the Sunday night my sister informed me that if I wanted to stay I would have to find a job and pay for my keep. It appeared she was now running the house and my mum was just agreeing with everything she said.

So, on the Monday morning I was up and out of the house before anybody else was even awake. I spent the whole day trawling the local area trying to find a job. I would have done anything. That evening I made a few bob dragging away the four-wheeled barrows from the market once trading had finished. But it was on the Wednesday that I finally managed to secure a proper job as a freezer man for the Dewhurst butchery chain, working in one of the giant freezer rooms of their massive sausage factory on the corner of the Walworth Road.

The job involved dragging pallets containing large boxes of wholesale sausages from the production line into the freezers using a small, unmotorised forklift. I would then drag the frozen ones out of the freezer to the loading bay and load them onto trucks for distribution to Dewhurst stores around the country. It was hard physical work. You were only allowed to work in the actual freezer for a maximum of twenty minutes at a time – if you managed to last that long – as the temperature was a constant minus thirty. But as I worked on my own, kept my nose clean and nobody hassled me, I was a relatively happy bunny.

I started work at six o'clock each morning, so left the house at about five-thirty. I finished when the last lorry was loaded, normally around four in the afternoon. I also had to work my first week 'in hand', which meant I didn't get paid until the end of my second week. This caused even more friction at home as my sister was convinced I had been paid at the end of the first week and was now holding out on them.

On that second Friday morning the foreman came around with everybody's wages. Everybody was paid cash in those days, as very few people had bank accounts. I kept working but watched him closely as he walked around the factory until he eventually got to me. He handed me a small square buff envelope with my name on it. It contained my very first wage slip, and my very first week's pay. I was so chuffed I didn't open it straight away. Instead I waited until my lunch break, and with a cup of tea beside me I sat on top of some boxes in the freezer room and opened the envelope. It contained just over £13. Shit, I'd never had so much money before.

At the end of the day I got changed out of the heavy duffle coat and steel-capped boots that the company had supplied on my first day, hung them in my locker and left for home. As I walked past the old Manor Place Baths I was already working out how I was going to spend the small fortune I'd been presented with. I even thought I might spend some of my first pay packet on a new pair of trunks and go for a swim. I loved swimming but hadn't been for ages. But right now I just wanted to get home and share the joy.

I got to the flat just as my sister was returning from school. She was fourteen now and had turned into a right little madam. As we entered the front room together the first words out of her mouth were, 'How much did you get paid?'

'I don't see what it's got to do with you, but just over £13.'

'Well, me and mum have discussed it, and we think you should contribute at least £10 a week towards your keep.'

I looked at my mum for some sort of support, but, just like that day at the Maudsley, there was nothing. I just stood there and shook my head. 'I'm going to get a cup of tea. Anybody else want one?'

As I walked out to the kitchen I could hear my sister following me, like a Jack Russell snapping at my heels. The initial euphoria that had accompanied my first pay packet was rapidly disappearing. Without saying another word – in truth I couldn't get a word in – I made myself a brew and a slice of toast, and sat down at the kitchen table. I was totally knackered. That toast was the first piece of solid food that had passed my lips all day and I just wanted to enjoy it.

But she just wouldn't let it go. 'So where's the money? You can't live here for nothing. Leeching off us like a parasite.'

I had no problem paying my way, but it wasn't as though I was getting anything in the way of keep. After two weeks I was still sleeping on the settee and living on tea and toast. My sister sat and nagged at me the whole way through what was to be my only meal of the day. As I sat there spreading marge on my toast I could feel the rage building in me. I had never hit a girl or woman in my life and I wasn't about to start now. I had witnessed my dad slapping my mum around when I was five, just before he finally left us, and it wasn't a pretty sight.

However, she was now pushing me to my limits, and without raising my eyes from my mug of tea I said, 'One more word and it's all over.'

'*And?*'

'That'll do.'

My right hand shot out across the table and hit her left shoulder. But I still had the knife in my hand. It was so blunt you couldn't have cut butter, or marge, with it. It didn't break the skin, but it probably hurt. Yet to hear the fuss she was making you'd have thought I was Jack the Ripper.

That was all the excuse she needed, and she was straight into my mum, telling her I'd stabbed her. There was now no talking to my mum and she shouted, '*Get out!* And don't come back. And you can leave the money you owe us. You've lived here for two weeks for nothing.'

I threw £8 onto the kitchen table, grabbed my duffle bag and started to leave. As I reached the end of the hall I met my little brother coming in from school. I ruffled his hair. 'See you later, mate. You take care.'

I would spend that first night, and many more over the next six months, walking the streets of south-east London. As I left the flat it was just starting to rain, so I headed for the subway complex at the Elephant and Castle. If nothing else, I could get some shelter down there.

There had been a lot of new development around the Elephant and Castle in recent years. It's where five of south London's major thoroughfares come together, and as a result there were now thousands of yards of tunnels criss-crossing the whole area. This maze of subways allowed the pedestrians to move around in relative safety, by avoiding contact with the road traffic. However, after dark it was a totally different matter. Then the subways became the haunt of drunks, tramps and the homeless. It was of this very select group of individuals that I was now about to become a member.

If I wanted to keep my job at Dewhurst I had to stay close to the Elephant and Castle and the Old Kent Road. So I spent that first week living in the subways and on bomb sites. I managed to carry on working for another week or so, until it became obvious to the foreman that I was living rough. Then I was out on my ear.

The next few months I spent living on the streets. I ate food from the bins behind the numerous cafés in the area – it's amazing just how much good food is thrown away – and collecting the 'spoils', bruised fruit, from the ground around the stalls in East Lane.

Living on the streets then was much the same as it is today: extremely dangerous.

The Second World War had been over for more than twenty years, but a lot of those living on the capital's streets were its damaged leftovers. These were men who had volunteered to do their bit and had carried the hopes of our nation for six years. But once it was over and they had served their purpose they had just been discarded. After the war, once it was found they couldn't cope with peace, they had simply been abandoned; condemned to spend their days running from nightmares or searching for friends who would never be found.

I can see the same thing happening again in the very near future, as those who have served in the Balkans, Iraq, Afghanistan and Britain's other 'little' wars become the new generation of abandoned heroes. Their services no longer needed, they will be left to end their days living rough on the streets of our major cities.

Now I was living in an adult world, and even though I was little more than a child there was no quarter given. I spent the whole time living on my wits and would regularly have to use my fists in order to survive.

That Christmas saw me living under some blue plastic sheeting in the railway arches at the side of Waterloo Station.

I had just met a big Irishman called David. Thinking back now, he was probably in his late fifties, but he looked much older. He had told me one night that he'd been a merchant seaman. It was bitterly cold, and we sat on a bench on the station concourse sharing a cup of lukewarm tea. We talked about all the places I wanted to visit, those that were being shown on the information boards above us.

He told me how lucky I was, and about how cold it had been sailing between America and Russia on the Atlantic convoys during the Second World War. Like any young boy, I was fascinated by war, and I asked him if he'd ever been on a ship that had been sunk. He suddenly went very quiet and seemed to drift away for a minute or two. Then he said, 'Let's go and find somewhere to sleep.'

I never asked him again. Dave took me under his wing and taught me how to get through the long days and nights. He showed me where I could get a daily meal from the Salvation Army, and how to earn a little money doing odd jobs for the various businesses in the area. The only problem with Dave was that he could become a real handful if he got a drink in him, but he was always good to me. In return I would make sure he got back safely to the arches every night. Then, once he'd fallen asleep, I would check that he was covered up against the cold and rain.

Given my experiences over the previous ten years, I found him the only adult I'd ever met who didn't have some form of hidden agenda. He was happy to give or share whatever he had without wanting something in return. Although our relationship was a little rocky at times, especially on the nights when we would both end up in a fight because he'd upset some other drunk outside a local pub, on the whole we worked well together.

That was until one morning in early March, just a couple of days before my seventeenth birthday. It was still dark o'clock, but the commuters were already starting to appear on the pavements as they made their way into Waterloo Station. Every now and again, as always, some arse would give your legs a sly kick and mutter obscenities as they walked past you. I leant over and gave Dave a shake. 'Dave, time to get up, mate. The normal people are out.'

He didn't wake up, though this was nothing unusual as he'd had a skinful the previous night. So I rolled up my blue plastic sheeting and tied a piece of string around each end of it. I then tied another piece in the middle between the two ends, making a sling, easier to carry. I then gave Dave another shake, but he still didn't move.

I tried to wake him a couple more times, but still there was nothing. First I put my hand on his face and then down the front of his shirt. His skin was cold. I mean really cold, like ice; a type of cold I'd never felt before. I guessed then that he was dead, that he'd died in his sleep. I was only about four or five years old when my granddad, my mum's dad, had died. He had also died in his sleep, but I remembered the adults talking about how the heat of my nan's body had kept him warm until the next morning. But Dave had died alone, and as a result his body was now ice cold.

When Dave and I had first become friends he had told me, 'If anything ever happens to me, you go and find a copper and tell him that you can't wake me up. But don't tell him that you know me. That will stop them asking stupid questions and you getting into trouble.'

So that's what I did. I covered him up against the cold. Then went into the station, found a copper on the concourse and told him about Dave. I took him back to where Dave was lying, then sat on a wall across the street and watched while the ambulance arrived and took his body away. I'd done the best I could for my mate and there was nothing more I could do, but now I was on my own once again.

A week later I made my way over to Bethnal Green and trawled the pubs – in fact I got thrown out of most of them because of the filthy state I was in – until I managed to find my uncle, my dad's brother. He then took me to the Roman Road and bought me pie and mash. That was the first hot meal I'd had in over a week, well, since Dave had died. While I ate he called my nan and granddad, who then took me in.

I lived with them for just over a year and, although I was still sleeping in the sitting room, at least it was on a Z Bed, a foldaway single bed, and not the settee.

For the first time in seventeen years I was enjoying life. I had even made some mates at a local boxing club where I trained three evenings a week. However, it wasn't long after that my nan was told that my granddad was really ill. He had been a heavy smoker for most of his life and now he had lung cancer. Although I now had a job working shifts at the Thames Board Mills, near Purfleet in Essex, and I was helping out with the bills the best I could, my living there was just putting even more stress on these two wonderful people.

I wasn't earning enough to rent a place of my own and I couldn't face going back on the streets. So, in desperation, I took the only other option open to me. I joined the army.

PART III: AN ACT OF DESPERATION

A Strange Breed

After years of being pushed from pillar to post I just needed somewhere to belong.

My grandson once asked me, 'Granddad, where do soldiers come from?'

This is not an easy question to answer as we soldiers are a strange breed. You will hear the uninformed say, 'He's a born soldier,' but this has nothing to do with our genetic make-up. There isn't a special chromosome that we inherit. One that will identify us as an individual who will eventually prove himself a natural fighter, a hero or a leader on the field of battle. In fact what they should say is, 'He was born to be a soldier,' as it has more to do with our origins and where we come from.

It also has a lot to do with the environment we were born into and our place in the pecking order during childhood. Since the beginning of time, whether it was in the Roman legions, at the Battle of Waterloo, during the First and Second World Wars, or today in the Middle East, those of us who make up the rank and file, the non-commissioned soldiers, the fighters, have mostly come from the poorer, lower classes.

When I first joined the army most of my fellow recruits, like me, came from poor and underprivileged backgrounds. They had been brought up in the poverty and slums of postwar Britain. For most of us at the time the choice was simple: you could excel at sport, turn to crime, or join one of the three armed services and try to lead a worthwhile life.

However, there were also others, those who came from good homes and backgrounds. They were the results of expensive public school educations, some of them the sons of very successful and wealthy businessmen. But, regardless of where we came from, whether it was a Georgian townhouse in Kensington or a tenement block in the Gorbals of Glasgow, the one thing we all had in common was that we were unhappy with our current situation and wanted to change it. Mind you, I still find it difficult to get my head around why, with access to an unlimited stream of cash and cars, anyone would ever willingly want to join the army. Although, that said, just like soldiers, unhappiness comes in many different forms.

In the past, the commissioned ranks, the officers, or 'Ruperts' as the men call them, tended to come from the wealthier upper classes, and this is still very much the case in today's army, especially in the cavalry and guards units. When I was a young trooper in the cavalry, any young officer who did not have a private income just would not survive, as his monthly mess bill alone would normally exceed his wages.

But, just because you come from a privileged background, it doesn't give you the automatic right to lead men. Even in my day all three of the services were still very much class-driven. A perfect example of how flawed the system can be is the rules concerning newly commissioned 'late entry' officers.

The rules at the time said that if you held a late entry commission – meaning that you'd come up through the ranks – you were not allowed to lead men into battle. And this despite the fact that, as a senior rank, you will have probably spent your working days leading patrols and managing contacts – basically, overseeing the daily lives of all those under your command both on and off the battlefield, and all without the help of an officer. However, win the ultimate accolade of being commissioned and suddenly you are no longer deemed fit to lead men in action. Who worked that one out?

All the same, I have the greatest respect for most of the officers I have served with, and especially those during my later years: the Airborne Brigade and Special Forces officers. But in the early days of my career I wouldn't have followed most of my young officers into the NAAFI (Navy, Army and Air Force Institutes, the organisation that runs all service bars and canteens), let alone into battle.

However, things are different now. Today's recruits are better educated and therefore have a greater chance of overcoming both their own background and those traditional class barriers to become commissioned officers. This is especially true in the Airborne Brigade and the Special Forces, where a privileged background counts for nothing.

East End Kid

With hair cut short so nurse can see the nits,
I play amongst the burnt-out buildings and debris of
   war.
My tattered clothes
hide the scratched and dirty bits,
as I climb over walls

and crawl through houses
without windows, roofs or doors.

I'm hidden by the shadows,
as they creep slowly across 'the square'.
Like shape-changing monsters they scurry from the
    light.
Squeezed behind these bins they won't even know I'm
    here.
Learning how to hide
is better than being drawn into a fight.

Today we're playing soldiers
and again I'm on my own,
there's no football or cricket for me,
I was born to fight.
Condemned to spend my future years wandering this
    world alone,
moving silently amongst my enemies,
a creature of the night.

Suddenly above the noise of the East End killing fields
comes a blood-curdling cry
as mothers scream from the balconies
'Come in for your tea.'

The battle ends,
my friends arise,
their wounds just disappear.

We won't all be so lucky in the coming years.

Basic Ingredients

The basic ingredients, at the end of basic training.

As in any walk of life, soldiers, like civilians, come in many shapes and sizes. Because of this we will also have quite different levels of skill and ability, and just as we won't all become Ruperts, we can't all become Apache pilots or Special Forces soldiers either. However, each and every one of us who takes the Queen's shilling, whatever our role, whatever our level of skill or ability, will all play an integral part in any successes that are achieved, whether they're on or off the battlefield.

Whether you're destined to become a Rupert or a Tom – a private soldier – there are certain qualities that you will need to possess, those that I call the 'basic ingredients', if you are ever going to make the grade as any sort of warrior.

During our early days as recruits we constantly hear the

phrase 'shit in, shit out'. It's regularly repeated by the non-commissioned officers, or NCOs, who are our instructors when referring to the calibre of new recruits they are given to train. Such a statement may come across as harsh and derogatory when you consider the efforts of these eager young volunteers, yet a saying never rang truer.

You cannot make a warrior from scratch: you can only work with the basic raw materials you've been presented with. Like a chef making a meal, if any one or more of the basic ingredients is missing, or any of them is of poor quality, then the finished meal will be of that same poor quality, regardless of how talented the chef is or how hard he works. It's the same with soldiers. If a recruit doesn't possess all of those vital basic ingredients, then he or she is not going to get very far in today's army.

In order to become a good soldier, each new recruit requires just four basic ingredients. He needs to be *dependable* and have an inbuilt *will to win*, a massive *sense of humour* and an inexhaustible willingness to *share* in both his brother's victories and pain. Everything else a soldier needs to be effective in battle can be taught. Given enough time you can improve anybody's fitness and teach them to shoot straight, but these four basic elements are either part of your DNA or they are not.

Dependability is probably the biggest asset any soldier has to offer. Whether it's just being there for his mates or as part of the 'big green machine' which is the modern British Army, this dependability will be a much treasured asset. For his NCOs, being able to give him a task to do with the confidence that he will do it first time, and to the very best of his ability, will take a great weight off their shoulders.

As a young recruit, your DS (directing staff) will begin testing your dependability from the very first day they get their hands on you. It starts with the simplest of things, like your corporal depending on you to turn up on parade each morning, on time, with clean boots and a freshly pressed uniform. Because if you don't it will reflect badly on him. It's he who will get bollocked by your sergeant, and as every soldier knows, shit rolls downhill.

Likewise, a guard commander will depend on you to remain awake and alert at three in the morning when you're on 'stag' (your turn to wander around the darkest, scariest parts of the camp on your own on guard duty), resisting the urge to duck into your accommodation block and get your head down for an hour or so. Even though you're soaking wet and freezing cold and you know the camp is totally secure. It might be simply turning up for a sergeants' mess fatigue on time, and then doing the best job you can, even if it's just washing dirty pans after a mess dinner. Tasks like these will be a basic test of your dependability.

As you rise through the ranks the complexity and importance of your responsibilities will grow, and with this will come even greater tests of your dependability. Your officers will look to you to ensure the smooth running of your section, troop or squadron. Your men will look to you for a fair, firm but friendly approach to their management. They will even depend on you to support and protect them against unfair or obsessive punishment when they do wrong.

However, the greatest test of a soldier's dependability will come when he is under fire and in the heat of battle. There is a unique bond that exists between an officer or NCO and his men. It's not the type of relationship that's given to you as part of your promotion package: it's something that has to be earned over time, it's not easy, and not everybody achieves it. As a young Tom you will depend on your officers and NCOs to give you the appropriate orders and guidance when under fire, those that will ensure you win through a 'contact' and survive.

Likewise, as an officer or NCO you will depend on your men to follow without hesitation the orders you give them under fire. Even when all hell breaks loose, you will still depend on them to remember and implement the things you have taught them during the previous months, even years, of training. If at any time either side feels they cannot depend on the other, then the whole thing begins to unravel at speed, and good men, Ruperts and Toms alike, will die.

The greatest compliment that a soldier of any rank can be paid is to be referred to as 'rock solid' and 'totally dependable'.

Yet no matter how dependable you are, if you are ever going to be considered a true warrior, you will also need an unstoppable will to win. It doesn't matter how intelligent you are, how fit you are, how much training you do, or how many courses you attend, without a strong will to win, your life, and those of your comrades, could be very short indeed.

The military begins the process of developing this will to win at any cost, at the same time as they begin to test your dependability: at a very early stage in your career. Even as early as basic training your DS will begin to build your competitive spirit through the introduction of simple sports competitions. Or such things as shooting range days and endurance events.

Even something as simple as having a 'stick man' when you are on guard duty will instil an increased desire to win in every man on duty that night. Being awarded the status of stick man – as the best turned-out man on parade – by the orderly officer is a huge bonus to any recruit given it. Basically it means your duty is over, you're no longer on guard and you are now free to get changed and disappear down to the NAAFI with the rest of your mates.

Then, when you get to your regiment, you will become involved in 'inter-troop' or 'inter-squadron' competitions. Each of these events is designed to build a sense of pride and team spirit within you, your troop, your squadron and the regiment. Whether it's a military themed event, such as an 'inter-troop gunnery' or a 'march and shoot' competition, or a sports event such as an inter-squadron football cup, the underlying purpose is to boost your team spirit and strengthen your will to win.

The next stage of the process in building this will to win is what I call 'making it worth your while'. Over time, and as your career progresses, you will be offered a chance to add extra military trades to your CV. For example, you may have left basic training, as I did, as a signaller in an armoured car regiment. Your next goal is to become what we used to call a 'crewman'. However, in order to reach this lofty level you will need to attend and pass a separate course for each of the two additional trades, 'gunner' and 'driver'. Gaining these two qualifications will earn you additional crewman's pay, and without them you won't get a shot at further promotion. This process is definitely a 'win-win' situation. Everybody gets something out of it: your regiment gets a versatile soldier who can jump into any seat in the vehicle and do his job to the required standard. The trained crewman gets more money to piss away on beer and birds and the chance of a promotion and yet more money.

But to earn that promotion you will have to demonstrate yet again your will to win. This you will do by attending a 'cadre course'. Normally this is a three- or four-week course – the length of the course depends on individual regimental policy. During this period around thirty or more candidates are formed into a separate sub unit and you are totally segregated from your troop and the rest of the regiment.

You will all live together in separate, dedicated accommodation and return to a basic training environment. Here you will also have to once again endure basic training-type room and kit inspections; attend extra military classes such as weapon handling, range days, first aid, map reading, field craft and regimental history. You will also spend count-less physically punishing hours in the gymnasium, running until you drop, and further endless hours on the drill square. Your goal during this time is simple: you need to shine out among all the other candidates, to be the very best on the course.

Although there may be thirty or more taking part – and the vast majority of them will 'pass' – the reality is that only those who finish in the top three or four will stand any chance of being promoted immediately. The rest will get that all-impor-tant tick in their promotion box but will have to wait their turn. At its heart, the course is just another demonstration of both your dependability and your will to win.

The actual format and the fine detail of the content of these cadre courses varies from regiment to regiment and corps to corps. In the Airborne Brigade you were required to attend a three-month junior NCOs' tactics course known as 'Junior Brecon'. This would involve candidates from all three of the Parachute Regiment battalions and you would need to pass with a really good grade to even be considered for promotion to lance corporal. Once promoted to lance corporal, and if showing further leadership potential, you would then have to attend a further three-month senior NCOs' tactics course (Senior Brecon) in order to be considered for further promo-tion to full corporal or sergeant. Both these courses were run at Dering Lines in Brecon, south Wales.

Later in your career, you may decide that you wish to test yourself to the ultimate by volunteering to join a Special Forces unit. There are many of these units, and some are well known, such as the Special Air Service (SAS) or the Special Boat Service (SBS). Then there were and still are other, lesser-known ones, in my day, for example, the 'Det' or 'Special Duties' (also known as 14 Int) – which was created for intelligence gathering in Northern Ireland – and many more. Each of these units has a very specific role and, although there is and will always be a high level of inter-unit rivalry between them, they are all greatly respected by each other, and each one of them has a very important role to play when the shit actually hits the fan.

However, whether you're being measured against the other hopefuls attending the Airborne Brigade's All Arms Pre-Parachute Selection Course – known as 'P Company' – or you're taking part in Special Forces selection, the one thing you can be sure of is that they will all push you and your will to win to the absolute limits.

Another basic but very essential ingredient if you wish to become a warrior is a massive sense of humour. Military humour is definitely an acquired taste. Soldiers tend to laugh at things that civilians just don't find funny. Most of it revolves around death, suffering, or somebody else's misfortune. It's not because we're sick or weird: it's how we cope with a life that will inevitably end in our death or that of friends.

I remember being on one fighting patrol when, halfway through the day, we got 'bumped', came into contact with the enemy. Heavily outnumbered, we returned fire and during the ensuing fire-fight one of our number was wounded. We were taking a lot of fire, and to be honest things didn't look good. It was then that the youngest man in the troop, a white Rhodesian who had been shot in the thigh, looked at me and with a big grin on his face, said, 'You know, colour [colour sergeant], it's times like this I wish I was an ice-cream boy.'

Ice-cream boys are the young blacks who peddle around a three-wheel bike with a large ice box on the front, selling ice cream to the locals. Now this may be seen by some as a somewhat flippant, throw-away comment, but this was a life-changing statement for this young white Rhodesian, someone who had been brought up on apartheid. His take on our current situation was obviously so bad that he was willing to change places with what his people considered to be the lowest form of life on the African continent. It's only then you realise just how deep the shit is – but the guy still managed to wrap it up in a joke. Although our current predicament was no laughing matter, his comment did bring a smile to my face. He was still a youngster, but men like him were worth their weight in gold. A sense of humour like this can be cultivated over time, though once again the raw basic ingredient needs to be there from the very start.

Being able to share is something else that should come naturally to a good soldier. We tend to share everything: our water, food, our ammunition, and even our money. Whether it's buying a cash-strapped mate a pint and a meal when you're on leave, or sharing out the last few rounds during a fire-fight, sharing should be second nature to a soldier.

As you read on through this book I hope you will come to realise just how important these four basic ingredients are to a soldier, and how it's impossible to do what we do without them. Each story you read will contain at least one of these ingredients and, in the majority of them, you will find elements of all four.

Basic

The day I boarded the train to begin my BMT (basic military training, or 'Basic') it was to be the longest train journey I had ever made. It would also take me the furthest I'd ever been from London. I left London's King's Cross Station bound for Darlington in the north-east of England and, from there, to nearby Catterick Camp and its Cambria Barracks, the training depot of the Royal Armoured Corps. Looking back now I have no idea why I joined a cavalry regiment.

In those days when you visited your local Army Careers Office and showed an interest in joining the army you would be required to sit an entrance examination, the results of which would determine which regiment or corps you joined. My results were good enough for me to join any regiment or branch I wanted to. But I was just eighteen and didn't want to be a mechanic in the REME (Royal Electrical and Mechanical Engineers), because I could fix vehicles in 'civvie street'. I didn't want to join the guards either, all that marching around and looking smart would drive me mad. In fact I was later told by one sergeant that even if they dressed me in an expensive Savile Row suit I would still look like a sack of shit. So I made the fatal mistake of asking the recruiting sergeant what he recommended.

I found out later that at that time recruiting staff earned a bounty (cash payment) for each man they recruited into their own regiment. As a result I was about to become a member of the 17th/21st Lancers, also known as the 'Death or Glory Boys'. A regiment steeped in history, their most famous battle honour was that they led the 'Charge of the Light Brigade' at the Battle of Balaclava during the Crimea War.

On reflection it probably wasn't the best choice I'd ever made and it was one that would be very short-lived.

Basic training really was pretty much a non-event for me. Four and a half months of room inspections, running, 'bulling' (polishing) boots, being punched and continually shouted at. Although it was a culture shock for most of the other lads, especially those who had come from good homes and caring backgrounds, it was already a way of life for me. It was what I'd been doing for the past twelve years. Shit, I was right back in my comfort zone: and after living on the streets, at least I was now getting three square meals a day, a place to sleep and a rigid timetable to build my life around.

We had two sergeants and two corporals; these were our intake DS. One of the sergeants and his corporal were great. They gave praise where praise was due, but if you overstepped the mark you knew you were in for a good bollocking. The other sergeant and corporal were nothing more than bullies. It didn't matter how hard you tried, or how hard you worked, it was never going to be good enough for these two muppets.

I remember that the corporal thought he was a bit of a boxer. One day I was sparring around with another recruit, Ginge from the RTR (Royal Tank Regiment), in the changing rooms before a PT lesson. The corporal came in, caught us, and went absolutely ballistic. As his blood pressure rose he shouted, 'Right, you two, get the gloves on, and you can show the rest of the intake what you can do – in the ring.'

The colour just drained from Ginge's face. He was no match for me. I had been fighting all my life and had boxed for a year before joining up. However, like when I was at school, I quickly saw an opportunity to level the playing field with the corporal. As we were having the gloves put on I told Ginge to throw punches, but I wasn't going to fight back

– unless he got carried away and started to put his weight behind them. My hope was that the corporal would get so frustrated with me that he would take the gloves off Ginge and put them on himself.

After about five minutes of me not attempting to throw a single punch, and whilst continually backing up, the corporal dutifully obliged. He ripped the gloves off of Ginge and put them on himself. As he vowed to teach me a lesson I would never forget, a perfect left hook, one that had travelled all the way up from my boots, landed on the point of his chin and dropped him like a sack of shit at my feet. Bullies are so predictable.

The Bully

Look at you,
standing there in all your finery,
your pressed uniform
and bulled boots,
chest puffed out like a peacock,
displaying an air of false authority
bestowed on you by rank
not respect.

Look at you,
shouting at anything that moves,
pushing and shoving,
swinging that bloody riding whip
like some Egyptian overseer
beating your charges.
This is tyranny
not leadership.

But my day will come,
the day when I'm no longer yours,
the day when I don't have to take it any more.
The day when you're not protected
by your position,
the two stripes on your arm
or those bloody Queen's Rules and Regulations.

On that day,
a left hook,
the one I have lovingly saved for you,
will make a bee-line for your jaw.

Well, today is that day.
Remember me, corporal?
Here, let me help you up
off the floor.

Basic training lasted until August 1970. Then, after passing out, we were all posted to our respective units. I was destined to join my regiment in Northern Ireland. It was the beginning of the Troubles. The army was initially sent to the province as a buffer force between the Catholics and Protestants, and in particular the 'B Specials', a highly effective armed Protestant reservist police force. There we would face riots, petrol bombs and chunks of paving stones. Deep joy, I thought: even more people whose sole purpose in life is to cause me pain.

It was then that I coined the expression, 'Always in the shit, it's just the depth that varies.'

No-win Operation

Ferrets moving through what was left of a Belfast street.

Home from home, typical example of troop accommodation in 1970s Belfast.

It was a quarter to seven in the morning and we'd been on the streets of Belfast for well over thirty-six hours. During this time we had faced a steady barrage of bricks, broken paving stones and petrol bombs. My regiment had been in Northern

Ireland for about eighteen months, but I'd been here for just a matter of days. I hadn't even had time to unpack my kit; I'd just left it lying on my bed in my kit bag and an army suitcase.

I had just turned eighteen, was fresh out of basic training and within an hour of arriving in Northern Ireland I had been issued with riot kit and shipped down to Belfast with the rest of my squadron's 'support troop'. Although I was now a member of an armoured regiment, I was also part of a troop that performed an infantry task.

Our normal combat role was clearing enemy infantry, machine-gun nests and minefields in support of the regiment's armoured reconnaissance Sabre Squadrons. However, there was nothing 'normal' about what was happening here right now.

There were about thirty of us standing in a large residential area between the Shankill Road and the Springfield Road, on what would in time become known as the 'Peace Line'. Behind us were the mostly friendly Protestants, the Unionists, those who considered themselves loyal to the British Crown and wished to remain part of the United Kingdom. In front of us there were about 200 rioters, those throwing the bricks and petrol bombs, the Catholics or Republicans, those who wanted to belong to a united and independent Ireland.

Of course it was nowhere as clear cut as that, but this was a unique situation for a British soldier. We were used to fighting in other parts of the world, and had been doing it since the early days of the British Empire. But these people were British, and although we got extremely angry when caught up in the heat of events, it was very hard to actually hate them.

There were huge social issues on both the Loyalist and Republican sides. But, underneath it all, 'the Irish' were a very friendly and extremely generous nation, and more to the point and whether they liked it or not, at the moment they were British, one of us and part of the UK.

We had arrived in the darkness two nights ago. By the time we had taken up our positions the road was already littered with half house bricks, chunks of paving stones and broken glass. The whole area had an eerie orange glow about it as huge bonfires lit up the night sky. Every now and again the burning tails of petrol bombs would carve their arcs through the darkness like comets, as they searched for their target – us. Within five minutes of our arrival the situation had become very tense and we were ordered to form a line abreast. We were then quickly marched down the street in support of two Ferret light armoured cars that had become trapped.

To the rioters, these two-man vehicles must have resembled a sort of mini tank. But they were only the size of a modern medium-sized family car, and their armour was very thin. We would find out later, as the Troubles progressed and the IRA (Irish Republican Army) became better armed, that it wouldn't even stop a well-placed heavy-calibre rifle bullet. The Ferrets had four wheels instead of tracks and a tiny turret on top which normally cradled a .30-calibre Browning heavy machine gun. Not tonight, though, because this was considered an internal security situation and therefore these heavy-calibre weapons had been removed, leaving the two Ferrets basically unarmed.

These light armoured cars were designed to move swiftly and silently ahead of the heavy tanks of the 17th/21st Lancers. Their role was to search out enemy formations and then report back. As a result they were hopelessly ill designed for use in riot situations. Even if their Brownings had been fitted, there was no way any British soldier was going to start machine-gunning civilians.

As a result these two unarmed Ferrets from my regiment were now under heavy attack from a mob of angry rioters. They had been sent down the street just minutes earlier, under orders to physically push back the barricades, clearing a path for an infantry platoon they were supporting. However, as they reached the barricades, with their hatches closed against the rocks and bottles which were now bouncing off their thin armour plate, a number of rioters had climbed on top of the vehicles and begun smashing their glass periscopes with metal bars.

These vital pieces of equipment allow both the commander and the driver to see where they're going when their hatches are locked down under combat conditions. But now, trapped and basically blind, the Ferrets were unable to move either backward or forward, their crews locked inside and at the mercy of the mob.

We were about twenty metres short of their position, dodging the rocks and bottles when two men jumped up on the furthest vehicle. They dowsed the turret with petrol and then set fire to it, turning it into a giant pressure cooker. If we couldn't get the crew out very quickly they would be roasted alive. I could feel the pressure from the shoulders of the guys on either side of me as we all squeezed together in our search for some sort of reassurance that the line would hold and we would not be left alone, at the mercy of the mob.

As our line approached, the rioters began to throw petrol bombs at the second Ferret. Both vehicles were now ablaze, flames covering both the main turret and the driver's hatches, making it impossible for either of the crewmen to escape. As we got even closer I could hear the commander of the nearest Ferret, which was burning furiously, screaming for help on his radio.

We took up a defensive position between the mob and the stranded Ferrets, and as we came together, shoulder to shoulder, the mob inevitably turned its attention to us. These were the early days of the Troubles and at that time we were still using cast-off police equipment. The small round metal riot shield had a wire-mesh section at the top which enabled you to look through it without exposing your head to the bricks and bottles. We were also using the standard police-issue fifteen-inch truncheon. It wouldn't be until much later that we would be issued with the full-length, purpose-made, Perspex riot shield and the long baton.

As a result our legs were totally unprotected and the majority of rioters were well out of striking range of our batons. Their first salvo was made up of bricks and broken paving stones. As soon as the rocks started bouncing off our helmets we lifted our shields in an effort to protect our heads and torsos. Although our ancient helmets deadened the effect of the missiles, the impact still rattled your brain. Then, as our shields came up to meet the airborne onslaught, another group began throwing petrol bombs at our legs. They were now working as a coordinated team.

They had also discovered, probably through trial and error, that if you added sugar and flour to the petrol mix before filling the bottles, this mixture, once alight, would stick to anything it splashed against, indeed anything it came into contact with.

Four or five flaming milk and beer bottles had smashed at our feet, splashing burning petrol over our legs and setting fire to our boots and trousers, to the cheers and delight of the mob. I'd seen my fair share of violence in the past, but this was a whole new ball game. As I felt the heat on my legs I instinctively lowered my shield in an attempt to put out the flames that were now rapidly creeping up my lower body. I knew it was a mistake the minute I started to lower it. As my shield started to come down towards my waist my corporal was already shouting, 'Stand fast.'

As the words left his mouth, a large piece of brick hit me square in the face. I was quickly covered in blood, and I had that soon to become familiar and very distinctive taste of iron in my mouth. I had gained nothing. I now had a broken nose, and my bloody legs were still on fire.

A Hell for Heroes

Using our line of bodies and shields for cover, the corporal had moved around behind us, removed the fire extinguishers from the front of the two Ferrets and was starting to put out their fires. Once he was sure that the fires on both vehicles were out and the crews were safe, he started working on our legs. With the fires out and with the help of the infantry platoon, we then managed to push the rioters back down the street some thirty metres or more. Far enough for the Ferret drivers to safely open their hatches and withdraw back up the street.

The rest of that first night, the following day and last night had been a continuous round of the rioters throwing missiles. Us driving them back. Them rearming and us getting battered again. A number of us had already been injured. I had seen two of my new friends get burned, one of them quite badly as his legs, torso and face were engulfed in flames from a number of petrol bombs that had smashed against his shield, spraying his whole body with blazing petrol. My body was covered in cuts and bruises. My nose was all broken and twisted, and although my corporal had tried to straighten it between his fingers as best he could, it was still killing me.

But for all this I felt proud of myself. I had overcome my initial feelings of fear and then, full of anger, I had stood my ground, shoulder to shoulder with my new mates. I didn't even know most of their names as there had been no time for introductions. But what I did know was that they were part of my regiment, my new family, and I would do everything that was expected of me to make sure they were safe.

Even my corporal had patted me on my back at one stage and told me, 'Well, Knell, you've fought and won your first battle, and you did OK. Well done.' But to be quite honest, as nice as it was to get a bit of praise, I did at times wonder what the fuck I was doing here.

The Troubles had started in earnest when I was still in basic training. Up to that point a tour of Northern Ireland had been

seen as a dream posting for the British soldier, with girls out-
numbering the guys around three to one (most young men
having left the province in order to find work on the mainland) and pubs that were open all day. However, by the time I
arrived it was rapidly turning into a nightmare.

My squadron had been sent to Belfast from our barracks
in the north-west of the province to help separate two communities, the Protestants and the Catholics, and to keep the
peace. And now, as dawn began to break over the rows of
terraced houses, that night's riot was starting to quieten
down at last.

'Do you think they're running out of ammo, corporal?' I
asked.

'You have to be joking,' he said with a knowing grin on his
face. 'This is Ireland. They have an unlimited supply of road-
building materials. Let's just hope they don't start digging up
the cobbles – those things will be bloody lethal. No . . . They've
probably just gone home for some breakfast and a kip. Talking
of breakfast, go and see if you can rustle us up a brew from
somewhere.'

To an eighteen-year-old from the East End of London,
someone who knew nothing about the complicated political
and religious situation in Northern Ireland, in fact someone
who until a few months earlier didn't even know that Northern Ireland was actually part of the United Kingdom, what
was going on here was totally ludicrous.

In the East End we had learned to live quite happily as a
cosmopolitan community. Ours was a diverse and complicated mix of different nationalities and religions. We even
married outside our own communities. As I've already said,
my grandfather was Italian and my grandmother Prussian.
My mum was a Catholic and my dad was Church of England,
a Protestant. Catholics lived and worked alongside Protestants. The Jews had shops in the Italian areas and now the

West Indians had joined the mix as well. This could never happen here in Northern Ireland – well, not in those days.

Although the Protestants for the most part saw us as friends, sometimes we would be caught between the two sides, with both Protestants and Catholics venting their anger and frustration on a convenient enemy: the British Army.

So, doing as I'd been bid, I propped up my riot shield against the wall, tucked my baton inside my American-issue flak jacket and set off down the street of terraced houses in search of a friendly face. It was just after seven now and most of the residents – well, those that hadn't been up all night rioting – were already heading off to work either in the Harland & Wolff shipyard or one of the many factories of East Belfast.

A woman was already on her hands and knees scrubbing her front step, a daily ritual in these parts. The women would scrub their front door step, which was either bleached white by the daily scrub or painted with 'red lead'. They would also scrub a large semi-circle of pavement in front of it, the size of which would be totally dependent on the length of the poor woman's arms. This was a demonstration to the world that her house was well looked after and clean.

'Excuse me, missus, any chance of a brew for me and my mates?' I asked.

She looked up from her chores, slightly surprised and with a big smile on her face. 'Certainly, son. How many of you are there?'

I hesitated, not wishing to take advantage of her kindness. 'About thirty, but anything you can manage would be really great, and very much appreciated. We can share a cup between two, three or even four of us.'

By now I was feeling slightly embarrassed about asking her for so much. These people weren't the rich and affluent, these were working-class, and just like most of us, they were always struggling for cash.

'Let me see what I can rustle up for you.'

Our conversation had brought other women out onto the street and the one I was talking to turned to one of them.

'Florrie, do you think we can get these boys a cup of tea and maybe some breakfast?'

The other women nodded enthusiastically, and then one said, 'You wait here, son, while we get you and your friends something to eat and drink.'

Did she say 'eat' as well? This should earn me some brownie points with the other lads.

They all disappeared into their homes, and shortly afterwards the woman I had started talking to appeared with a large mug of tea.

'Here you are, son. You drink this while we sort out something for your friends.'

I took the tea, thanked her, then sat down on her step; it wasn't until I took the weight off my legs that it suddenly dawned on me that I had been standing up all night. Shortly after that I also realised that I'd sat down on her still wet step. But I was too tired to care. As I sat there with the water soaking into the arse of my combat trousers and drinking my tea, my eyes wandered down my legs to my boots, both of which had been quite badly burned. Luckily, thanks to the double lining in my combat trousers, the flames hadn't had time to do much more than scorch my legs, although it would be a week or so before the shrivelled hairs would start to grow back and the redness would finally disappear. My boots were a different matter, though. I wasn't going to be able to fix them with a quick lick of polish.

I then started to look up and down the street. All the kerb stones – what the locals call 'cribbies' – were painted red, white and blue. A Union Jack, a red and white Ulster flag, or an orange flag with a star on it (a Protestant Orange Order flag) hung from nearly every house in the long, narrow street.

But the road was now littered with lumps of paving stone, half house bricks and shattered glass.

What a mess, I thought. It will take them hours to sort this out and then it will all kick off again. But what I didn't know at the time was that within days most of these good people would be homeless. Every one of their houses, along with their precious possessions, would be burned by the mob.

About ten minutes later I had just about finished my tea, when the street suddenly came alive with women carrying trays laden with pots of tea and plates of buttered toast. They had got themselves organised, pooled their resources and were now following me down the street towards the barricades. I felt like the Pied Piper. The look on my corporal's face was absolutely priceless. It was the first time I'd seen him smile in two days. I was the new boy on the team and desperate to be accepted, but this was definitely going to help.

'Well done, Knell. Only a bloody cockney could go off in search of a cup of tea and come back with a banquet.'

As we stood drinking our tea and tucking into what seemed to be an endless supply of toast, I had no idea that later that month we would be in a similar situation on the Springfield Road, a Republican area. But on that occasion our tea would be laced with petrol, and the cheese in our sandwiches would be mixed with crushed glass.

Suddenly there was a little old lady tugging at my sleeve. 'Excuse me, son, you look like a nice lad. Do you think you can help me?'

'I don't know about nice, but what can I do for you, darling?'

She smiled at me, her face so clean it was shining. 'It's old Mr McClean, who lives next door.'

Her look said I should know who she was talking about.

'What's he done, darling?'

'Oh, he hasn't done anything, but you see he walks down to the paper shop at the same time every morning, at about half past six. But nobody's seen him for a few days. I've told the police, but they say they don't have any time, they say they're too busy with all these silly riots. Do you think you can take a look for me, just make sure he's OK?'

'You wait here and I'll go and ask the corporal for you.'

I explained the situation to the corporal and, with a mug of tea still in my hand, we returned to where the old lady was standing. After she'd told him the story yet again, all three of us, the old lady leading, made our way down the street to where the old chap lived. The curtains were still drawn, and although we banged hard on the door and windows for well over five minutes we couldn't get any answer.

'Right, Knell, get one of the others, then go and case the joint, try and find a way in.'

'Why me, corporal?'

'Because you're a bloody cockney. You're used to breaking into houses. It's a national sport in the East End. And Knell, don't leave a mess. Try not to break any windows, or anything else. The old boy could just be off visiting.'

'Yes, corporal.'

I collected one of the other troopers to watch my back and we made our way down a side alley into another one which ran along the rear of the houses. Each house had a back yard with a gate onto the alley. We found the right house and luckily the gate was unlocked. As we entered the yard I could see that one of the upstairs windows was open. But how do I get up to it? On the left side of the yard, set back from the house, was a small brick-built shed. I opened the door.

'Bloody hell, it's an outside shit house. I haven't seen one of these since I was a nipper in the East End.'

It's funny how, when your brain's unexpectedly presented with a toilet, you suddenly have an urgent need to piss. Suddenly it occurred to me that I hadn't had one all night, and once I started it seemed to last for ever.

Finished and feeling about three stone lighter I moved outside, only to find my mate practically cross-legged and dancing
on the spot. The sound of running water had started a chain
reaction and he was now busting for one too. I left him to it
and climbed onto the roof of the outhouse. Once up there I
walked along the narrow wall that separated the yard from the
house next door, and up to the back of the house. I shinned
up the drainpipe, then, hanging onto the gutter with one hand,
and with one foot on the window sill, I managed to pull down
the top half of the old sash window and climbed in.

I stood motionless on the window sill while my eyes became
accustomed to the limited light in the room. I then jumped
down onto the bare floorboards and walked towards the door.
I opened it slowly, and as I moved gingerly onto the small
landing at the top of the stairs I shouted, '*Hello, is anybody
there?*'

Nothing.

So I shouted again.

Still no answer. So I started to make my way down the
narrow staircase which opened out onto a small lounge. As I
rounded the bottom of the stairs I was stopped dead in my
tracks. Sitting in an armchair next to the fireplace was a little
old guy. He looked like he was asleep. I walked over and shook
his arm. Nothing. So I put my hand on his cheek. It was the
end of August and not very cold outside, but his skin was
freezing. A type of cold I'd felt before, under that railway arch
at Waterloo. I shook him again. Still nothing. It was then that I
noticed the large wet patch on the front of his trousers. He'd
wet himself. I found out later that that's what happens sometimes when you die.

The poor old guy must be dead, I thought.

I just stood and looked at him; he looked peaceful enough,
but still incredibly alone.

What a shit way to die, I said to myself, I wonder if it hurt, if he knew he was dying, or did it just happen quietly, while he was asleep? Let's hope so.

I pulled myself together and made for the front door. As I swung it back to the wall I was greeted by the old lady, who tried to get around me and into the house. I put my arm out and placed my hand on the wall of the porch, blocking her way. As she ran into it I pulled her in close. 'I'm sorry, darling. He's passed away.'

She pulled herself together, straightened her hair and her pinny and then gently patted me on both cheeks. Then, holding my face with both hands and looking me straight in the eyes, she said, 'Thank you, son.'

I put the latch on the door so that it couldn't lock itself and pulled the door to behind me. I left my mate outside the house to stop anyone getting in and walked down the street towards where I'd last seen my corporal. Somehow I felt older, a little more mature. The events of the past few days had forced me to grow up very quickly. My nose had stopped bleeding, but had now swelled to twice its normal size, making it increasingly hard to breathe, and it hurt like shit. My eyes had also started to go black, and I now resembled a racoon.

When I found the corporal I told him what I'd found, and he began to soften. 'Are you all right, mate?'

This was another, milder side to the man who had chewed my head off on that first night.

'Yes, corporal, I'm OK, thanks.'

'Good. Now go and find a telephone and get an ambulance down here to remove the body. And don't be all day about it. It looks like they've finished their breakfast and are starting to come back for round two.'

I set off down the street in search of a phone. Our communications weren't synchronised in the early days. At that time the army couldn't talk directly to the police or the ambulance service, so in most cases you had to use the public telephone system. As I reached the old boy's house I bumped into the little old lady, still hovering outside, worrying about her friend, and asked her, 'Excuse me, darling, has anybody in the street got a phone? We need to call an ambulance to come and get your friend's body.'

'Mrs McConnell at number twenty-three has the only one. I'm sure she will let you use hers.'

Three minutes later, with the phone call finished, I was on my way back up the street to report to my corporal.

'Corporal.'

He turned and looked at me. 'What's the score on the ambulance, Knell?'

I took a deep breath. 'They weren't very helpful, corporal.'

'So what did they say?'

'Their actual words were that after last night's riots you can piss off. They're not coming down here for someone who's already dead. You'll have to wait until it gets quiet.'

He looked like he was going to explode. 'Right. Well, we can't just leave him where he is. This might go on for days and apart from the fact that it isn't right, he'll begin to stink. Go and find me one of the guys who can drive a Land Rover, someone who knows their way to Musgrave Park Hospital.'

I was getting pissed off with this. I had joined the cavalry because I didn't want to walk everywhere, but I'd done nothing else all bloody morning. Eventually I found a driver, Danny, and we went back to the corporal.

'Right. You two get the old boy into a Rover,' he said. 'Cover him up with something, and take him out over the waste ground at the end of the street to Musgrave Park. They can deal with him. Get someone to ride shotgun on the back, and don't be all day about it. I can't afford to be three men down if this all kicks off again.'

However, when we tried to lift the old chap out of his chair to lay him on the floor, his body just wouldn't bend. He was as stiff as a board. I looked at Danny. 'What the fuck are we going to do now?'

Danny looked at me and shrugged his shoulders, then said, 'Well, let's just go and tell the corporal we can't do it. And why's he all wet?'

'It's a long story. And you can fuck off. The corporal's about to blow and I'm not going to be on the receiving end when it happens. Let's just lift him into the Rover in the sitting position. We can sit him in the front between us.'

Danny wasn't too keen on driving through Belfast with a dead body sat between us, but the alternative, telling the corporal we had failed, was even less appealing. We loaded the old boy into the front of the Land Rover, sitting him in the centre seat with one leg either side of the gear stick. This meant Danny was going to have to brush up against him every time he shifted gear. He was not a happy bunny.

We picked up our third man, another trooper. He thought the whole thing was totally hilarious, but that was because he was stood on the tailgate at the back and didn't have to deal with the problem directly. We drove the four miles to Musgrave Park Hospital without incident. On our arrival Danny parked the Rover while I went and got a wheelchair from the reception area.

Once we'd loaded the old boy into the wheelchair we took him into reception. As we went through the double doors we nearly ran over a QARANC (Queen Alexandra's Royal Army Nursing Corps) sister, dressed in her smart grey uniform and red shoulder cape. She looked like she'd spent most of her life chewing wasps.

'Where are you two going?'

Danny just looked at her; young troopers like us were just a source of fresh meat for these dragons. She was also a major, so as far as we were concerned that made her God's sister, and a terrified Danny blurted out, 'He's dead.'

A Hell for Heroes

She half smiled. 'No kidding. How did he die?'

Danny panicked. 'We didn't do it.'

I quickly spoke up. 'I think it was just old age, ma'am.'

'OK, well, I can't spare anybody, so you two will have to take him down to the morgue. Just follow the signs, and make sure you bring that chair back when you're finished.'

As we set off through the maze of hospital corridors, I smiled at Danny and said, 'We didn't do it!'

He just scowled at me. 'Well, I bet that old bag haunts houses when she's on leave.'

Eventually we found the morgue; I took a deep breath and pushed the old boy in. It was the first time either Danny or I had ever been in a morgue and it wasn't pleasant. As I pushed the wheelchair through the swing doors and entered the room proper, we were met by what might best be described as Lurch's big brother. The spitting image of Lurch from *The Addams Family*, he must have been well over six foot tall with a massive forehead and a mouth that looked like it was filled with far too many teeth.

'What do you two want?'

Danny beat me to the punch again. 'He's dead.'

Lurch just looked at the old boy and then at the two of us. 'You think so? OK, lift him onto that table so that I can get him undressed, washed and into a cold drawer.'

Danny and I lifted him out of the wheelchair and laid him on his back on the metal table, but he was still more or less in the sitting position. Lurch just looked at the dead man and then at the two of us. I could see what was coming.

'He's no good to me like that. I can't get him into a cold drawer in that shape – you'll have to straighten him out.'

'*What?*'

'You'll have to straighten his legs so that he's flat. It's the only way he'll fit in the drawer.'

'Well, how do we do that?'

Lurch just smiled. 'You'll have to stretch or break the tendons and ligaments in his legs.'

I didn't like the thought of that, but I thought Danny was actually going to pass out. He then said, 'Can you not just lay him on his side?'

Lurch shook his head and said, 'I'll be back in a few minutes. Best you two get on with it.'

I looked at Danny. The colour was rapidly draining from his face, so I sat the old boy up as best I could.

'OK, mate, listen. You get up on the table and push down on his knees while I pull back on his shoulders. It shouldn't take a lot and then we can get out of this place.'

Danny climbed up onto the polished metal table and got himself in the kneeling position at the old boy's feet. As he started to very gingerly put both his hands on the old boy's knees he said, 'So why's he all wet?'

It didn't seem fair to tell him right now. 'I'll explain it later. Now start to push down on his knees.'

As Danny pushed down I grabbed hold of the old boy's shoulders and started to pull back. You could feel and hear the tendons creaking as we both put more and more pressure on his knees and shoulders. Danny now had all his weight pushing down through the knees, when I had a wicked thought. I opened my hands, releasing the old boy's shoulders.

Without me pulling back, and Danny still pushing down with all his weight on the old boy's knees, the corpse sat up and smacked Danny in the head with his chest. As the two collided I shouted, 'It's alive'!

Danny looked up, terrified. Practically foaming at the mouth, he jumped off the table. He must have gone around the room three or four times, with his hands brushing along the wall like a demented mime artist as he searched for the door. At last he found it and almost knocked Lurch over as he pushed past him. I don't think he stopped until he hit the car park.

I was practically crying and couldn't breathe for laughing. Even Lurch saw the funny side of it. And although it probably wasn't the correct way to behave in these circumstances, it was as though all the weight and tension of the previous three days had been lifted off me, and at last I could breathe again, although not through my broken nose.

My reward? Well, I spent the next thirty minutes working with Lurch, trying to straighten the old boy's body. However, I think he started to warm to me, as he offered me a cup of tea and a piece of his ham sandwich when we'd finished. Little did I know at the time that sitting eating and drinking among the dead would become commonplace in future years.

I spent the next eighteen months in Northern Ireland, during which time the Troubles quickly escalated. Along with the riots we soon found ourselves dealing with the shooting and mutilation of off-duty soldiers, running battles with snipers, and having to face the terrorist's most effective weapon: the bomb. A weapon which the IRA and Provos (Provisional IRA) used to great effect for over forty years, and one that has now been exploited with devastating consequences in Afghanistan.

Whether it had been left in a parked car on a busy high street, its purpose was to terrorise innocent shoppers, many of them likely to be women and kids. Or it was hidden in a lamppost and detonated as an army or police patrol passed by, showering its targets with brick-size chunks of concrete moving faster than the speed of sound. The result was always the same: death and mutilation on a massive scale.

Like a Demon at My Shoulder

It was now the beginning of 1971, and as the Troubles escalated in Northern Ireland, so did the number of troops deployed. It wouldn't be long before all of the major cities in the province would be crawling with British soldiers desperately trying to keep the peace between the Protestant and Catholic communities. At the height of the conflict there would be over 21,000 troops regularly operating in Northern Ireland. Naturally this number would grow during times of increased tension, such as the start of 'Operation Motorman', the programme of internment of terrorist suspects which began in August 1971, when troop numbers would reach close to 30,000.

The infantry were much better suited than us to this new urban anti-terrorist role, as our armoured cars were large and cumbersome and found it hard to manoeuvre through the narrow city streets. Although we had had our uses up to this point, in providing armoured cover against snipers, performing as rolling roadblocks or acting as troop carriers for the infantry, it wouldn't be long before the infantry were using their own armoured transport in the shape of the ancient Humber 'Pig'. These vehicles were purpose-built by the now defunct British car manufacturer for dealing with civil disturbance.

No longer needed on the crowded streets of the towns and cities, we moved out into the countryside and back to our traditional role of looking for trouble while patrolling the dangerous border areas. At the time we were the only armoured regiment based in Northern Ireland, and, located in County

Tyrone in the west of the province, we had a huge operational area to cover.

One time, as our small four-vehicle armoured patrol, which consisted of two lead Ferrets followed by a Saladin armoured car, with another Ferret bringing up the rear, began to climb the mountain road towards the TV mast that stood on its summit, my mind began to wander. I stood on the radio operator's seat of the Saladin with my head and shoulders proud of the hatch on the left side of the turret. A major piece of armoured hardware, the Saladin weighed in at just over eleven and a half tons. Unlike the smaller Ferret it actually resembled a real tank, with a large turret which housed its main armament: a 76mm gun which fired High Explosive and anti-tank shells. It also carried two .30-calibre Browning machine guns, but unlike a real tank it had six large wheels instead of tracks. Very imposing but not in fact of much use in an urban environment, since we were never going to use our main armament within the confines of a built-up area, as the Syrian army are doing in Homs even as I write today.

As we rumbled up the narrow mountain road I thought about how much my life had changed over the previous ten months. In little under a year I had left the comfort and safety of my nan and granddad's home in the East End of London and had completed five months' basic training at Catterick Camp in North Yorkshire, before joining my regiment here in Northern Ireland. Within hours of my arrival I had been sent down to Belfast, where I had spent nearly a fortnight being pelted with bricks and petrol bombs, had my nose and right hand broken and been set on fire while dealing with mobs of angry rioters.

Suddenly I was brought back to the here and now as I heard the Saladin commander, my troop leader, shout over the IC (internal communications) radio, 'Pull over to the left, Briggs. One of the Ferrets has had a puncture.'

Danny, our driver, did what he had been told and pulled the massive six-wheeled vehicle over against the small grassy bank that ran along the left side of the road.

As we waited for the Ferret crew to change their punctured wheel everybody except for the Ferret gunners and the troop leader dismounted and took up defensive positions on both sides of the narrow road. We were now in what we called 'Bandit Country' and being caught in an IRA ambush was a very real possibility.

We had been dismounted for about five minutes when we heard a vehicle approaching. Unlike those initial few weeks during the riots in Belfast, the Browning heavy machine guns had now been refitted into their turret mountings on the Ferrets, and as the noise of the approaching vehicle grew louder I heard the commander of the rear Ferret disengage the manual turret lock and swing it and its .30-calibre machine gun around to face any potential threat that might be coming along the road behind us. As the vehicle came around the bend we could see it was a long wheelbase hard-top Land Rover, what was referred to as a safari-type Land Rover.

It obviously wasn't one of ours as it was a solid dark green all over, whereas all of our vehicles were painted in a green and brown camouflage pattern. Nor was it an army Land Rover. In those days the army didn't use hardtops. Also, it was alone, and at that time no military vehicle went anywhere in the province on its own. But as it came closer we could clearly see the government livery on the side. It was then that the driver of the Land Rover saw the rear-guard Ferret with the barrel of its .30-calibre Browning looming down on him. He flashed his headlights on and off three or four times in a desperate demonstration of friendship.

After the Land Rover's driver explained to the Ferret commander his reasons for being there, he was allowed to pass, and drew up alongside the turret of the Saladin. Still being tracked by the rear Ferret's commander and the heavy Browning, the front seat passenger wound the window down. There were five men in the vehicle. The troop leader then lifted one side of his headset and leaned down towards the Land Rover, before saying, 'Morning, gentlemen. What are you doing up here, and where are you going?'

I was crouched on the edge of a ditch on the other side of the road and had already made eye contact with the driver of the Land Rover. I could see the apprehension in his eyes and in an effort to control the situation I held his gaze. We didn't want him panicking and trying to drive off, because if that happened we would be forced to open fire on him. Then, in a shaky voice, the man beside him replied, 'Morning. We have some maintenance work to do on the TV mast at the top of the mountain. It should only take us a few hours.'

'No problem. We'll be up there shortly to take a look around. One of our vehicles has had a puncture, and as soon as it's fixed we'll follow you up.'

With that the men said their farewells. We soldiers were ever fearful of some kind of surprise attack, not knowing whether the apparently innocent might in fact be part of something much nastier, for the IRA had already started to hijack cars and use them to mount surprise attacks. There was a very real possibility that these harmless-looking civilians could indeed be IRA terrorists. Perhaps the real government contractors were even now lying tied up in a ditch a mile or two away. We watched the Land Rover intently as it drove off up the hill.

It had just disappeared from sight around the next bend in the road when the ground beneath my feet shook violently. The tremor was so powerful that it felt like the whole planet was coming apart below me. I then heard a huge explosion which came from the direction of the Land Rover, and as my ears struggled to cope with the enormous noise and the massive shift in air pressure, my world suddenly fell silent. A split second later I was knocked off my feet as my body was hit by a hurricane-force gust of burning wind. As I picked myself up and collected my senses I glanced instinctively to the top of the Saladin and my troop leader.

Although he looked shaken, his hearing had been partially protected by the large rubber earpieces of his radio headset, which totally covered his ears. But shaken or not, his automatic pilot had kicked in and he was already on the radio sending a contact report and our current location.

Meanwhile the troop corporal took control of the situation and shouted to the commander of the rear Ferret, 'Tommy, pull your scout car across the road. Cover anything that comes up it with your Browning. Nothing gets past you unless I say so.'

'Roger that.'

As the rear Ferret started to pull across the road the corporal turned his attention to me. 'Knell, you and Robertson come with me, and be careful, there may be more devices out there.'

Both of us shouted up together, '*Corporal.*' I slid the bolt of my SMG (Sterling sub-machine gun) to the rear, re-engaged the safety catch and looked into the now open ejection port, where I could see the first 9mm round in a magazine of twenty as it waited to be fed into the chamber. Now ready to return fire if it was needed, Titch Robertson and I followed the corporal up the hill in the direction of the explosion. I could see the plume of thick black smoke rising into the air but had no idea what awaited me as I walked along that narrow road, but I instinctively knew it wasn't going to be pleasant.

As I rounded the bend the scene in front of me resembled something straight out of hell. The Land Rover had triggered a massive landmine. A blanket of thick acrid smoke hung just above head height over the whole area. The wooden posts that had previously supported the barbed-wire fence that ran along both sides of the road had been ripped from their footings and completely disappeared. Pieces of vehicle debris were spread over what remained of the road and out into the surrounding area.

A crater, twenty feet wide and well over six feet deep, had ruptured the road, making it impassable to normal vehicles. My first concerns were for the five men who had been travelling in the Land Rover, but I couldn't see anyone. In fact I couldn't see their vehicle either. The only piece of it that was left was its stripped steel chassis, which was lying half in and half out of the deep hole in the road, twisted and blackened by the ferocious blast.

But where were the five men? I could see no sign of them; it was as though they had just disappeared into thin air. As I got closer to the crater and the centre of the blast I noticed something lying in the grass beside the road and bent down to pick it up. It was soft and warm, but I quickly dropped it again as I realised it was a human arm. It had been severed just below the elbow and I could see, protruding from one end, the heads of the two bones that make up the lower arm.

Titch had found another piece: an arm with part of the shoulder still attached to it, and he was now throwing up violently on the grass verge at the side of the road. Although they had initially been invisible, as I now looked around me it became apparent that what I had thought were pieces of rubble were in fact human body parts, arms, legs and chunks of raw flesh. As I took in what lay before me the corporal said something that shook me to the bone.

'That landmine was meant for us. The Ferret getting a puncture and that Land Rover coming along the road when it did was the best bit of luck we'll ever have, although the same can't be said for them.'

The front Ferret, with its wheel now changed, had started to move up the road behind us but had been forced to stop as it reached the first human remains. Its commander, ever aware of the threat of a secondary ambush, was now working furiously, sweeping the open ground on both sides of the road and the area immediately to our front beyond the crater with the Browning in an effort to provide us with what little cover he could.

'Right, guys, put everything back where you found it and touch nothing else,' he said. 'We'll now have to wait for the police team to get here.'

The whole area resembled an abattoir floor, with body parts everywhere, and we were finding it difficult to move around without stepping on something that had once been human. Very carefully we withdrew slowly back down the road, set up a defensive cordon and just watched and waited. There was nowhere you could look that your eyes didn't fall on a piece of a human body. Talk about feeling totally helpless.

It's funny how the human mind works at times like this, but crouched at the side of the road all I could think about was, what happens if a flock of crows turns up? How do we stop them from flying off with the smaller bits?

It was well over an hour later when the police forensics team arrived, and although the adrenaline was still coursing through my veins the initial rush that had been there in those first few minutes following the explosion had now dissipated. I was now left with the raw reality of what I saw in front of me. I think that if we had been allowed to get on with the job of clearing up immediately, the task that now lay ahead of us wouldn't have been so daunting. But crouching there, surrounded by the carnage, for close to two hours while we waited for the forensics guys to arrive, that grisly job was now playing with our minds.

There were very few visible signs of blood, considering that five men had been literally blown apart, but the smoke, with its smell of iron mixed with cordite, had now invaded my nose, mouth and throat and still hung mercilessly all around us.

Once the forensics team had finished their initial inspection and taken what seemed to be a thousand photographs, it was time to start the clear-up. Our orders were simple: we were to concentrate only on the human material, and put the large body parts – two arms, two legs, a torso and a head – in one huge plastic bag. The smaller unidentifiable pieces of flesh were to go in another.

I remember the police ME (medical examiner) telling us, 'Everything has to be recovered. Don't walk past anything. If you don't have room in your bags, then stand still and call for one of the police team and we'll bring you another. Also, don't bother trying to match up the individual body parts at this point. I will do that when I get them back to the lab. We just need you to make sure that we have five bags each containing one complete body, and ensure that nothing is left out here when we're done.'

Armed with two clear plastic bags and my bare hands (no nice white rubber gloves in those days), I took my place in the line of police and soldiers which stretched across the road and out into the open ground on either side. The Ferrets had positioned themselves as best they could to provide us with cover as we went about our grim task.

My position in the line was neither an accident nor a random act. I had chosen it purposely. In fact I had squeezed into the line, roughly pushing a policeman out of the way. I knew exactly where the arm that I had found and picked up earlier was lying, and that's what I needed to find again if I was going to make it through this carnage. My theory was simple: I'd picked it up once, so I knew what it felt like, and if I could just do it again it might make the rest of this madness bearable.

As we moved slowly forward down the road I started picking up the bits of raw flesh that had been lying there for close to three hours now. The heat of the body that they had once belonged to had now gone, leaving them nothing more than cold wet lumps of meat. It was just like picking up the large lumps of fatty stewing steak when I worked at Dewhurst, and I put them into the 'bits' bag as quickly as I could.

I was fighting back my body's natural urge to puke as I came across the arm that I had found earlier. Steeling myself, I bent down to pick it up. In an effort to get to grips with my fear I grabbed at it, and after getting a firm grip on the wrist I lifted it off the grass and put my hand in the plastic 'body parts' bag, but I couldn't release it. It had taken all my resolve to pick it up a second time, so much so that I now had an iron grip on it and couldn't let it go.

I quickly said to myself, get a grip, man, you've picked it up and put it down once already. Now just let go of it. With that I slowly let it fall from my fingers and into the bottom of the bag. I brought out my hand and I stood and stared at it as the blood ran off my fingers and back into the bag. The corporal, who was walking slightly behind the line armed with an SMG, had been watching me. 'Are you OK, Knell?'

'I think so, corporal. It's just a bit weird.'

'I know, son. It doesn't get much weirder than this.'

I carried on moving forward, picking up more and more pieces of shattered body, but it wasn't getting any easier. The line of police and soldiers had now progressed to the far side of the crater and as I moved on I noticed that Titch and one of the police team were being taken away by the corporal and another policeman. Titch looked like a broken man, although given his smaller size he looked more like a young boy. He had thrown up so many times that the front of his flak jacket and trousers were now covered in puke. He was so weak he could no longer stand up straight unaided.

I'd covered about another five feet when something in the ditch caught my eye. As I began to focus in on it with eyes that were so sore that they had lost their ability to create any more tears, I realised it was a human head. I could only see the back of it as it was lying face down in the mud of the ditch. I hesitated, but the police ME was there like a demon at my shoulder, spurring me on. 'Go and pick it up, son.'

Letting my two plastic bags settle on the ground, I climbed down into the ditch, and after taking a deep breath I crouched down to pick it up. My first instinct was to just grab it by its lengthy brown hair and drop it straight into the bag, but I couldn't do that; it would have been disrespectful. So, placing one hand on each side of the head, I lifted it gently and climbed out of the ditch. I was totally shocked by how heavy it was. I don't know how heavy I was expecting it to feel but it certainly wasn't that heavy. For what seemed like an age I stood there with the severed human head in my hands, but now, having retrieved it from the ditch, I was totally torn.

On the one hand I just wanted to drop it into the plastic bag and run off down the road, just get out of the area altogether. But on the other hand I desperately needed to see this man's face. Using my thumbs and fingers I slowly rotated the head back towards me. The severed neck was the first thing that came into view. I could see everything: bone, muscles, arteries and all. As I continued to turn it, this was followed by his chin and mouth.

The next thing I saw was the nostrils, and as the bridge of his nose came into view I could see that his deep brown eyes were still wide open. As our eyes met and I locked onto his, I realised it was the Land Rover driver. I now wished I had shown him more kindness earlier, but I just stood there and stared into them, transfixed by his lifeless stare, unable to turn away.

Suddenly I felt a hand on my shoulder. It was the ME again, and in a soft, almost fatherly voice he said, 'Just put it in the bag, son. The person he once was has gone now.'

Although I had just dropped the other lifeless body parts

into the bag I couldn't do it with a man's head. It had a face, and somehow that gave it a soul, so I crouched down next to the bag and gently laid it in the bottom. Then I closed his eyes with my fingers before standing up and handing the half-full bag to the ME.

I was eighteen years old and that day my life changed for ever. No matter how much I longed for the old days of boarding school and living rough on the streets, as bad as they'd been at the time, it would never ever be the same again. Even so, in the future I would feel no sorrow or pity when it came to the men that I killed in battle. And in the case of terrorists I would only ever feel contempt bordering on pure hatred as they hid behind the civilian population, for they were the enemy and it was either them or me.

However, witnessing the death of my close friends, valued team members or innocent men, women and children would continue to scar and haunt me for the rest of my days.

Titch was also a changed man. He never again spoke about that day, and was killed some three months later when he drove a car headlong into another car on a deserted road. Given what I know now I often wonder if his actions were his way of escaping his memories of that day and the nightmares they conjured up, the results of PTSD. But as, like most of us, he never spoke to anyone about his feelings I don't suppose we'll ever know.

Northern Ireland was also the first place I ever got shot at. Part of my regiment's duties were supporting the RUC (Royal Ulster Constabulary) by jointly manning roadblocks and providing extra protection for rural police stations – a favourite target of the IRA and Provos in the early days of the Troubles. Attacking isolated police stations, especially those in south Armagh and Fermanagh, on the border with the Irish Republic, was a very effective tactic, and one which they would continue to use for the next forty years.

One of these police stations was in the sleepy little town of Belleek, the home of a world-famous porcelain factory. It was as if the town had been purpose-built for the terrorist. You could simply drive over the border from Ireland, shoot the place up in 'drive by' fashion and then, without turning around, leave by the other side of town and head straight back into the Republic. Normally, by the time we reacted it was too late and the terrorists were safely across the border. Of course we weren't allowed to follow: diplomatic relations and all that shit. A problem I was to come up against many times in the future.

Hate

A tiny border town awakens from a less than peaceful
    night.
The sangar on the police station roof gets a new tenant,
one who minutes before
had been dragged wearily from the clutches of a giant
    green maggot
to spend the next two hours
sweeping the countryside through a rifle sight.

A mixed Army-Police patrol moves quietly through the
    town
while locals go about their business.
A young woman,
not much more than a girl,
danders in front of me with a child.
I watch them laughing
and for the briefest moment I forget where I am,
the flak jacket and the gun in my hand.
A screech of tyres forces me back to reality,
turning around

just in time to see the rear window of a car being slowly
   wound down.
Automatic gunfire shatters the fragile peace.
Grabbing the young mother and her child on the run
I bundle them into a shop,
and as I fall on top of them
I am showered with broken glass and stone chippings
as bullets smash through windows,
and crash into the brickwork of the tiny store.

But before we can respond,
return fire,
they are gone
back into the South
and it's over.

I help the mother and her unharmed child up off the
   floor
but am totally unprepared for her reaction;
as she heads quickly towards the door
with hatred burning fiercely in her eyes,
she spits in my face and shouts loudly

'Take your hands off me, you British bastard.'

Then pushing me aside
she quickly leaves the shop
uninjured
with her precious child.

I remember thinking,
'Just how much do these people hate us?'

PART IV:
JOINING THE BROTHERHOOD

On the Move Again

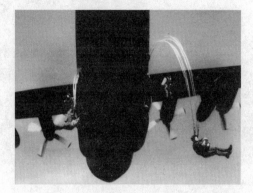

Green on – Go. Troops jumping from a C130.

A head for heights, the 'Shuffle Bars', the Para Trainasium at Aldershot.

It will be over soon, the Steeple Chase – P Company Aldershot.

At the end of its three-year tour in Northern Ireland the regiment moved to West Germany (as it was then) to take up its Cold War role as an armoured reconnaissance unit. After all the excitement and experiences we'd had in Ulster, all we had to look forward to now was a mundane life on the tank park. It soon became clear that if I stayed where I was I would spend the remainder of my time in the army servicing and repainting armoured vehicles, while carrying out exercises that were becoming more restricted by the month.

I also felt that any potential I had would be stifled as, being an outspoken cockney in a cavalry regiment – as one young officer put it, 'a guttersnipe' – I wouldn't get very far at all. But where do I go? In those days there were only two transfer requests that couldn't be blocked by my regiment. But I was still too young to volunteer for Special Forces (you had to be a minimum of twenty-one years old), so it looked like I was off to the Airborne.

However, it wasn't going to be a case of just turning up and jumping out of an aircraft. No, first I would have to pass the All Arms Pre-Parachute Selection Course, or 'P Company' as it was known in the Parachute Brigade. This involved four weeks of hell as I perceived it at the time, although I have since revised my opinion. Four weeks that would change my life. Four weeks when I would be run, marched, punched and kicked into the ground.

The aim of the first two weeks was to drive you on until you collapsed from pure exhaustion and frustration. You would then be picked up and driven on until you dropped again. This process was repeated time and time again until, in the end, you would fall, pick yourself up and drive on alone. This is what makes an Airborne soldier what he is. An animal that is so determined not to be beaten that he will die trying to achieve the goal he's been set. They are the pit bulls of the British Army.

One hundred and twenty-seven officers and men started my course. Twenty-four of them were from the APTC (Army Physical Training Corps), supposedly the fittest men the army had to offer. Only three of them would eventually complete the course and pass.

The rate of attrition during the initial two weeks was enormous. Of the 127 of us who started my course, less than half would make it to week three and Test Week One, where the real selection process began.

Test Week One consisted of a number of high-speed endurance tests conducted in the Aldershot area and on the rolling hills of the South Downs. It also saw me taking part in the 'steeplechase' – a timed four-mile run across country, over both man-made and natural obstacles including water jumps – and all without the help of a horse. I would also be required to pass the airborne assault course test. Then there was 'milling'. This involved standing toe to toe with another man of equal weight and size for three minutes. In order to pass the milling test I needed to continually throw punches while standing my ground and giving no quarter. To take just one step backwards could mean I would fail the test. But, although I wouldn't fail the whole Pre-Parachute course at this stage, it would cost me valuable points, which in the end might also cost me my Airborne beret.

I also had to pass the Para Confidence Course, or Trainasium. This entailed running along a series of narrow walkways that were built high up in the trees. As you ran along the narrow planks you would have to negotiate a number of running jumps and see-saws, take 'leaps of faith' – jump large gaps – and climb scramble nets and rope swings. All of this would be done thirty feet in the air, and all without the aid of a safety net. Walk instead of run, stop or hesitate in any way when given the order 'Go', and you failed. This was a very important test as being able to operate efficiently at heights is a must for an airborne soldier; and the Trainasium was no place to be if you had a fear of heights.

The final test on the Trainasium was the 'shuffle bars'. Here I had to traverse along two ten-foot scaffolding poles that were set shoulder width apart. About halfway along there were two six-inch-high metal cleats (large metal brackets used to fasten one piece of scaffold to another), which I had to lift my feet over before proceeding to the end of the bars. It sounds easy, doesn't it? That's until you put them eighty feet in the air and you're told you must remain standing upright and on no account are you to use your hands. The man who took the test immediately before me froze as he reached the cleats. He just couldn't get his feet to move; it was like they were welded to the bars. My emotions at this point were very mixed. On the one hand I felt really sorry for him as this would spell the end of his career in the Airborne before it had even started. On the other hand it gave the test real value. It wouldn't be a test if everybody passed.

I then stood and watched as two members of staff climbed up on the bars and tried to get the man down. Little did I know that only a few months later it would be me who was climbing up on the bars, then walking along them in an effort to recover another guy who had frozen and failed to meet the required standard.

Week four, or Test Week Two, took place in south Wales, on the Black Mountains and the Brecon Beacons. During this phase I would take part in a series of long, high-speed marches (one of which was across Llangattock Bog in the dark) while carrying a heavy pack and a rifle. Members of staff designated 'hares' would lead these marches, which had to be completed in a set time. We were all very conscious of the fact that, if we finished more than just a few minutes behind the hare, we would fail that event and probably the whole course as long, high-speed arduous marches were the bread and butter of the Airborne.

The last march of the week would take us from the top of Talybont Reservoir, down into the forestry blocks on the valley floor, up the old Roman road, around the front of Cribyn (a large, cone-shaped mountain) and onto the top of Pen y Fan (pronounced 'penny fan') before dropping down 2000 feet to the Cwmgwdi (pronounced 'cum goody') ranges. I remember passing a number of guys on their hands and knees, totally exhausted and close to tears, as I made my way up the steep side of the 'Fan'. I also remember that as I reached the top a member of staff grabbed me and told me to go all the way back down to the bottom and drag one of these flagging men back up to the summit. On reaching the top for the second time, I was then told to make sure my new buddy made it back to Cwmgwdi, and if he failed the march, so would I. This wasn't victimisation: looking after your mates regardless of the personal cost was all part of being an airborne soldier.

The final test was a stretcher race. Here I was expected to work as part of a twelve-man relay team, and take my turn to carry a 170lb stretcher over a nine-mile course which ran from the Cwmgwdi Ranges to the Storey Arms. The Storey Arms had once been a pub, but was at that time a Youth Hostel. I always wondered just who would have used it when it was a pub as it was set beside the road below the summit of Pen y Fan and so in the middle of nowhere.

Even though this was the final test in what had been a nightmare of a four-week course, once again no quarter was given. As the test progressed a number of our team fell by the wayside, broken and too tired to carry on. They would now fail the whole course. What a waste. However, it also left only four of us to carry the stretcher the last three miles uphill to the finish, but even though you were short-handed and totally fucked – there's no other word for it – the staff would not allow you to drop the pace.

Of the 127 officers and men who started my course, only around thirty of us managed to pass, go on to earn our 'wings' and join our units as airborne soldiers. I obviously made an impression on someone as, shortly after passing, I was posted back to the Para Depot at Aldershot as a P Company instructor. I was the first person to achieve this and, as far as I am aware, the only one ever to do so, even though at the time I wasn't even parachute-trained.

On arriving back at the Depot my first task was to complete and pass my Basic Parachuting Course at RAF Abingdon, and earn my wings. This was a high priority for me as, until I had them, I would be referred to as a 'penguin'– a bird that had no wings and therefore couldn't fly – and, of course, that was all the more embarrassing as I was now also an instructor.

I spent the next four weeks at RAF Abingdon while completing the eight jumps I required to earn my wings. After more than a week's intensive ground training, in which I learned how to perform para rolls, or parachute landings, from a huge number of swinging contraptions that would throw me repeatedly to the floor at all manner of speeds and from a number of different directions, it was time for my first jump.

The first jump is always done from a balloon, as it provides both the instructor and jumpers with the closest thing you can get to a controlled environment. The balloon itself resembled a Second World War barrage balloon and had a large wooden box, known as a 'basket' or 'cage', suspended below it. This is capable of carrying five men: four jumpers and a PJI (parachute jump instructor). It's open at one end – well, apart from a very flimsy safety bar – and the whole contraption is tethered by a strong steel cable to a winch truck.

As a newly promoted Airborne SNCO (senior non-commissioned officer) I would now be expected to lead from the front. Yes, you got it. I would be the first one of the entire course to jump.

Your first balloon jump is a very strange experience. You stand in the basket looking at the faces of all those around you. Nobody looks over the side on their first jump: it's too bloody scary. Once everybody's in, the winch truck begins to slowly pay out the cable that tethers the balloon to the ground. As the balloon begins to climb higher you become aware of the noise of the wind and the breathing of all those in the basket. But, apart from these faint noises, your world is now totally silent. As you progress even higher the basket begins to swing unnervingly in the wind.

Once at the required height, around 800 feet, you begin to get a grip of your fear, and as you lift your eyes from the wooden floor of the basket you're presented with a fantastic 360-degree view of the countryside below. But these feelings of peace and tranquillity are very short-lived, as it's at this point that the PJI lifts the flimsy bar that stops you from accidentally exiting the cage (like that's ever going to happen) and calls the first man forward to the door.

As I stood there alone in the doorway with the whole world stretched out beneath me, I could hear someone behind praying. But before I had time to turn around and tell him he was wasting his time, the PJI shouted, '*Red on.*'

After weeks of training I instinctively let go of the bars on each side of the doorway and folded my arms across the top of my reserve chute. A split second later the instructor slapped me on the shoulder and yelled, '*Green on. Go.*'

I pushed myself out of the door and into space, to be immediately hit by a feeling of helplessness as I began to tip forward and fell the first 200 feet straight down. It's at this point you struggle to look up and watch as your canopy slowly opens, only to be overcome with fear as it starts to close again; it's what they call breathing. Then as you pass the 600-foot mark, indicated by a small red and white wind sock attached to the steel tether wire, your canopy finally opens and you begin a controlled descent towards the ground.

At this stage I was relatively happy, as my chute was open and I had performed all my drills. But this feeling of happiness began to rapidly disappear as I reached about fifty feet from the ground and experienced the 'ground rush' effect for the very first time. It was then – when the ground seems to race up to meet you – that I realised just how fast I was falling.

Seconds later I hit the ground like a sack of shit. As I lay there on the grass I quickly ran my hands over my body in an effort to make sure all my body parts were where they should be and nothing was broken.

I completed my next seven jumps from a C130 Hercules. Three were 'clean fatigue' (without carrying equipment), although one of them was at night, followed by four equipment jumps where I would jump carrying a container.

After completing our final jump we were all formed up – placed in three ranks – on the DZ (drop zone) and presented with our wings by the chief instructor of 1 PTS (No. 1 Parachute Training School). Later that afternoon I was on my way back to Aldershot.

Owing to some bad weather I'd spent just over four weeks at RAF Abingdon, and as I walked into our house my wife looked at me and said, 'How did it go?'

I smiled and handed her ten sets of Para wings. 'Great, thanks, darling, but I now need a pair of those sown on everything, including my underpants, before work tomorrow.'

Of course I was only joking about the underpants, but I was so chuffed to get my wings I think I would have put them on my pyjamas. Well, I would if I'd worn any.

Armed with my crimson beret and new wings, I soon settled down to begin a three-year posting in Aldershot. Although my time at P Company would be a relatively happy one, it was also incredibly hard work. Each four-week course would see me cover at least 450 miles carrying a 40lb pack, while at the same time trying to get as many young hopefuls through Airborne selection as I could. My daily life would revolve around Aldershot and the Brecon Beacons. As well as giving 100 per cent while performing my daily role, I also had to ensure that I stayed free of injury.

Even if I were injured I couldn't contemplate going sick, unless it was with something close to life-threatening. Anything less than a traumatic amputation of the lower leg would leave you open to an enormous amount of merciless abuse from the rest of the staff. Slacking of any kind, even with a valid excuse, just wouldn't be tolerated.

Although we members of staff were regarded as animals by most, I can honestly say that each of us worked as hard as humanly possible to get as many through P Company and into the Airborne Brigade as we could. And there wasn't one of us that would have dreamed of lowering the standards just to keep the numbers up.

A lot of the soldiers I took through P Company would later prove themselves beyond doubt at the Battle of Goose Green and on Mount Longdon during the Falklands War of 1982. During both these engagements members of the Parachute Regiment were involved in bitter hand-to-hand fighting, and as a result members of the Parachute Regiment were awarded two Victoria Crosses and countless other awards for gallantry.

New Name Same Dog

Action stations,
stand in the door,
red on,
green on, GO.

Like stepping off a hundred and fifty mile an hour train
into the slipstream of the Fat Albert for a forty-second
    ride,
a sky crowded with a thousand men,
there'll be no place to hide.

Chutes billow in the half light,
like giant jellyfish they float on the air,
men hanging helpless beneath them
like small fish caught in their tentacles.

But unlike the fish, most will win their fight,
stuffing their captors into big green bags
to be left on the DZ
for collection later that night.

Casually he dismisses the sound of aircraft approaching,
'That will be the heavy drop
delivering the equipment we need to carry the war to
    the enemy.'
But tonight it sounds different,
closer.
He looks up.

'The stupid bastards,
they're dropping their load right on top of me.'
With no place to run he stands his ground
waiting for something to land.
Alone in the darkness he hears voices

'Dig faster.
No, deeper, you idiot,
before we get hit.'
He turns to see two young Toms
digging a hole for all they're worth,
both of them covered in shit.

'What are you doing?'

The pair look up surprised,
as if they expected to be alone.

'We're digging a hole, sergeant.'

'I can see that, but why?'

'We need a place to hide.'

'Well, wait for something to land and get under it.
That's of course unless you wanna die.'

He drags them from their unfinished grave
just as a pallet lands on top of it with a thump
and without pausing
they scramble back under it.

'Now stay there until it's done.'

As he walks away
he hears one of them say

'That sergeant just saved our lives.'

'Yeah, but he took me through P Company

so he's still a bastard.'

Para Pay

Apart from the guts and tenacity needed to be part of an airborne operation, you also have to deal with the fear that comes from the parachuting or 'delivery phase' as it's called. Airborne troops are what are known as shock troops. Their primary role has always been to shock the enemy into submission, and as a result all airborne missions are high-risk. Airborne troops are not normally assigned to low-risk missions.

As an airborne soldier you were at the time required to complete at least eight jumps per year in order to collect your 'Para pay'. It wasn't a lot – only about £12 a month – but back in the 1970s £12 went a hell of a lot further than it does today. For starters, my wife could get us a week's shopping for close to that. If you were a single soldier it would buy you fifteen pints of beer. There was no need to worry about food as that came from the fairy that lived in the cookhouse.

However, this additional payment should in no way be viewed as a freebie, or some sort of bonus, as nobody likes military parachuting. If you find yourself sitting next to someone that does, then quickly move away. He's an idiot. No, worse than that, he's dangerous. Not even the free-fall guys – those who paid to jump at the weekends for fun – liked military jumping.

Military parachuting is an extremely dangerous environment. Sixty-four guys are crammed into the back of a 'Fat Albert' (C130 Hercules), thirty-two on each side. Each man is wearing a parachute weighing 55lb on his back. He also has a container (a Bergen rucksack, a weapons valise, or both) weighing anything up to 160lb. Once he's stood up and about to be deployed, this container will be hooked on his front. It will be suspended from two quick-release hooks situated just below his reserve chute, giving him an all-up weight of well over 200lb.

This was also not a good time to be part of Support Company, and especially not the mortar platoon. A mortar base plate would weigh 60lb on its own, and then there was the tube and the ammo: the mortar bombs that would be shared out among all the other members of the team.

Parachuting was bad enough if you were a big guy like me, as your chute would struggle with the extra weight and you would hit the ground really hard, but it was really rough on the little guys. Because of their smaller size and lower body weight their chute could take a much larger, heavier container. Although its contents would be shared out once you hit the ground, some of these containers were so big and heavy it would take two or three men to carry them onto the aircraft. Once at action stations (standing) and hooked up, I've seen these poor sods being lifted to the door and then stand there while being supported by the number two and three in the 'stick': a line of parachutists waiting to jump from an aircraft. Then as the green light came on, they would be literally pushed through the door and out into the slipstream.

However, once you're standing up and your container is attached you may be expected to stay in one spot, at action stations, for anything from thirty minutes to an hour while you wait for the RAF to get their act together, the green light comes on and you can finally get out.

But just because you're standing there, laden with kit in a dark, stuffy aircraft full of aviation fuel fumes, it doesn't mean that your body stops functioning; in fact, once the nerves kick in it's quite the opposite. If you're sitting down and need to puke, then the dispatcher will pass you a sick bag. If you need a piss, he will help you work your way through the melee of men and equipment that covers the floor of the aircraft, before helping you to climb up the steep tailgate to where the toilet is situated, on the starboard (right) side of the tailgate.

But there was no door or curtain on this deluxe bathroom, so we all made sure there was never the need for a crap. If you were unfortunate enough to be frantic for a crap – well, normal troops are bad enough, but airborne troops will actually sit and watch you while you die of embarrassment, then cheer when you're done. In this type of environment everyone is a potential target, and anything goes in a desperate attempt to break the tension.

But once you're standing at action stations, well, that's a whole new ball game. If you need a piss, then you just piss where you stand, and hopefully no one will notice. And with any luck your trousers will dry off as you fly down the slip-stream and complete your descent.

But the most unsettling thing is standing there cramped up against one another, wedged in so tight that you can't move, and hear the guy behind you start to retch. He won't even be able to turn his head, so you know if he does puke it's going to hit you square in the neck. If there's sufficient force behind it it will go up into your helmet and may even make it round to your face. But there's nothing you can do: you just have to stand there and take the hit.

With the green light on you will leave the aircraft in a 'sim stick' formation, 'sim' being short for 'simultaneous'. A 'sim twelve', for instance, is twenty-four men, twelve on each side of the aircraft, with one man in the port-side stick leaving from that door, followed by one from the other, starboard stick leaving by the starboard door. The SOP (standard oper-ating procedure) for this method of deployment is a full second between each man in the stick. This means one man and his kit will leave the aircraft every half-second. The first man to exit will be from the port side (the left side as you face the front of the aircraft) then a half-second later one would leave from the starboard side, then back to the port, and so on. In theory it should take you around thirty seconds to empty an entire aircraft, but I've been on jumps where it's been done a hell of a lot quicker than that.

The whole process would be controlled by the RAF dispatcher or the PJI. With the green light on he would slap each man on the back as he took his place at the door, controlling their rate of exit. However, after the first three or four guys have left the aircraft this procedure would normally turn to a bag of shit, as desperate men just pushed their way out of the aircraft as fast as they could. The slower the rate of exit, the more chance there was of the red light coming back on again, as the pilot ran out of DZ.

If that happened the drop would be stopped immediately and you would be forced to hang around while the pilot circled, joined the end of the queue of aircraft and started another run. In an attempt to avoid this, once the dispatcher got rid of the first three or four men he would normally just stand back against the hull of the aircraft and let you go. Any attempt on his part to slow things down could result in him getting pushed out of the door as well.

Although he wore a safety belt known as a strop which anchored him to the bulkhead of the aircraft by means of a ten-foot tether, and wore a lightweight chute, the last thing he wanted was to get pushed out of the door. If that happened he would spend the rest of the drop hung up outside the aircraft, in the slipstream, getting battered between the parachutists jumping out and the hull of the aircraft itself. In such a situation his chances of surviving without sustaining a serious injury were virtually nil.

But the number of men in a sim stick will be totally dependent on the length of the DZ being used. There are very few

DZs in the UK that are long enough to take a full 'sim thirty-two' – under normal conditions this would require approximately 2000 yards. The only times I ever jumped a full sim thirty-two was at Fox Covet, on Salisbury Plain.

As you step through the door and begin your journey down the aircraft's slipstream at close to 200 miles per hour – your chute's rigging lines are dragged from their bag and the last tie (a piece of thread with a 15lb breaking strain) securing your canopy to its bag is broken. The half-inflated canopy then flies over your head and shakes you like a rag doll as it struggles to support the massive weight of you and your container while trying to inflate. The scene that then confronts you is awe-inspiring.

Slightly behind your aircraft and around fifty feet higher are another three C130s spewing out their human cargo. Then another three behind that, fifty feet higher again, dropping even more troops, and so on. The theory is that the oncoming aircraft will fly straight over the chutes of the troops which have already been deployed. The troops they drop will then land at the same place on the DZ as the troops leaving your aircraft. But there comes a time when the ground becomes totally saturated with men and equipment, and it's not long before troops begin to land on one another.

Within minutes there could be well over 1000 men in the air. You will spend the next forty seconds, from 800 feet, the standard height for training drops, trying to avoid countless men who are totally out of control and could drag you to your death as they go to theirs. Being there, under what is in reality an unresponsive parachute canopy (these aren't steerable free-fall canopies: their sole aim is to get you on the ground as quickly as possible), watching aircraft fly over the top of you, delivering hundreds more troops into the air above you, used to frighten the shit out of me. I could only imagine what it would feel like to be an enemy sentry, standing alone in some corner of a deserted airfield, or some other strategic target, during an airborne assault. Standing there, just you, your rifle and a very limited number of rounds, with a cold wind whistling through your clothing (airfields are always windswept) as you realise that you're totally alone and you don't have enough ammunition to kill them all as more and more of these airborne killers fill the sky above you, would scare any man shitless.

Once you were clear of the aircraft, you would check your canopy. If it was fully deployed, you would then perform your 'all round observation drills', and as long as you were clear of everybody else, you would pull your feet back out of the way, flip the quick-release hooks under your reserve and drop your container. It would then fall away and hang at the end of a thirty-foot length of rope that was attached to your parachute harness at your hip by a quick-release strap. This was done in an effort to remove this massive weight from your body and stop you breaking both your legs when you landed, which would have certainly happened if you had tried to land with the container still attached to its hooks.

However, there was always the risk that some idiot, in a state of panic and far too eager to get rid of his container, would not look below him before releasing this huge dead weight, and it would come crashing down on your canopy, collapsing it. Or, instead of the container just hanging there inert beneath him, it would begin to swing on the end of its rope like a pendulum and then get entangled in your rigging lines.

Both of these scenarios would seriously diminish the efficiency of your canopy, which could result in you having an extremely rough ride and a high-speed crash landing. If you were lucky you might only break both legs.

I only saw a tangle like this happen once, but as I was normally preoccupied with my own survival I probably missed a lot more. On that occasion the poor guy whose chute it was, was only about 300 feet from the ground when a container got entangled with his rigging lines and collapsed his canopy. He could do little at this point to save himself. He tried everything to get it reinflated, kicking his legs and shaking his rigging lines, and he even tried to deploy his reserve chute but without success. Unable to help, I just had to hang there and watch as he accelerated into the ground. He was killed instantly. I didn't even want to think about the mess he would have had to deal with if he'd survived the impact.

I count myself lucky that in over eighteen years of parachuting the worst injury I suffered was a few twisted ankles and sore arses, but others weren't that lucky. We would regularly have guys with broken legs, whiplash and other neck injuries, and occasionally even a broken back. I have also been on jumps where good men died, but this is all part of being an airborne soldier.

Being part of an airborne operation has always been a risky business. Even in the early days of such operations, at Arnhem during the Second World War, then at Suez, and still today, the acceptable level of casualties for an airborne operation, either through parachuting accidents during the delivery phase, or from enemy fire during the following battles, was and is close to fifty per cent. It sometimes makes you wonder why men would volunteer for such a role.

But if you were lucky enough to avoid all this, you would then hit the ground like a sack of shit. Not a strictly technical term, but in eighteen years of parachuting I never once had one of what the instructors called a 'side right' or 'side left' landing as taught at the Parachute Training School. But I had loads of what we used to call 'sack of shit' landings.

If the winds were high and you were one of the smaller guys it was at this point you would be thankful that your container weighed as much as it did, as it would add extra drag and maybe even anchor you to the ground while you wrestled to collapse your chute as it tried to drag you across the DZ and off to God knows where.

I think you'll admit it's a very hard way to earn an extra £12 a month, and it's only when this phase is over that the real battle begins.

I always thought it quite ironic that the motto of 1 PTS was 'Knowledge Dispels Fear'. It was obviously thought up by some arse who had never ever jumped.

And I often also thought about how my predecessors must have felt sitting in those old Dakota DC3s on their way to Arnhem. Our modern-day chutes were more reliable than theirs, but we now carry all of our equipment with us when we jump, whereas theirs was either delivered in gliders or dropped in containers. Later in my career I would find out at first hand what it felt like to jump from one of these ancient aircraft, sometimes from as low as 350 feet and into a hot DZ. At one time we were routinely dropped at low altitude into the middle of fire-fights in support of a troop that was heavily outnumbered. But that was one for the future.

Manna from Heaven

Now the good news was that there were a number of ways in which you could complete your eight jumps per year and collect your 'Para pay'. Yes, you could go through the torture of what's just been explained. Or you could do a 'clean fatigue' descent, at somewhere like Hankley Common, a small DZ on the south side of the ridge known as the Hog's Back, between Aldershot and Farnham. You would still jump as part of a 'sim six or eight' but normally without equipment, so no container. Or you could get three or four jumps done in a single day by doing balloon descents on Queens Avenue, a large area of parkland behind the Para Depot in Aldershot. Mothers would regularly bring down their kids, and then, armed with a bag full of sandwiches and pop, they would spend the whole afternoon watching us idiots throw ourselves into the air like lemmings.

However, this was a much slower process. It involved just four jumpers and the PJI in a basket that was suspended from a tethered barrage balloon, jumping one at a time. But again it was clean fatigue, because without a slipstream you automatically dropped 200 feet straight down before your chute even began to open and slow your descent.

But the preferred option for most – and especially for us senior ranks, as I was now a sergeant – was to take the whole day off work and pitch up at the Parachute Training School, which was then at RAF Abingdon but later moved to RAF Brize Norton. You would then have a really nice lunch in the RAF sergeants' mess – RAF food was always far better than ours – and volunteer to act as a 'drifter' for a basic training course whose participants were jumping at Weston on the Green, a small RAF basic training and free-fall DZ just outside Oxford.

Being a drifter involved jumping on your own from the side door of a C130 and doing absolutely nothing: not trying to control or steer your canopy in any way. This would allow the DZ party (the RAF ground staff) to assess the wind strength and the subsequent drift. The pilot would then make any adjustment needed to ensure that all the novice jumpers would land along the centre of the DZ, and not in the pig farm, or on the railway line which ran down the side of the DZ.

The candidates on these occasions were normally Parachute Regiment recruits or 'All Arms' candidates who had recently passed P Company and were now on their basic parachute course. Trying to earn their wings.

As trained airborne troops we were basically gods to these guys. I had taken most of them through P Company only weeks before. Sat there in the aircraft they would search your face for any sign of fear. Most of them were crapping themselves, especially if it was their first aircraft jump. It only took one of them to refuse to jump and you would get a chain reaction that would knock on all the way through the aircraft. If you did get a refusal in the door, or even a hesitation, the dispatcher would drag the offender out of the stick and throw him without pity back to the tailgate. He would then rush the others out of the door as fast as he could in an attempt to stop the rot from spreading.

As soon as the drop had been completed, the guy who had refused would be flown straight back to camp. His kit would be packed, and his bed space cleared before anybody else retuned to barracks. He would never be seen again.

On this particular day Bob and I were acting as drifters for a basic course whose intake were making their very first aircraft descent. The aircraft was – as it normally is – dimly lit by a sort of orange-red glow. The doors were tightly shut in preparation for take-off, and as a result it was becoming increasingly stuffy, as aviation fuel fumes rapidly filled the fuselage, adding to the feelings of nausea.

Bob and I took our seats at the tailgate end, in the central row of red web seats. We were facing the port door and started to chat. We had just started to taxi when Bob tugged on the left leg of the dispatcher as he walked past us on his way back towards the port door. He then pointed at the sick bags which were tucked behind the hydraulic pipes which ran the full length of the fuselage. The news of Bob, an experienced para-chutist, asking for a sick bag before we'd even taken off, spread like wildfire throughout the aircraft and all eyes were now on us. Bob sat in what looked like deep thought for a moment or two, then shook his head and tucked the bag into his smock. We carried on chatting for a few minutes, while taking sly glances around the aircraft.

All eyes were still firmly fixed on the two of us. They were obviously all waiting for the re-emergence of the dreaded sick bag. After about thirty minutes of flying the red light flashed on and off, and the dispatcher held up both his open hands, signal-ling we had ten minutes to drop. You could feel the tension in the aircraft rise as he cracked the door and slid it up in prepara-tion for the drop, giving us a perfect view of the Oxfordshire countryside as we rolled over it at around 1000 feet.

At this point Bob removed the sick bag from his smock and began to retch violently. He then brought the open bag up to his mouth and began to puke into it, while I patted him sym-pathetically on the back. All through the aircraft elbows were being dug into ribs.

'Look, he's puking.'

When Bob was sure he had everybody's attention he removed the bag from his mouth and looked into it, gently shaking it while examining the contents. He then dug me in the ribs and offered me a look. I looked into the bag, then put my hand in and pulled out a large piece of the contents. I put the piece into my mouth and began to chew it, while at the same time nodding my head in approval.

What nobody else knew was that earlier, before getting on the aircraft, Bob had got hold of a sick bag, broken up some dry biscuits from an army ration pack and placed the pieces in the bag. He had then placed the sick bag in his smock. Later, when he had asked the dispatcher for a bag, he had simply swapped it with the biscuit-filled one already in his smock.

The sight of me chewing on what they believed was a large piece of Bob's regurgitated lunch was more than these poor sods could take. And, even above the noise of the aircraft, you could hear them beginning to retch.

The youngster sitting on the opposite row of seats and to the right of me, and who'd had a perfect view of the whole proceedings, was in the final throes of submitting to his feelings of nausea. Then, all of a sudden, a steady stream of vomit left his open mouth under pressure and fell into the lap and all over the legs of the guy sitting opposite him. That was all it needed. Like dominoes they all started to throw up. Within seconds the deck of the aircraft was awash with hot, steaming vomit, which then started to slide up and down on the composite metal deck in sympathy with the roll of the aircraft.

It was at that point that the dispatcher shouted, '*Stand up. Action stations.*'

Bob and I stood, hooked up our static lines to the overhead wire and moved to the door. The dispatcher knew exactly what had happened. 'You pair of bastards can come and clean this mess up when we get back to the airfield.'

I just smiled.

'*Red on Green on. Go.*'

My parting shot as I stepped into the slipstream: 'Yeah, right. In your dreams, mate.'

As we hurled ourselves through the open door and into space, the floor of the aircraft was swimming in puke.

Later, as we lay on the short grass of the DZ, drinking tea while we waited for the bus that would take us back to the airfield and watching the rookies complete their first aircraft jump, you could still see the string of puke flowing down the slipstream like a long, shiny trail of snot. Oh happy days.

Mad Dogs and Paras

Since the beginning of time, drink has always played a big part in military life. Whether it's at a mess dinner, celebrating a promotion, the return from a successful operation, or the loss of a brother soldier, the one thing you can always be sure of is that it will involve copious amounts of alcohol.

Within the military, alcohol is also used by all ranks as a great leveller. Heavy drinking at a mess dinner, or a company or squadron social, will normally lower the barriers created by rank. Subsequently anything that is said or done while under the influence at these events will in most cases be forgiven. If it can't be forgiven, at worst the penalties for any such indiscretion will normally be greatly reduced. In garrison towns such as Aldershot even the local police force have been known to be more sympathetic, and even turn a blind eye, at such times. However, no matter how drunk they are, most soldiers know exactly where the line is, and although they will push up against it, they will normally avoid crossing it at all costs.

That's not to say that all soldiers have a drink problem. Far from it. Most operations, and definitely all Special Forces operations, are termed 'dry', regardless of their duration. Although, once the operation has finished and you're back in the lines, the debriefing is over, and the equipment has been squared away, it's normally straight down town to your favourite pub and the celebrating or commiserating begins.

Some sessions go on for days at a time while you try to drown out the bad events associated with the previous four or six months. But this is also the time when any frustrations or bad feeling come to the surface and old scores need to be set-tled. However, once these issues have been laid to rest there will also always be the inevitable repercussions of alcohol-induced stupidity to deal with and, on such occasions, most of us just accept what we've done was wrong and take our pun-ishment on the chin.

A military funeral will normally bring out both the very best and the very worst in soldiers. During the service and burial, I have seen even the hardest and bravest of men, although in the public eye, reduced to tears as they watch a wooden box, which now contains the empty shell that was once their friend, lowered into the ground.

But once it's over and we're all back behind closed doors and the drink begins to flow freely, those feelings of anger and frustration, those that have been suppressed since the event itself, will begin to emerge. It's then that any blame that can be apportioned will be dropped squarely into the lap of the guilty party. That said, I don't think I've ever seen a soldier openly blamed for the death of another.

I've seen plenty that blame themselves. But, when they can't get their hands around the throat of some arsehole – normally a politician or very senior officer who richly deserves it – sol-diers will strike out at the nearest target – normally their greatest friend – and the fists will start to fly in an attempt to ease the anger and frustration. This is also the time when most of us will try to shed the enormous burden of guilt which comes from having been there but surviving when a close friend has been lost on an operation. Shedding the guilt that comes when a brother soldier is killed in combat is not like getting over a bad hangover. It can't be sorted out with another drink, a few pills or a good night's sleep. It's something that will stay with you for the rest of your life, day in, day out, and in a lot of cases most of your nights as well.

While having a drink is part of most serving soldiers' lives, it's normally when we leave the military that drink takes on its truly demonic shape. It's then that the ritual of getting drunk with our mates, drinking to celebrate or commiserate, loses its primary purpose, and, if not confronted, it can become a dark and lonely habit.

The following story tells of an event which took place in Aldershot in the late seventies following a particularly bloody tour in Northern Ireland.

My head's banging and, as my eyes slowly open, I am temporally blinded by the light from an unshaded fluorescent tube. My back is stiff and I'm cold, the result of spending the night lying on a rock-hard bed without a pillow or blanket. There are no windows in the room and the walls are covered with shiny grey gloss paint. Shit, I'm in a cell. I must have had a skinful last night.

I can hear the heavy door opening, followed by footsteps as whoever it is walks slowly across the uncarpeted floor. Darkness creeps over me as a faceless dark blue uniform with three silver stripes on the arm blocks out the light. It's a civilian police custody sergeant. Bugger, I think, I'll need to come up with something quickly if I'm going to get out of this one.

So, tilting my head slowly to one side, I smile shyly and in my best wounded toddler voice say, 'You're not my mummy.'

Far from defusing the situation, my comment just seems to enrage the sergeant. His face quickly reddens as his blood pressure rises, and he covers me in spit as he shouts at the top of his voice, '*I'm not your fucking mummy!*'

Grabbing me by the collar, he drags me from my bed and pushes me roughly across the floor. Then, without loosening his grip, he bounces me first off the walls, then against the door frame, before finally pushing me unceremoniously out into the custody suite. As I hit the counter I collide with Bill, who's arriving from the cell next door. The Glaswegian, who's as wide as he is tall and never knows when to shut up, suddenly bursts into that old Glasgow Saturday night favourite, 'What's the charge, officer?'

The sergeant's face is now turning dark with rage and he roars, '"*What's the fucking charge, officer?*"'

I resist the urge to remark on how impressed I am to find that the sergeant also knows the words to this much-loved Scottish hymn.

Without taking a breath he then starts to tell us his side of the story, which is handy as both Bill and I have no idea what the fuck has happened.

'At two o'clock this morning you and your mate here were on all fours, crawling up Middle Hill, barking like dogs.'

Bill misreads the sergeant's softening tone as a sign of weakness and replies with an arrogant 'And?'

At this, the sergeant's voice quickly rises again, 'And one of my officers, out of the goodness of his heart, stopped to give you two idiots a lift back to the Lines.'

Bill thinks he can now smell a victory, and retorts, 'And he should be commended for his kindness and generosity. But I still don't see what the problem is.'

The sergeant composes himself and takes a deep breath. 'The problem is, dickhead, that as he was patting you on the head telling you what a good boy you were, your Rottweiler mate here bit him on the leg.'

'Dickhead, *moi*?' A guy with a broad Glaswegian accent trying to act sophisticated and talk French at the same time pushes me over the edge and I burst out laughing as Bill continues, 'Well, you can hardly blame us for that. Did his mum never tell him not to approach strange dogs?'

The sergeant's face gets blacker by the second and I think to myself that this is not going to end well. The sergeant is either going to have a heart attack and we'll get done for manslaughter, or he'll just throw away the key and we'll never be seen again. So I stamp on Bill's foot, the pain taking him straight to the floor.

Now on one knee and clutching his injured foot, Bill looks at me with a tear in his eye and says, 'What the fuck was that for?'

'If you don't shut up we'll never get out of here.'

As we start to rise slowly above the desk, like a couple of 'Whatnots' – the cartoon character we all drew at school where you see the top of the man's head, just the nose and the eyes, and a hand on each side, as he peers over a wall – the sergeant's face slowly returns to its normal colour, now with just a hint of rage. The bad news is that he's scribbling furiously and his report has already progressed to a third page.

Time to intervene, to try to save the situation. 'Sergeant, if we promise to be good and not to get into any more trouble – well, not for a week or two anyway – do you think you could see your way to letting us off, with a really good bollocking, of course?'

Bill just can't resist it any longer, and before the sergeant can answer, blurts out, 'And maybe you could throw in a handful of Bob Martin's [dog biscuits] and a big bowl of water? We missed breakfast this morning.'

Tonight's Target

The first pint tonight will go a long way
to cooling you down at the end of a long hot day,
start a conversation with a total stranger,
piss the wife off,
even raise her to anger.

The second pint is easier to swallow.
It will take you that little bit further,
make stupid orders easier to follow.

One more and you're well on your way
to another forgotten night
followed by another painful day.

The fourth pint is easier to sink.
It's the point where old scores will need to be settled,
helps you tell others what you really think.
Just one more and you're about to cross that line,
that line where nothing really matters,
where you'll drink anything that's going,
except the posy wine.

Six pints or maybe even more
and your target's finally reached.
Just getting here has deadened the pain,
softened the loss,
hidden the guilt and anger,
well at least until you're sober again.

The stupor,
the one which now engulfs your body,
will eventually provide that much-needed sleep,
the one where you'll lay
comatose on the NAAFI floor
until dawn the next day.

Fighting for Food

It was Tuesday morning on week two of the All Arms Pre-Parachute Selection Course. That meant that we started the day with a six-mile run in 'belt order': OG (olive green and lightweight) trousers, boots, T-shirt, web belt with a full water bottle weighing about 5lb. It wasn't the traditional long, hard P Company run; it was designed purely as a loosener following the hard tab (the Airborne Brigade's term for a forced march) of the previous afternoon.

The route this morning would take us first along the towpath beside the Basingstoke Canal, past the now derelict Malta Barracks, across the Fleet Road and up to the top of Miles Hill. Here the front runners would get a short rest, although they would spend it doing press-ups and sit-ups while they waited for those who were lagging behind to catch up.

Once all of us on the course were together again we would head off down the steep, sandy sides of the hill, before making our way across the sand and mud of Long Valley. This whole area was like something from the land time forgot. Even during the very hot and drought-ridden summer of 1976 you could still find more mud here than was healthy. The only thing missing was the dinosaurs. We wouldn't stop again until we reached the Trainasium area situated behind the Rushmore Arena.

Although the run was short – a maximum of seven miles – it was still fairly hard, and, by the time we had reached the floor of Long Valley and started making our way across its three miles of sand, mud and two-foot-deep tank tracks, we would be strung out again. By this stage the air would be thick with shouting and swearing as members of staff tried to encourage the Airborne hopefuls to pick up the pace and join the main body up ahead.

Few of them understood that, although it's hard to stay at the front, it totally defeats the object to lower your pace in order to get a short breather, as you then have to work twice as hard to catch up again.

The other problem was that, by this point in the proceedings, the daunting sight of Flagstaff Hill had loomed into view. Flagstaff Hill is the highest point in the Aldershot area and it dominates Long Valley. Around 700 feet high, it has a large white flagstaff on top which used to fly a red warning flag when the old Church Crookham Road rifle ranges were in use. It is covered in grass and rough gorse and criss-crossed by a network of rough sand and stone paths cut out by countless troops running up and down it over the years.

The prospect of having to climb it yet again, while pursued by a pack of rabid dogs (the P Company staff) snapping at their heels, was often more than some of the runners could handle. The weak would begin to fall by the wayside, like olive green dominoes.

Eventually we reached the Trainasium area and, in an effort to slow down the greyhounds at the front, while allowing the stragglers to catch up, on their arrival we would make the front runners climb to the top of the sixty-foot 'death slide tower', cross the wooden platform on the top and then scramble down the other side using only the corner scaffolding poles. This was just another test of a man's confidence and his will to win, as one false move or a lapse in concentration would put you in free fall. If you managed to survive the landing you were certainly on your way to hospital.

I was standing on the far side of the tower, shouting and screaming at those who had just completed the climb and descent phase and were now doing countless press-ups, when Sammy, a short Irishman, calmly grabbed my elbow. In a quiet Celtic lilt he said, 'Come here, mate.' As he pulled me firmly to one side, a body hit the ground right where I'd been standing only moments earlier. Automatic pilot kicked in and without taking a breath I shouted, 'Where the fuck did you come from?'

The poor lad was lying flat on his back and was so winded he couldn't say anything, so he just pointed at the top of the tower.

Sammy burst out laughing. '"Where the fuck did you come from?" Where the fuck do you think he came from?'

The medic, who had seen the whole incident, ran over. I undid the injured lad's belt, which carried his water bottle, and slid it from underneath him. He had hit the ground with such force that he had flattened the metal bottle and, although the top was still tightly screwed on, the bottle itself had split down both sides as the weight of his falling body had forced the water out.

With the medic's help we splinted his whole body and moved him onto a stretcher, before loading him into the back of a Land Rover ambulance in preparation for his short trip to the Cambridge Military Hospital in Aldershot. As we were about to close the ambulance doors, the sergeant major, another mad Irishman, pushed to the front and yelled at him, 'You guys will do anything to get off a tab.'

I couldn't believe that the lad actually said, 'Sorry, sir.'

We found out later that day that he had cracked his spine in five places. Although he returned to full fitness and to his unit, and stayed in the army, he didn't come back to try again.

With the first part of the morning over, we got ourselves cleaned up and headed over to the sergeants' mess for NAAFI break, a well-earned cup of tea and slice of toast. The Airborne Brigade had always had a fearsome reputation among the rest of the 'green' army. We were classed as 'animals', a reputation that had been hard earned by our forefathers in operations such as Market Garden, the airborne assault on Arnhem back in 1944, in the last year of the Second World War.

The Airborne were renowned for being the first into a fray, fighting like demons, and then being the very last out. Individuals who were so determined to win through that they would die trying to achieve the goals they had been set, or face anything rather than give up.

Most of the regular green army, or 'crap hats' as we called them because they didn't wear the coveted crimson beret of the Airborne Brigade (the Military Police, or 'monkeys', wore red berets), would avoid the Airborne at all costs. Our reputation was such that if we couldn't find anybody else to fight with, then we would fight among ourselves. But getting stuck into a few crap hats, especially if you were outnumbered, was a much more attractive prospect. Like I said, the Airborne have always been the pit bulls of the army.

However, this reputation was taken to yet another level when it came to the P Company staff. We were considered to be even bigger animals by the rest of the Brigade. Dressed in our distinctive dark blue tracksuit tops – which carried our rank and of course our Para wings on the right sleeve – our OG trousers and crimson berets, we were easy to spot and avoid.

But while we were viewed as supermen by some, we were also treated as pariahs by most members of the Brigade, and referred to as the 'P Company animals'. Those who had made their lives hell for four weeks. Even in our own sergeants' mess we would sit on our own at NAAFI breaks and mess dinners, although we were always given a great deal of respect by those around us.

It was now 1977. I was twenty-five and had already been a sergeant for two years. By now I had a wife and small son, but still nowhere near enough money coming in to support them. This wasn't because I drank it away. In fact I very rarely had a drink. It also wasn't because I wasted it on stupid things that weren't needed. It was purely a consequence of low wages. I had to find a way to overcome this problem and provide my wife and son with the food and clothing they needed.

The answer was simple: I would have to find a second job. The only problem was, I still had to carry out my normal day-to-day duties. This meant that any second job I managed to find would need to be done once normal working hours were over. Mind you, given the enormous amount of energy I expended every day, I didn't know how I would also manage to work most of the night as well. Yet I had to do something to ease our situation.

I wasn't on my own, though; we were all in the same boat. Even the sergeant major, who was two ranks above me, was struggling, and nothing has really changed over the years. Even today young soldiers struggle with money, many of them living in sub-standard accommodation, fighting desperately just to keep their young families above the poverty line, while spending months away from home, fighting wars.

Most of us had sacrificed our summer leave to chip the old cement off bricks for a penny a brick when they were pulling down the nineteenth-century cavalry barracks on the Farnham Road. This was hard physical work and after a day or two your hands would be cut to ribbons, but it would earn you a few badly needed extra quid every day, so you just had to grin and bear it. However, leave was now over and, as the demolition phase had also finished, the work had dried up and our second job choices were now limited. It would have to be perhaps bar work, or stacking shelves overnight in one of the new-fangled supermarkets.

As a consequence of these problems, once the post-mortem of that morning's run had been completed, all the talk at the morning's NAAFI break revolved around the fact that we were all struggling to find that extra couple of quid.

One time Tommy had just put a fresh pot of tea down on the table when Pete appeared. 'Hello, lads, listen to this. You know my mate Glynn, the one who owns the car dealership in North Camp. Well, him and his partner Tony have just taken over a nightclub in Farnham.'

Sean, the sergeant major, who was not the most patient man in the world, just rolled his eyes and said, 'Pete, are you not listening? We don't have enough money for food, let alone enough to go clubbing.'

'No. I know that, Sean, but he has a problem with a group of locals and wants to know if I can find half a dozen guys to resolve it for him.'

Tommy, being Irish, and always game for a fight, then piped up, 'What's he paying?'

Pete smiled. 'Well, it will mean that we will have to work on the door every night that the club's open. We will need to be there from seven-thirty until two-thirty, but he's willing to pay us £8 a night each.'

Back then, £8 a night, cash in hand, working on the 'if you don't tell the tax man then neither will I' basis, would put food on the table and clothes on our children's backs. I smiled back at Pete. 'I'd fight the Devil himself for eight quid a night.'

Even if it was only three nights' work a week, that money would make a huge difference to all our families' way of life, so I was definitely up for it.

'So what's the score, Pete? What do we have to do to get in on this?'

Pete smiled again, then said, 'I take it we're all in then?'

Everybody nodded their head, and Pete said, 'Right, meet me tonight outside the Pegasus at 1900 hours.' The Pegasus was a pub the P Company staff used.

Frank spoke up, 'What's the dress, Pete?'

'A plain shirt, preferably white, smart trousers and a bow tie, and shoes – no "desert wellies" [tan suede desert boots worn by most of the Airborne Brigade when off duty].'

We all looked blankly at each other, then one man said, 'Where the fuck are we going to get bow ties?'

Pete had anticipated this question. 'Er, you all have mess kits, don't you?'

We'd all forgotten that our mess kit, the military equivalent of a dinner suit, came with a bow tie. I spent that afternoon, like most of the others, pounding the tank tracks on Long Valley in full kit, trying to convince the weak and needy that they really had to raise their game and try harder if they were ever going to make the grade and join the airborne brotherhood. Of course it wasn't put quite as politely as that, but you get the drift.

At seven that evening the four of us were stood outside the Pegasus, opposite the park in Aldershot, waiting for Pete, who, as usual, turned up five minutes late. As he walked towards us his face dropped. 'Where are the bow ties, boys?'

Frank just looked at him in disgust. He couldn't believe that he'd even asked such a stupid question. 'Do you really think that we're going to stand around in the middle of Aldershot in a bow tie? Do we look that stupid?'

With that we all piled into two cars and headed for the centre of Farnham, about six miles away.

We arrived at the club at around seven-thirty, parked and made our way over to the front door. In fact it was more of a side door, consisting of large double doors at the top of three steps that ran off a wide alleyway between the club and the building next door. A brand-new sign on the front of the building read 'Mr Kip's'. As we reached the doors Pete pushed his way to the front. 'Let me do all the talking, lads. I know these guys.'

'Fucking hell, Pete, it's not rocket science,' said Frank. 'They're not looking for diplomats. They only want some heads breaking.'

We all stood just inside the doors while Pete went and found the two bosses. The entrance area was about twenty feet long and six feet wide, with a cloakroom counter on the right side just as you entered. On the left there was another counter, six feet long, which ran partway along an outside wall. Stretching out from the right-hand edge of the cloakroom there was a three-foot-high barrier which extended about fifteen feet into the club proper.

The club comprised two fairly large areas which melted into each other in a sort of twisted figure of eight. The bigger of the two contained a long bar which ran along one side of a large dance floor. On the other side of the dance floor there was a small seating area with tables and chairs. Tucked away around a corner there was another, smaller bar, which served an area that was laid out as a type of lounge with seating for around thirty to forty people. The club could hold around 250–300 on a good night.

We had been standing there for about five minutes and, as I looked around at the others, I had to smile to myself. Everybody was doing the same thing: surveying the surroundings and working out a suitable strategy. One that would allow us to contain the problem at the door, while at the same time enabling us to get stuck in.

It was then that Pete returned with the two bosses, Glynn and Tony. Talk about being typecast: you couldn't find two guys that looked more like second-hand car salesmen if you tried. They both looked like a cross between Frank Butcher and Arthur Daley, a sort of educated-looking Laurel and Hardy. We introduced ourselves and then Glynn, who seemed to be the boss, filled us in on the problem.

They had recently bought, refurbished and then refurnished the club. It had always been a nightclub and, although they didn't know it at the time, they had also bought the trouble that came with it. Aggro was pretty much part of the 'fixtures and fittings'. While the place had always been a bit of a rough house, the main problem now was that the local rugby club had moved in.

They normally drank at the Lamb, a pub about a mile away in the centre of town. But once the landlord called last orders, they would all head straight over to the club. They would force their way in, giving the door staff a good hiding, then help themselves to drinks and manhandle the female staff. This had been going on for about six weeks now. In fact ever since Glynn and Tony had taken over. They had tried talking to them without any success. Now it was our turn. Although there wasn't going to be a lot of talking done.

Glynn went to great lengths to explain that they had spent a lot of money getting the premises up to scratch and turned into the type of place where people would want to spend the night with their friends. He finished by stressing the point that they didn't want all the furniture broken either. He then asked us if we would like a drink. But, before anyone could answer, Sean shouted up, 'Yes, thanks, Glynn. Five coffees would be really great.'

While Glynn appeared a little surprised, as he was obviously expecting all of us to have a beer, Pete looked like he was going to go into anaphylactic shock. But once Glynn and Tony had left to get the drinks, Sean said, 'We need to be professional about this. There will be no drink until we get this problem sorted. Understood?'

Everybody agreed. It didn't matter that we were now all off duty. It also didn't matter that we were all senior ranks either, he was our sergeant major. He was a lot older and more experienced than most of us, so whatever he said went.

It was now about eight-thirty and the first punters would start arriving around nine, although the numbers had dropped off drastically since the lot from the Lamb had started performing.

Once Glynn and Tony had brought the coffees, they disappeared into the club and left us to it. We had been stood there drinking our coffee for about five minutes when Sean said, 'If we only opened one side of the door, how many guys do you think it would take to fill it?'

The overall opinion was probably two, three at a push, but no more. I could see where this was going; Sean was going to employ the Spartan approach. In 480 BC 300 Spartans had denied passage to over 200,000 Persians by blocking off a narrow pass at Thermopylae, forcing them to fight on a front that was only fifty feet wide. By doing this they had reduced the odds from over 600-1 to 1-1.

If we could keep one of the double doors closed, we would also reduce the odds, from four or five to one down to 1-1. It didn't matter how many of them there were outside; the maximum number that could get involved in the fighting at any one time would be limited by the size of the entrance to around two, or three at the most.

Sean was the first to speak again. 'Right. We need to keep this in the entrance area. That way we can contain it. If it spreads into the main club area we've lost. It will just turn into a running battle that will also involve the punters and we'll end up wrecking the place before we can get them out. So, this is what we're going to do. Theo, you and Tommy take the point.'

Pete, who was always eager to get his name on the team sheet, butted in. 'Why not let me take the lead, Sean?'

'Because Theo and Tommy are both boxers. They're used to keeping their punches short and fighting at close quarters. That doorway is quite tight.'

Pete wasn't going to give up. 'Well, why don't we just take it outside, into the alley?'

Sean was now getting aggravated. 'For two reasons. Firstly,

we're going to be outnumbered by at least three or four to one. Fighting a holding action in the doorway means we reduce the odds. Secondly, once it moves out of the club and into the street the police are obliged to get involved. If we can keep it in here, it's none of their bloody business. Any of them that manage to get past Theo and Tommy will be taken out by Frank, Pete and me. Any questions?'

Of course there weren't any. It was a good plan. We'd all been in such situations many times before when involved in riots in Northern Ireland. The only difference this time was that there would be no bricks, petrol bombs or the threat of instant death from a sniper.

We spent the next hour or so introducing ourselves to the bar staff and making sure that the half of the door that was to remain closed would stand up to the battering it might have to take as those that weren't involved in the hand-to-hand fighting struggled to get in.

Tony agreed to stand at the rear of the entrance area and give us the nod regarding those who shouldn't be allowed in, although he made it very clear he didn't want to get involved in any of the physical stuff.

That suited us. The last thing we needed was a civvie who had the physical attributes of a ten-stone rent boy getting in our way. We would have our work cut out looking after ourselves, let alone him as well.

It was just after ten-thirty that the first of the bunch from the Lamb arrived. Sean stood at the open door, with Tommy and I standing slightly behind him, as the first four of them came up the steps.

I turned and looked at Tony, who nodded. I then leant in towards Sean and whispered, 'Game on.'

Sean raised one hand like a copper on point duty and, in his quiet Irish voice, said, 'Sorry, lads. It's members only tonight and as you're not members you can't come in.'

One of them retorted, 'How do you know we're not members?'

Sean just smiled. 'Because we don't have any yet.'

'And I suppose you're going to keep us out. The last lot tried that, we sorted them. What makes you think you're going to do any better?'

'Because fighting is what we do for a living.'

With that, in one smooth movement, Sean stepped back between Tommy and me, and we moved forward to fill the space.

The guys from the Lamb had their one and only chance to leave quietly and now it was time for our hands to do the talking. As we moved forward my hands were already coming up, my feet were shoulders' width apart and my knees were slightly bent, giving me a well-balanced platform from which to launch my attack.

As one of them tried to push his way past us, I unleashed a short left hook to his unprotected chin. My fist couldn't have moved more than eight inches. But, as it had travelled up from my boots, the punch had all my weight behind it, and when it connected with his open mouth I heard a snap. My first blow had broken his jaw. His legs gave way and, as he started to fall, Tommy reached over his crumpling body and hit the guy behind him square in the face with a straight right, knocking him back into the guy standing directly behind, and the two of them fell backwards down the stairs.

Within moments the stairwell was full of bodies. A mixture of those fighting, those trying to get in, and those who had already failed and been knocked down.

Sean's plan was working perfectly. Tommy and I were holding our own at the door, although Pete, who didn't want to be left out, was stood behind us constantly saying, 'If you need a break, guys, just shout. I'm ready to take over.'

We stood our ground and exchanged punches with them

for over thirty minutes, after which they carried away their wounded and it all went quiet. Not one of them had managed to get over the threshold and surprisingly, apart from a small mouse (the boxing term for a swelling) under my right eye, Tommy and I were unmarked.

Tony was over the moon. 'Well done, guys. That's the first time we've been able to keep them out in six weeks.'

I thought to myself, what's with the 'we'?

We had a stand-up battle every night the club was open for the next five weeks. At the end we had a large collection of knives, rounders and baseball bats and iron bars, which the muppets had left behind them. We had also built up a fearsome reputation as a no-nonsense team, and the club was turning into the type of place where people could come for a good, trouble-free night out, a rarity in those days.

The P Company team worked the door at Mr Kip's for over three years. As one member of staff was posted elsewhere, his replacement automatically took over.

I personally worked there for just over two years, but it took a terrible toll on both my body and my relationship with my wife and small son, as I saw so little of them. I would start work at P Company at seven-thirty each morning. I would then spend my day running and tabbing over Long Valley and the hills around Aldershot. At five I would go home and have my dinner. I would then be at Mr Kip's from seven until two-thirty the next morning, before coming home and grabbing three hours' shut-eye, then going back to work at seven-thirty.

But that's what being a husband and father is all about. You work as hard as you need to, to ensure that your family gets everything they need, whatever the personal cost. It was also good training for my next job working with Special Forces.

With or Without?

Bollocks are funny things.
They come in many sizes
but they're nearly always round.
The other strange thing is
that sometimes they come with a dog
and sometimes they don't,
but they never ever make a sound.

When they come with a dog it's a good thing.

like 'the dog's bollocks' of a

car
suit
haircut
or even an arse.

When they come without the dog, it's bad,

like hitting your thumb with a hammer.
'Bollocks, that hurt.'

Or, backup won't get here for thirty minutes!
'Bollocks, we'll all be dead by then.'

Other statements like

We've run out of beer money
He hasn't turned up
You've missed dinner

You're parachuting tomorrow
or
You've been dumped

will all elicit a simple 'Bollocks' (without the dog).

So, as you can see,
if your bollocks come attached to a dog
you're going to be a hell of a lot happier

than if they don't.

No Second Chances

'You two OK back there in the cheap seats?'

It was Steve, the operation commander. I shifted again as I tried to get a little bit more comfortable: not easy given the cramped conditions in the rear of the beat-up Datsun. I shifted one last time, nearly kicking Tommy in the face with my right boot. 'It's a bit tight back here, and the cabin service in cattle class is shit. How much further is it?'

'About another five minutes, mate.'

'Great. If we have to spend much more time down here, not only will me and Tommy know far too much about each other's anatomy than is healthy, but I'll be good for nothing.'

Tommy and I were lying across the back seat and on the floor of the old Datsun 180 which was being used for the drop-off. Even though it was late, just after one in the morning, we couldn't run the risk of being seen as we were driven through the tiny back streets to our eventual drop-off point. If anybody clocked a car with four occupants coming into the area and then saw it again as it left, but now with only two in it, even at this time of the day word would quickly spread and the operation would be over even before it began.

'About thirty seconds, Theo.'

Steve then turned his attention to the driver. 'Bill, just let the car roll to a stop around the next corner, don't use your brakes. We don't want anybody noticing the glow from the brake lights indicating we've stopped and giving the game away.'

As the car slowed to a halt I pulled down the door handle which had been digging into my head for the last twenty minutes, before pushing the door open and sliding out onto the road. It was now starting to rain. Staying low and shielded from prying eyes by the vehicle, Tommy passed me the two weapons and the Bergen before joining me beside the car. We had practised the car exit procedure a number of times that day and as a result the whole process was over in less than thirty seconds.

Once we were clear of the car we took shelter behind a low wall and waited until it had moved away before starting to head across a patch of waste ground which sat at the back of a row of small terraced houses. There were no street lamps – well, none that were working – but as the rain got heavier you could clearly see it bouncing off the road like bullets dancing as they hit water. Now clear of the open ground we were hidden in the shadows as we made our way into a long, narrow passageway that ran along the backs of the houses. The alleyway was around 150 metres long and its walls now shone black in the moonlight as the heavy rain ran down the old brickwork. As the two of us moved quietly along it I could see the glow of house lights shining over the walls at the end of the back yards.

Tommy and I had worked together on a number of occasions over the years and after fighting our way through a series of tight scrapes, we had formed that unique bond that can only exist between soldiers. We were now alone in an extremely hostile environment, hunting an experienced killer with no immediate backup if it all went wrong. What happened over the coming twenty-four to thirty-six hours could, if it went pear-shaped, test our friendship to its limits.

I had finished my Snipers' course some four months earlier and although I had achieved a high grade and been practising regularly, I still had a lot to learn. If we managed to find the mark (the enemy sniper) it would be the first time I had fired my L42A1 rifle in anger.

After the adoption of the 7.62x51mm ('7.62 Long') round as the NATO standard rifle round in the 1950s, the round which was now used in our SLR (Self Loading Rifle), the British RSAF (Royal Small Arms Factory) at Enfield Lock had developed a conversion for a number of the surplus Second World War .303-calibre British Lee-Enfield SMLE No. 4 rifles. The conversion included a new heavier floating barrel, which had been chambered to take the now standard-issue 7.62 Long NATO ammunition. It also had a shortened fore-end and hand guard. Later, with the addition of the No. 32 scope mounted on a bracket to the left side of the receiver, it had become known as the L42A1 Sniper Rifle.

The mechanism was the old-fashioned 'manual rotating bolt' action, which meant you had to lift the curved cocking lever that sat flush on the weapon and pull it back. This would eject the empty cartridge case that had been fired earlier from the chamber. Then, as you slid it forward again, it would pick up the next round from the top of the ten-round box magazine and feed it into the chamber. You would then lock the cocking handle back into place and the rifle was ready to fire again. As every single round had to be individually loaded into the chamber, the weapon was a lot slower to load than our modern SLRs but its punching power and accuracy at anything from 400 to 800 metres more than made up for this inconvenience. It must be said, though, that the limitations on the rifle's maximum effective range had more to do with the efficiency of the No. 32 scope than the rifle itself.

The whole rig – rifle, sight and a full magazine of ten rounds – weighed just over 5kg, a bit over 11lb. Although it was heavy and the conversion was now well over twenty-five years old, it was still the best weapon for the task and as a result it was in use by a number of armies around the world.

Tommy was armed with a standard-issue L1A1 SLR, the British version of the Belgian FN (Fabrique Nationale) rifle. We also both carried a 9mm Browning pistol with two nine-round magazines in a holster attached to our web belt in case we were compromised while in the confines of a building. Under these circumstances the two rifles would prove cumbersome as we would need to act fast and shoot on the move.

Tommy was one of the good guys, even when the odds were stacked heavily against you. You could always count on him to stand his ground and have your back.

We were about halfway along the narrow passageway when Tommy whispered, 'How much further, mate?'

'It's the seventh house along, so one more.'

'Are we sure it's definitely empty?'

'Well, if it's not, someone's in for a nasty surprise.'

Although my answer had been flippant, I had left nothing to chance. The previous day I had borrowed a smock that had been stripped of its rank and joined a regular foot patrol as a Tom in order not to draw attention to myself as I recced the whole area. The location had to be perfect if we were to stand any chance of succeeding in our mission of keeping the target alive while at the same time removing the mark, the ambush predator who had been assigned to kill him.

The house I had chosen and the one we were about to enter was ideal. It was on the same side of the road and about three doors down from the target's house. It had been empty for a few months; the front door and all the ground-floor windows at both the front and back had been sealed with breeze-blocks in an attempt to keep out squatters and thieves who were after building materials. However, the back door had been left unbricked, in case the fire service needed to gain access, I assumed. But it now had a hefty padlock.

Pausing at the back gate, I said, 'This is it, Tommy.'

'About bloody time. I'm pissed wet through and fucking freezing.'

Although it was now easing off, as a result of the heavy rain we were now both soaking wet.

I laughed quietly. 'Just be thankful we're not wearing Yeti suits on this job.'

'Why's that?'

'Because you'd be pissed wet through, fucking freezing and with a soaking wet Yeti suit you'd be about 30lb heavier as well.'

We entered the back yard of the small two-storey house through an old wooden gate, closing it quietly behind us. As we reached the back door of the property Tommy reached into his pocket and pulled out two lengths of thin wire and got to work on the padlock that was now securing the door. Although it was a substantial-looking lump of metal its internal workings were fairly basic. I had made a note of its make and size during my recce the previous day and given this information to Tommy. He was our MoE (methods of entry) specialist and he had spent most of the previous night and earlier today practising on a lock of the same make and model in order to ensure we would have a quick and smooth entry.

While Tommy worked on the lock I was crouched down beside him, covering the back gate with my pistol, and after about three minutes he quietly said, 'We're in, mate.'

Thanks to Tommy's lock-picking skill, getting into the house had been pretty easy, but we now faced another problem. We wouldn't be able to replace the padlock once we had entered the building, leaving a tell-tale sign that it had been entered. Therefore, working on the basis that an empty hasp would draw attention to the fact that a padlock had once been there but had now been removed, Tommy unscrewed the two parts from the door and the frame before we entered the house, closing the door behind us.

Picking up the Bergen, I moved quickly through the small kitchen and into the front room, leaving Tommy to wedge an old plank between the door handle and the stone-slab floor in an effort to stop anyone getting in. With the back door shut and as secure as we could make it, the ground floor was now in complete darkness, so we both stood motionless for a minute to accustom our eyes to this.

The house had been left partly furnished, indicating that those who lived here had left in a hurry. The last thing we wanted to do was bang about, tripping over furniture in the dark and waking up the residents of the houses on either side.

'You OK, Tommy?'

'Yeah. But it's bloody pitch in here.'

It was now just after 0200 hours. 'Right, let's get upstairs,' I said. 'We have a lot to do before the sun comes up. I don't want to be moving about too much once it's light and the locals are moving around.'

We made our way carefully through the front room and up the narrow stairs that led to the first floor. As I reached the top I could see that the bedroom doors on either side of the landing were wide open. The rain had now stopped falling, leaving a crystal-clear sky, and as I moved slowly towards the right-hand door I could see the moonlight streaming in through the curtainless windows, lighting up both rooms.

There were a number of bricked-up houses in the street, but this was the only one where some of the top-floor windows had been broken, probably by the local kids. If Tommy and I wanted to remain invisible to the outside world I wouldn't be able to start opening windows or breaking glass in order to get my shot in. It's little things like a window that's been shut for months suddenly being open that get you noticed.

Like the sitting room downstairs, both bedrooms had been left sparsely furnished. It was the right-hand one of the two rooms that interested me as it faced out onto the street at the front of the house and the pane of glass in the bottom half of the window had already been broken.

'Wait here, Tommy. I need to make sure I can see every-thing from here before we waste time getting set up.'

Tommy didn't say anything, just tapped me on the left shoulder to let me know he understood, and I made my way into the room. As I crossed the bare wooden floorboards they creaked under my weight. In the dead silence of night it sounded to my mind as loud as an elephant walking across a corrugated-iron roof.

The rooms were really quite tiny and within three strides I found myself flat up against the front wall of the building, and I began to slowly slide down it. Now down on one knee at the left side of the window, I looked through the broken glass at the bottom of the frame, across the large area of waste ground and onto the houses that stood on its far side.

The waste ground directly in front of me had a road run-ning along either side of it and had once been the site of a busy outdoor market. It was the type of place where every-body from both sides of the community could come to work and shop together quite happily and in relative safety. How-ever, that was before the civil unrest that had split the nation in half. Once the market had ceased to function properly, it had become deserted and was eventually closed down. As a result the area had now become a sort of ghostly no man's land. Although there were no physical barriers, nothing in the world would entice the members of either of the two commu-nities to venture across it.

I had a good view of the whole area through the window, but the triangular hole through which I would make my shot was very small and down in the bottom-left corner of the frame, so it would limit my field of fire. It would need to be enlarged if I was going to widen my 'arc': the distance my rifle could travel from left to right. I turned to look at the doorway. Tommy was also down on one knee, watching me.

I put my hand on top of my head to signal him to join me

and he started to come over. As he reached me I whispered, 'OK, mate, this is it. We have a complete view of the whole area.'

Tommy raised his head and took a good look through the window. 'Great spot, mate. The recce was obviously well worth the effort.'

'Yeah. The only problem is, the firing aperture is too small. I'll need to make it larger if I'm going to make the shot. However, the glass around the hole is nicely cracked, so with any luck I should be able to remove it without making too much noise. Let's get set up.'

'No probs. Oh and by the way, while you were checking out the five-star accommodation in the front room I checked out the kitchen sink. Not very hygienic. In fact I've had a dump in cleaner toilets, but we do have running water.'

'Great.'

Although we had each brought two water bottles, if we had to stay more than twenty-four hours we would need to replenish our supply.

Tommy rested both weapons against the wall, being extra careful not to knock the sight on my weapon and ruin the zeroing. He then began to unpack the Bergen. Meanwhile I carefully examined the broken window pane. The hole in it close to the left side of the frame had a number of cracks fanning out from it, although the upper half of the glass had been left virtually intact. As I worked out what I was going to do I heard Tommy switch on the radio, and with it turned to 'whisper mode' (so you could talk in a whisper at our end but still be heard normally at the other) I heard him call for a radio check. 'Hello, Zero, this is Alpha Two Two. Radio check. Over.'

'Zero. OK. Over.'

'Alpha Two Two, we are in position. Over.'

'Zero, roger that. Any problems. Over?'

'Alpha Two Two, negative. Out.'

Although I don't wear gloves when I shoot as I like to have direct contact with the trigger and feel the pressure, I always carry a pair to keep my hands warm while waiting for my target to appear, and I removed them from my pocket and slipped them on. Then I started to work one of the cracked shards of glass backwards and forwards so as to loosen it and then remove it from the frame. I had to take out each piece separately and as silently as I could, making sure that none fell out of the window and dropped onto the pavement below and gave the game away.

Ever conscious of the noise, I took close to thirty minutes to clear away all the glass along the bottom edge of the window, leaving an eight-inch-high gap.

With the glass removed, I now had another problem. The remainder of the pane now had nothing to support it. Nothing to stop it slipping down the grooves in the frame and refilling the gap I had so painstakingly cleared. But how to stop it? I couldn't prop anything underneath it as our 'friend' the mark might see it when he did his visual recce at first light.

'Tommy, you got any chewing gum in your pocket?'

Tommy was always chewing gum, which at times infuriated the shit out of me.

'Yeah. Why? Do you want a piece?'

'Yeah, and can you chew a piece as well?'

'Sure.'

Tommy removed two pieces of gum from the packet that had been in the breast pocket of his smock and handed me one. As I unwrapped it and slipped it into my mouth I reminded him that we needed to police (pick up) everything, leaving no trace that we had been here. We sat and chewed on the gum for a few minutes before I held out my hand just below his chin, saying, 'Right. Spit it out.'

'What?'

'Come on, Tom, spit it out. I need it for the window.'

Without any further argument he spat the well-chewed gum into my hand. I began to roll this and then my piece between my palms until each was about the length of half a matchstick. I then pushed a piece into the groove that ran down each side of the window frame, just below the pane of glass. Tommy had been watching me and as I finished he commented, 'Smart arse. It'll go hard and stop the window pane dropping down. Correct?'

'Correct. You're a lot smarter than you look. OK. The next thing I need is a comfortable firing platform. I can't kneel in front of that window supporting the full weight of the rifle for what might be close to an hour.'

Tommy smiled. 'I think I spotted a chest of drawers in the back bedroom earlier. Give us a hand?'

'Sure.'

Keeping low we crossed the room and the narrow landing before entering the room opposite. We then carried the small chest of drawers into the room we were intending to use for the operation and pushed one end of it up against the window to form a rough 'T' shape. Luckily it was slightly lower than the window frame, which would allow me to kneel behind it. I could then rest my elbows on top of it while waiting to take the shot, without exposing any of my body.

I had the best end of the deal here. The mark was going to have to be standing in order to get the downward elevation to his target, who would be stood at his front door on my side of the street, whereas I was going to be shooting horizontally. I picked up my weapon, knelt down behind the chest of drawers and rested my arms on top of it, then looked through the sight. It wasn't ideal, but beggars can't be choosers and it would get the job done.

'Tommy, go around the other side and check the barrel length. We need to make sure the end of it stays well inside the window.'

Going around behind me, staying low and out of the moonlight that was now streaming through the window, Tommy moved to the front wall. 'We probably need to shift you back about six inches to be sure.'

I scratched the top of the chest to mark my firing position. 'OK, great. Does that give you enough room to spot as well?'

'Yeah, I'll manage.'

'No, let's not manage, Tom. Let's get it as best we can. There'll be no second chances here.'

Once we were both happy with the position, I laid my weapon on top of the chest of drawers and joined Tommy at the window. 'How far do you think it is from here to the houses on the other side of the waste ground, Tom?' Tommy had been part of 3 Company's Mortar Platoon for many years, and so he had a nose when it came to working out the range to a target, to within a couple of feet.

'About 200 metres in a straight line. No more.'

'Yeah, that's what I thought.'

He was also very cool under fire, which was a must when working as a spotter for a sniper. It's not everybody's cup of tea. Most soldiers feel very vulnerable with only a pair of binos in their hands when being shot at, but not Tommy: he was rock steady under fire. He now crouched down, looking through the aperture that I'd made earlier.

'There's an awful lot of houses over there, mate, and a lot more windows. Do we have any idea where the mark's likely to be shooting from?'

I joined him at the window. 'Can you see the red door, slightly right of twelve o'clock, near enough opposite to where we are now?'

Tommy strained his eyes in the dark. 'Yeah.'

'Well, that's practically in line with the target's house. His front door opens inwards and from the left to right when he's standing inside. He's been aware of the threat for a while now, so he won't want to open it very wide, and the mark will know that. I think for the mark to get his kill shot in, he will have to be somewhere to the right of that red door as we look at it. Given the fact that the hit will be taking place in broad daylight he also can't risk a member of the public getting in the way at the last minute, so it will also be from an upstairs window.'

Tommy nodded. 'So, we're only really interested in the upstairs windows of the houses immediately to the right of the red door?'

'Yeah. Because of the way the target's door opens and the fact that he will be close up against the left wall of the entrance, the mark won't be able to see him if he's firing from the left of that red door. If it was me, I would want to see as much of the target as possible. So I reckon the perfect position would be from windows two to five on the right.'

'That makes sense. How are we going to spot this?'

'OK. If we use the red door as zero, for each window to the left or right you will either add or subtract one. For instance, the third window to the right of the red door will be plus three, the second window to the left of the red door will be minus two. Using a scale map and a sketch I made after my recce yesterday morning, and given the distance and angle of the shot, I reckon he's going to be pushed to get in a kill shot outside of plus five to minus two. So we'll concentrate on that area.'

'Great. Do you think he'll be on his own?'

'Yeah, it's a single-handed job. Unlike us he knows exactly where his target will be. He doesn't need a spotter.'

Although it would be me pulling the trigger, Tommy was a very important part of this operation and I wouldn't get it done without him. When a sniper is given a clearly identifiable target and a definite location he can be pretty sure of where to find him. Even if he's working on opportunity, selecting random targets from the civilian population or patrolling troops, he is more than capable of working alone because his target is whatever falls within the 'cross hairs'. But in a situation such as ours, where we are not sure of where the mark will be, we will basically have to hunt him down, and identify his firing position from a number of possibilities. And given the narrow field of vision that my No. 32 scope provided, I would need an extra pair of eyes.

'Right, it's three twenty-seven. Let's get some shut-eye. I'll take the first stag and wake you up at around five.'

'OK.'

Although there was an old iron bed frame in the room the springs and mattress had been removed, so Tommy propped himself up in the corner to the left of the window. He removed his pistol from its holster and laid it in his lap before nodding off. We had both chambered a round in our pistols and then returned them to the half-cocked position after leaving the car. That way, if anything happened we would only have to pull the hammer back half a click and pull the trigger to start firing.

Tommy always amazed me as he could sleep on a clothes line. He was the only bloke I knew that could actually fall asleep on a Hercules C130. We'd flown to Cyprus for an airborne exercise some years earlier and the whole journey had been a serious assault on your eardrums. It was like spending six hours in a dustbin with a punk rock band, but Tommy had slept the whole way there and back.

As I sat there alone in the darkness I started to think about what lay before me. For my first operation as a sniper it didn't get more critical than this. Working on military intelligence (now, there are two words that should never be used in the same sentence), I knew the mark's intended target was a prominent religious leader. Because of the potential threat to his life he'd basically been under self-imposed house arrest for close to a month. In the past, in situations like this, the bad guys would normally have chosen the up close and personal approach. Two guys would knock at the target's front door and, when it was opened, they would open fire at point-blank range, killing him immediately. But in this case the target lived in a very tight-knit and supportive community, so this approach just wasn't possible. It had to be a sniper: someone who would be capable of performing the kill with a single shot and at long distance.

We had it on good authority from an undercover operator that the terrorists had sent a registered letter by commercial courier to the target's home address which, of course, would have to be signed for. As a result, and for his own safety, we had subsequently replaced the target with one of our own guys, basically removing him and his family from harm's way. Even though the target's replacement would be armed and wearing an anti-ballistic (bulletproof) vest, he would still be taking a huge risk. Back then bulletproof vests were nowhere near as efficient as they are today. Kevlar was still in its infancy and there were no ceramic plates. At best they were what would later become known as 'second chance' vests. If I didn't get to the mark before he pulled the trigger, our guy Pete, my mate, would probably be dead.

Rumour had it that they had brought in an outsider to perform the hit. The word was that he was either a Russian or East German, so I would be up against the very best, a professional killer who knew exactly what he was doing. As opposed to a local fanatic, he'd be someone who had perfected his shooting skills through a mixture of natural ability and trial and error.

The more I thought about it the more convinced I became that the shot would have to come from the plus side – the right-hand side of the red door – as the shooter would also have to get his shot past the delivery man. He wouldn't have time for a second shot.

I looked at my watch: 0515 hours. Time to rouse Tommy.

Moving across to where he was sleeping I shook his right boot. You never wake a soldier up by shaking his shoulder, not unless you want to end up with a mouthful of loose teeth. 'Tommy, your turn, mate.'

Tommy was quickly up on his feet, making sure to stay away from the window. 'OK, mate, you get your head down for a few hours. What time do you want me to wake you?'

'Just before first light, about six-thirty. If we're lucky we might even catch our friend setting up. And we need to shut the door on the back bedroom in order to keep this room as dark as possible.'

I took Tommy's place in the corner and fell into a restless sleep. I was tired enough to sleep for a week, but the adrenaline was already beginning to flow through my veins. As I started to drift off I turned over in my mind all the possible outcomes of the coming day's events.

I felt my left boot move on its own, then again, and as I opened my eyes I saw Tommy crouched at my feet. 'Time for work, mate.'

'OK, Tom. No problem.'

I looked over at the window on my left. It was starting to get light and I thought to myself, you stupid, lucky bastard.

I was really annoyed with myself. I hadn't taken into account the direction of the sun rise. It was the type of mistake you would expect a novice to make, but on this occasion I'd been lucky. The sun was rising from behind us. If it had risen from the front, from behind the houses opposite, we would have been in trouble as it would have practically blinded us as it rose in the sky. But thankfully it was coming up from the other side, from behind the house we were in, and hopefully into the eyes of the mark. That's if he was even there.

Tommy handed me a half cup of strong black coffee from

a flask he had pulled from the Bergen and I took a mouthful. 'Tommy, that tastes like shit, mate.'

'I'll have it back if you don't want it.'

I smiled at him. 'No, you're OK. I'll get used to it. Is there anybody about?'

'No. It's like a bloody grave out there. I've had a thought, though.'

'What's that, mate?'

'What happens if this courier fella pulls his van right up to the door, blocking the mark's line of fire?'

'He won't. Our man on the inside says the courier is working for the baddies. That's how they gather most of their intelligence and track troop movements. He's been told to leave his van at the end of the road and walk down. Now let's get set up.'

Tommy had started to put everything back in the Bergen so that we would be ready to move if something happened and we had to bug out.

I moved over to the window and took a look. Tommy was right: the place was deserted and the sun's rays were already starting to bounce off the windows of the houses opposite. I picked up Tommy's binos, then, staying low and back from the window, I began to sweep the row of houses on the other side of the waste ground. Apart from just one which was too far to the right for the shooter to get the right angle, all of the upstairs windows were closed.

It was now 0655 hours. 'Time to call the office, Tom.'

'OK.'

Tommy switched on the radio and after giving it a minute or two to warm up and settle down he whispered, 'Hello, Zero, this is Alpha Two Two. Radio check. Over.'

There was a little static, what radio operators call squelch, followed by, 'Zero, OK. Over.'

After getting a sitrep (situation report) from the ops room Tommy switched the radio off and propped it up against the front wall of the room. The latest information we had was that the courier wasn't due to arrive at the target's address until after ten, so we would switch the radio back on for a final update around 0930 hours. There was no point in wasting the battery, as we might need it later.

It was only a couple of hundred metres from our location to the houses opposite, and while Tommy had been practising on the padlock, I had spent yesterday morning on the ranges zeroing my weapon at 300 metres. At that distance my three-round grouping was really tight – only around an inch and a half – and I was happy it was now spot on. Given the opportunity I would always go for a head shot as opposed to the body. But, depending on the mark's location and how much of him I could see, I might not have a choice. As for the tightness of the grouping, it simply confirmed the accuracy of the weapon and my own ability. This would all be over with one shot: there would be no time for second and third chances.

'Do you want another drop of coffee, Theo?'

'No thanks, mate. The last thing I need is to overload my system with caffeine and get the shakes. I'll stick to water, but you carry on.'

The next two hours seemed to drag on for ever and while Tommy started to search the houses opposite for any sign of the mark, I checked my weapon and ran through my drills in my head.

'Oh-nine-forty, Tom. Time to call the office again.'

With that Tommy switched on the radio and called the ops room, and although I could hear him, the words weren't really registering. After a minute or two he brought the radio over and rested it against the front wall. 'The courier has left the depot and is being tracked by an unmarked car.'

'Great. Our boy should be set up by now if he's coming, so it's game on, mate. You need to stay sharp now, Tom. We can't afford to miss anything or make a mistake. Any error, no matter how small, could cost both of us our lives.'

Tommy picked up the binos and moved towards the window. He took up a position about a foot back from the sill and began to search the houses opposite for any signs of life.

It was just after ten and Tommy hadn't taken the binos from his eyes in over fifteen minutes when he said, 'I think we may have a result, mate.'

I stopped what I was doing and moved up behind him. 'What you got?'

'Plus three. The window is open. It had been closed up until a minute ago. There's also another one open down the road at plus five, but that one's been open since first light.'

'Give us a look?'

I took the binos and lifted them to my eyes. Tommy was right: the window at plus three was open about six inches but it had a net curtain behind it. 'That could be our man.'

I then turned my attention to the window at plus five. It was open about ten inches, but I had initially dismissed it as, given the angle, the shot would be really tight from there. As I looked at it again I wondered if it was open wider now than it had been earlier?

As I continued to watch I thought I saw a movement, just the flicker of a shape as it moved across the window, but I couldn't be sure. Tommy now had the radio headset on, although he had left his right ear uncovered so that he could still hear my instructions.

'The courier is about ten minutes away, Theo. They will give us the heads up when he parks up and leaves his van.'

'Great.'

Although I'd responded positively, the lack of movement on the other side of the waste ground worried me. But it wouldn't be too much longer before we would find out if the mark was there or not.

I got down on one knee and, after picking up my weapon, I leant against the chest of drawers to steady myself. The distance to the window at plus three was around 230 metres, with the window at plus five another fifty metres further on, and both windows were well inside my pre-prepared range.

There was no significant wind, so keeping both eyes open I put my right eye to the eyepiece on the sight. I then lifted the cocking handle with my right index finger, hooked my finger around it and drew it back before pushing it gently forward again. As it slid forward I felt a slight resistance as it connected with the top round in the magazine that I'd inserted into the bottom of the weapon. It slipped the round smoothly into the breach and then I pushed the cocking handle back down until I heard it click into place. Now loaded, all I had to do now was flick off the safety catch with my thumb and I was ready to go.

I had the whole window at plus three in my sight, but couldn't see anything. Something didn't feel right.

I ran it over and over in my mind and eventually I put myself in the mark's position. I pictured myself standing there behind the net curtain with the window open just six inches and, as I looked through his scope, it finally hit me that there was no way the mark could fire from there. If he was using a scope, that curtain hanging so close to it would appear as just a blur, a sort of fog, totally obliterating the target area. Also, he would have to be higher than the window to get the downward elevation, and the bottom of the thick wooden window frame would form a barrier straight across his line of sight. He would either have to shoot from below the window frame, exposing more of himself and his weapon, or open the window even wider.

Although we couldn't see what was happening on our side of the street, Steve the operation commander, who had dropped us off earlier that morning, had now started to feed

Tommy the real-time commentary from the OP (observation post) car parked some distance away, and Tommy was in turn feeding it to me.

'The courier has parked the van and is now beginning to make his way down the street. Eighty metres from the target's door.'

'Seventy metres.'

I was still fixated on the window at plus three as that was the prime position for the kill shot. Something's not right here, I was thinking. Where's the shooter?

'Fifty metres.'

'Forty metres.'

'Thirty metres.'

My gut was telling me that there was no way the mark could get a shot off with that net curtain and the window frame three feet in front of his sight.

'Twenty metres.'

'Fifteen.'

'Ten metres.'

'He's at the door, Theo.'

There was still no movement from behind the net curtain at plus three. Where the fuck is he?

'Tommy, the open window at plus three is a distraction. The mark is at plus five.'

As the words were leaving my mouth the fore-sight of my weapon was already sweeping smoothly from left to right. I quickly switched my focus to the window at plus five, just in time to spot the sunlight bounce off the end of the shooter's rifle muzzle.

Now I had located the mark I began to focus in. As I strained my eyes the area behind the window slowly became clearer and I could now see the dark shape of a man standing on the right-hand side of the window frame. I now began to separate his shape from the darkness of the room and pick out the shape of his torso, head and the rifle in his hands. His head was buried behind the scope, with his cheek pressed hard up against the stock, reducing the size of the target area. His left arm was supporting the rifle and blocking a clear shot to his chest. I couldn't run the risk of hitting him in the arm and only wounding him, so, moving the cross hairs on my sight up to the area just beneath his chin, I steadied myself.

It was then that I heard the heavy metal knocker on the target's front door crash into the metal button.

Thinking aloud, I heard myself say, 'Just give me two seconds before you open the door, Pete.'

I took a deep breath and exhaled slowly.

With my lungs totally empty I stopped breathing, and as the cross hairs settled just below his chin, I felt my heart slow and I gently squeezed the trigger.

Totally fixated on the mark and in some sort of dream, I heard the weapon fire and felt the recoil as the heavy wooden butt of the rifle punched hard into my right shoulder. It was done: the round was on its way. If I was on target he would never hear the shot that killed him.

Without disturbing the aim of my weapon my index finger quickly lifted the curved bolt, pulled it back and, as the empty brass cartridge case flew silently through the air to my right, I was already pushing the bolt forward, and I felt that slight resistance as the breach block picked up the next round and guided it into the chamber. Ready to fire again.

My eye hadn't left the scope and now, as if in slow motion, I watched the muzzle that had initially given away the mark's position drop down below the window frame and out of sight.

Tommy, who had watched the whole incident through his powerful binos, calmly said, 'Target. That's a kill. Great shot, mate.'

Cat or Mouse?

Hello
I see you across the canal,
I see you over the fields,
their sparse grass blowing gently in the wind,

I see you
sitting amongst the ruins of the compound,
its crumbling walls providing little respite against the
    heat of a midday sun.

I see you
crouched low behind a pile of mud bricks,
your rag-covered head,
your cheek resting on the Dragonoff,
your eye glued to its sight,
while you try to see me.

But you don't see me
lying in this hole
half covered by stinking mud,
quietly watching the dust swirl across the track,
judging the wind,
the range,
continually adjusting,

I take a breath
exhale
hold it
and squeeze.

Another place
another time
maybe you and me be mates

Goodbye.

PART V: NEW CHALLENGES

Can It Really Be That Hard?

The Brecon Beacons, a second home for most of us.

Joining Special Forces is the obvious progression for an air-borne soldier. First serving and currently living in Hereford, even now I have men come up to me in the street and say, 'You don't remember me, do you, staff?'

The outcome to such a question will go one of two ways. He's either going to shake your hand, or punch you in the mouth. Luckily it's normally the former, followed by, 'You took me through P Company in nineteen-seventy so-and-so, and thanks very much for all your help.'

However, no matter how obvious a progression it may be, most of those who volunteer still have no idea what they're letting themselves in for. If you're looking for fame and fortune, forget it. Not even the guys who led the Iranian Embassy operation, those whose actions were photographed by the world's press and then plastered across the front pages of every newspaper on the planet, have ever received any public recognition. Likewise, if you're looking for some nice new shiny medals to wear, then it's best you stay where you are.

Joining a Special Forces unit, whether it be the SAS, the SBS, the 'Det' (14 Int) or one of the other, lesser-known but still highly effective clandestine organisations, is not something to undertake lightly. It should not even be considered without first doing a great deal of research and being in possession of all the facts.

If you're a married man you should think long and hard before making such a decision as it will put enormous strain on both your marriage and your family, much more than you could ever imagine.

Deciding to become a Special Forces soldier will also take you to places you have never been before. I'm not talking about an all-expenses-paid world tour, courtesy of the British taxpayer. No, I'm talking about taking your body on a journey of pain and destruction, the effects of which will stay with you long after you've left the service.

Your mind will also travel: to some of the darkest corners of human experience, to places very few of us have ever even imagined, forcing you to confront and overcome your innermost fears.

A lot of soldiers think that once they have overcome the initial hurdle of Selection, then that's it and it's all over bar the shouting. However, many will find out at first hand that this is not the case and, let's be honest, nothing worth having is ever going to be that easy.

First, there's the small matter of Selection to pass. Each Special Forces unit conducts its own process of Selection, tailored specifically to the type of operations it carries out. SAS Selection lasts approximately six months. On day one, regardless of your previous accomplishments or honours, you will be just another unknown face among around 120 officers and other ranks. At this point all those attending Selection will be divided into squads of a manageable size: between twenty and thirty.

The first three weeks are designed specifically to allow the staff of the training wing to assess your personal fitness, map-reading skills, determination and self-confidence. The course is not designed to build or improve your personal fitness to a level which will enable you to pass Selection. That should have been done before your arrival in Hereford.

This initial period begins with a number of squad runs and marches that will have you trying to keep up with some of the fittest men in the world. We're not talking about men who can run a sub-ten-second 100 metres, or a two-hour-ten-minute marathon. No, we're talking about men who can cover forty miles of the roughest mountain terrain in the world, carrying a 60lb pack and a 9lb rifle, while in the dark and totally alone.

The individuals who lead these events will be selected for their natural ability. In my day these 'hares' were international-standard fell runners, or those who had been recently involved in, say, Everest expeditions. Their purpose was not to break you, but to push you to your limit without actually pushing you over the edge. During these early stages nobody is 'binned', or told to leave. If you want to leave the course and return to your regiment you have to go to a member of staff and 'VW' (voluntarily withdraw).

The training wing staff will also steadily reduce the number of men working in each group, until, by the end of week three and in preparation for the start of 'test week', you will be left working on your own.

Test week finishes with what is fondly called 'Endurance': a forty-mile trek across the highest peaks in the Brecon Beacons. During this you will carry a 60lb pack and a rifle, and be expected to do all your own map reading and time manage-ment (time and distance). You will have only twenty hours to complete the course. A lot of it will be done in the dark and you will be totally alone throughout. The only human contact you'll have when involved in the tests during the whole week is with the staff at the checkpoints. Here you will pick up a new grid reference for the next checkpoint, maybe five miles and three mountains away. They will ask you if you are fit to continue, but there will be no deep and meaningful conversation.

Once test week is over, those who are left – and this can be thirty or even fewer – will take part in four weeks of intense weapons and tactics training in the depths of Wales. Here you will be taught how to use the Regiment's (from this point onwards 'the Regiment' refers exclusively to 22 SAS) vast array of weapons and equipment, while working in four-man patrols in preparation for the six weeks of jungle training that follow. You will hear the 'old and bold' say, 'The jungle is where the real selection is done.'

The jungle phase is extremely hard work. It involves long patrols through dense jungle, live firing exercises, ambush drills and demolitions, while living in the very worst of conditions. When the course was being run, in the jungle in Belize, which is renowned as one of the world's 'dirtiest', candidates would regularly return with some dangerous but little-known diseases or skin conditions.

Of the thirty or so that go to the jungle, maybe only six will actually pass. On their return to the UK these join students from other units in the British Army to take part in the All Arms Combat Survival Course. Here they spend the first two weeks being taught how to live off the land in preparation for the 'escape and evasion' phase.

The escape and evasion exercise lasts a further five days. Here participants will be released into the wilds of either Wales or Scotland with nothing more than the clothes they stand up in. They will then be expected to avoid capture (evade) by what could be a company-size 'hunter force'. These hunter forces are normally provided by one of the Parachute Battalions or another top-shelf infantry unit. If you're captured you should expect no quarter, as none will be given.

Each day you manage to stay free you will have to make your way miles across country, using only the stars and a rudimentary map to find the next isolated checkpoint.

Normally checkpoints are set in the middle of an isolated forestry block halfway up a mountain. Here, in the dead of night, you will meet a solitary agent who will give you fresh instructions and your next RV (rendezvous point). Fail to find the checkpoint, or turn up late to meet the agent, and basically it's over. You can go no further as you don't have any more information to work with.

But it doesn't matter how good you are, everybody gets caught in the end. It's set up that way.

Those who are caught are then taken through a 'resistance to interrogation' phase, while the others, after a debrief, will go back to camp for a shower and some scoff. The resistance to interrogation exercise is extremely realistic. After going without sleep and being subjected to other unmentionables for over twenty-four hours, it doesn't matter how many times you tell yourself, 'It's only a training exercise, and it will be over soon.' Even the strongest among us will start to question the reality of it all.

All those who make it through this harrowing event and go on to pass Selection are then expected to give up their current hard-earned rank and be reduced to the rank of trooper (private soldier). However, all is not lost, for in most cases, as long as he continues to perform well, an SAS soldier's rank will continue to rise in his parent unit. I knew men who had reached the rank of SAS corporal (no mean feat given the calibre of men you're up against) who also reached that of warrant officer (sergeant major) in their own regiment or corps.

Those who are already Para-trained will now be ready to be 'badged': receive their gravel-coloured beret and SAS wings. Those who are not Para-trained will have to wait until after they've attended the basic parachute course at RAF Brize Norton.

It's easy for anyone outside the Regiment to assume that, with Selection over, it's plain sailing from then on. But it's only just the beginning. Yes, you've passed six months of Selection, a considerable achievement in itself, but you still have no experience of Special Forces warfare. Apart from your basic infantry skills you have no specialist skills to offer, nothing to contribute to your troop or patrol.

At this point you will join one of your squadron's four troops and start to learn your trade. You will then be assigned to an Air, Boat, Mobility or Mountain troop. Each member of these troops is trained to the very highest level. The Air troops are trained to the very exacting standards needed to perform HALO (high altitude low opening) jumps. This means exiting an aircraft at 25,000 feet (five miles high) and free-falling for two minutes. The Boat troops will all be expert canoeists, boat handlers and divers. The Mobility troops will be able to drive and repair any vehicle they come across, regardless of its size, whether or not it has tracks, or the number of wheels it has.

The Mountain troops will all be very experienced climbers, many of them attending 'mountain leader' courses with German, Austrian and Swiss alpine troops. Some will eventually go on to conquer some of the highest and most dangerous peaks in the world, including Everest and K2.

Once you have reached the required standard for your designated troop, you will then be expected to attain a specialist skill, in medicine, communications or demolitions. Most will also learn to speak at least one other language.

Becoming a Special Forces soldier will totally change your way of life. You will have to learn to function efficiently in a totally different world. Learn to keep secrets from your nearest and dearest whilst learning new skills and languages in order to try to keep pace with an ever changing world.

But whether you're part of a two-man OP team working undercover in Ulster, watching the IRA conduct weapon training, or practising section attack drills in the 'bandit country' of south Armagh and Fermanagh, or become part of a full-size troop working deep behind enemy lines in the Middle East, there are only two things that can be guaranteed. First, you will always be outnumbered. Second, if you get 'rumbled' you'll be up against it and fighting for your life

Why?

Why do we choose such a role?
Leave the comfort of our homes and family,
expose our ears to such brutal rantings,
suffer the abuse
and ridicule.

Why do we train so hard?
Run until we drop,
our muscles aching,
throbbing head
and lungs fit to burst.

Why do we volunteer?
To expose ourselves to such scrutiny
in the hope that we will be selected
while countless others fall by the wayside,
our reward
to be the first into the breach,
the first to meet the enemy.

Why are we always outnumbered?
Living in the dark
for days, sometimes wèeks,
run the risk of being wounded
even killed,
watch our friends suffer and die,
returning home quietly in secret,
hiding our dead,
our feats and fate unknown.
Why?

Because we're soldiers, and for the same reason a dog
    will lick its arse.
It's what we do.

Strictly Need to Know

Secrecy and security are probably the most important aspects of all Special Forces operations. Because of this there is one phrase you will continually hear: 'That information is on a strictly need-to-know basis.'

Some people are under the impression that being part of a Special Forces unit will give you unlimited access to all of the highly sensitive or secret information on the activities carried out by these specialist units. However, in reality all information about Special Forces operations both past and present is a closely guarded secret and hopefully it will remain that way. Well, at least until all those who took part in them are long gone.

This level of security is necessary if we are to have any chance of protecting the very sensitive, and in most cases highly valuable, information that has been gathered at great personal risk by individuals working deep undercover, sometimes for years at a time. These undercover operators will work in some of the most dangerous environments on the planet, and some will end up paying the ultimate price.

So, in order to protect the various undercover teams such as the 'Det' and military intelligence agencies such as MI5 and MI6, while at the same time safeguarding the anonymity of those who have already taken part, or will take part, in such operations in the future, all the information surrounding Special Forces operations is always handled on a 'strictly need-to-know' basis.

However, this level of security is applied not only to the serving soldier. It is also rigidly applied to our wives and families: not because we don't trust them, but because it's safer for everybody concerned, including them.

In the early years, if I told my wife I was going on a trip, she would always ask, 'Where are you going?' And I'd reply, 'Sorry, but that's on a need-to-know basis, and you don't need to know, darling.' To begin with, this answer would infuriate the life out of her, and would be met by a very angry, 'But I do need to know. It's me that's left here looking after our son for months on end, not knowing where you are, or if you're even going to come home.' So one day I sat her down and explained to her in great detail why it had to be this way. That it was not only for our security, but for her safety as well. It wasn't that I didn't trust her or was being deliberately obstructive. We never even knew what our mates in the other squadrons were doing, or where they were going, and you never asked. If you needed to know, someone would tell you.

Even after an operation was over, as far as we were concerned you would never talk about it again as your casual chatter could easily put at risk those who were still involved. This attitude to security is deeply ingrained in everybody who is part of the unit, regardless of their job or position, and remains with you even years after you leave.

In the early days, before the mobile phone and when even the traditional pager was still in its infancy, the SP (special projects) team would carry an early numeric version of a pager, not unlike those carried by doctors in hospitals. These little blue plastic boxes, no bigger than a ten-pack of cigarettes, would be with you twenty-four hours a day for the duration of your time on the team, normally six months. Of course in its day the device was state of the art, yet it would only display a simple three-figure code. These codes, of which there were about ten, were pre-set by the 'head shed' – that is, any officer, but especially those at HQ – and their meanings would range from a simple order to 'phone camp' through the various levels of 'training exercise call-out', to the full-blown, no duff 'operational call-out', 'no duff' meaning it was for real.

Receiving an operational call-out could mean that the shit had already hit the fan somewhere in the world, but it would normally relate to a terrorist incident somewhere in the UK. Each three-number combination had to be memorised by the operator. Writing it on a piece of paper in the form of a list and then sticking this to the back of the pager was definitely a no-no.

The day WPC Yvonne Fletcher was shot dead outside the Libyan Embassy in London, we were on 22 SAS's training ground, about thirteen miles outside Hereford. As pagers were very expensive and not particularly robust, it was common practice for only one or two of us to carry them on our person when we were involved in any sort of training where they might get damaged. The rest of us would just leave them in our bags.

It was about halfway through the morning when the bleepers started going off. One of the guys hurriedly reached into the pocket of his ops waistcoat to stop the noise but, even before he had the pager in his hand, he was bombarded with shouts of, 'What's it say?' He looked at the three red numbers displayed on the long narrow blue screen, then said, 'It says "666".'

There was a deathly silence as the same thought ran through everybody's mind: there isn't a code 666. It was then that it hit home and a lone voice broke the silence. 'You prat, you're reading it upside down. It's "999". It's an ops call-out.'

The words had barely left his mouth when one of the team was already heading for the office of the MoD 'plods' – Ministry of Defence Police – at the main entrance to the training ground, and the nearest telephone.

With the head shed – the squadron leader and officers – already in the process of climbing aboard the chopper that would take them back to camp for a briefing, the rest of us quickly loaded all our gear into our fleet of Range Rovers and Transit vans in preparation for a high-speed dash back to camp.

On our arrival in Hereford we were quickly briefed and then set about getting our shit together for what could have been another Iranian Embassy-type operation. The IA (immediate action) team with all their kit, including two Range Rovers, were immediately loaded into the back of a Chinook helicopter and flown down to an airfield on the western edge of London. The rest of us were given an ETD (estimated time of departure) to leave camp and drive down to the same airfield.

At that time I was living in army quarters very close to the back gate of the camp. So, once all my kit was loaded, I took the opportunity to dash home for some extras. I came through the front door of our house like a whirlwind and, as I leapt up the stairs three at a time, I shouted to my wife, 'Can you do me a flask of coffee and a sandwich, darling?'

She knew straight away that something was up. 'What's happened? Where are you going?'

'Switch on the TV.'

The story was already making the news and I hadn't broken the need-to-know code by telling her. With that I grabbed the flask and small pack of sandwiches, kissed her on the cheek and disappeared out of the front door. There was no further contact between us until the operation was over, just over a week later.

Angel of Death or Mercy?

In order for a Special Forces unit to be 100 per cent effective, it has to be totally self-sufficient for what can turn out to be months at a time. Once a patrol is away from the main body, doing what it does best, gathering intelligence or causing havoc behind enemy lines, its members will have no access to hospitals or other medical services if one or more of them is wounded, injured or falls ill. However, there is also no room for non-Special Forces personnel, such as an RAMC (Royal Army Medical Corps) medic, in a hostile environment.

In such a small and tight-knit unit everybody must be a fully trained Special Forces soldier. Each man must pull his weight and contribute fully in every aspect of the patrol. All those involved must also be capable of carrying an enormous amount of weight in their pack and suffering immense hardship without complaint. Overcoming any obstacle, whether it be physical or mental, that is put in front of them, they will stand their ground against overwhelming odds.

We are unable to carry passengers, and the only alternative is for one of the troop to take responsibility for all the patrol's health and welfare needs. This is a very complex role. For, as well as taking responsibility for the day-to-day health needs of all those present, this individual will also have to deal with any injuries that are sustained under fire: complex bullet wounds and blast injuries. But it doesn't end there. Most of the reliable intelligence we gather in the field will come to us through either observation of, or direct contact with, the local population. Experience has taught us that the best way to get these people to open up and share their valuable information is to provide them with the things they desperately need. In short we have to play the 'hearts and minds' game.

However, 'hearts and minds' is no longer the old-fashioned ideal of dishing out chocolate bars and sweets to the local kids, or silk stockings to the womenfolk. These days you need to provide these people with the type of help and support they can't get anywhere else, the type of things that will improve their quality of life. This means anything from basic medicine for everyday ailments such as infected cuts, bruises and burns to the treatment of childhood diseases such as measles and whooping cough, and in some cases we would treat whole villages who were suffering from outbreaks of dysentery. You will also be expected to provide much-needed education in disease prevention and water purification techniques. Although we still give out sweets to the kids if we have them.

Once you have earned people's trust they will also begin to bring you their children for the treatment of traumatic amputation from landmines and other war-related injuries. On occasion, though, they will be looking for miracles which you are unable to perform.

You will also be expected to help deliver babies and even treat sick animals. Yes, you've got it: all of this falls on the shoulders of the patrol medic.

But where do you acquire these valuable and very necessary skills? Well, first you will have to complete the troop medic's course in Hereford: the very intensive, three-month paramedics' or REMT (Registered Emergency Medical Technician) course. As with most internal courses provided by Special Forces units, if you are enrolled on this course you are expected to pass first time, and pass well, and, as with everything else, there is no quarter given for failure. If you can't keep up with the workload, or you fail to meet the required weekly grades, you're off the course, and there's no coming back.

The troop medic's course was generally recognised as being the most demanding trade training course the Regiment had to offer. The day was broken up into hour-long periods during which the instructor would provide you with a brief outline of the specific elements to be covered. Then, at the end of the day, and armed with a sack full of textbooks and medical manuals, you would head home and spend the rest of the night going into depth on each of the subjects covered that day.

I would regularly sit at our dining table and work alone until three in the morning. I saw hardly anything of my wife and small son for the whole three months. In fact, to them, I was just a ghostly figure that came into the house at six each evening and sat at the dining room table surrounded by my books. I was still there when they went to bed, but was always gone by the time they woke up the following morning. My wife would bring me my meals and cups of coffee and then leave me to it.

During the first period the next morning you would sit an exam. It would last around an hour and would cover all of the subjects you were supposed to have covered the previous night on your own. You couldn't afford to fail. At the end of that first week we had a three-hour exam which was the equivalent to A-Level Human Biology. If you failed it was all over. You wouldn't be allowed to resit the exam or apply to take the course ever again.

Over the next eleven weeks we would study in minute detail the human body and the cause, prevention and treatment of diseases and ailments. Each subject would be approached in exactly the same way, and using the same format. A rough outline from the instructor, then you would do the hard detailed work on your own that night, followed by a fresh exam the next morning.

We would practise our suturing (stitching) skills on oranges and surgical felt because they tear in the same way that human skin does if you pull it too hard. Our dentistry skills were sharpened by drilling, filling and pulling the teeth out of pigs' heads because their teeth closely resemble a human's.

We would also practise on each other, for instance when inserting nasal-gastric tubes. You would thread the long flexible plastic tube up your own nose and then swallow as you pushed it down your throat and into your stomach, taking care to avoid the bronchial tubes (the access to the lungs), before drawing off acid from your stomach with a syringe. We would also have lectures from a number of outside agencies, such as midwives and anaesthetists, all of which would prove invaluable before long.

Friday afternoon of each week would see us sit yet another exam, and again, if you failed, there were no second chances: you were just gone. Although most would manage to scrabble through the initial few weeks, as the course progressed we would lose the odd one or two. On the Friday of week twelve we sat two three-hour exams. The first one was on 'A&P' (anatomy and physiology). The second exam was on trauma procedures – the immediate action and management of tropical diseases, gunshot and stab wounds, burns and bomb-blast injuries – along with mundane day-to-day medical care procedures that we used to call 'tailboard medicine'. This was followed by an hour-long practical session which concentrated on suturing, CPR (cardiopulmonary resuscitation), breaks and burns management. Then there was a thirty-minute oral exam on drugs and their uses. During this you would be expected to know all of each drug's indications and contra-indications (the conditions it could be used for, along with what it couldn't be used for, and its side effects) and the recommended dosages of over fifty drugs.

The pass rate for each exam was 80 per cent. If you failed

to reach the required standard in any one of them you were off the course. There were no resits or second chances. My overall pass mark was 97 per cent. All of those who sat the final exams on the last Friday passed. To be honest, most of us would have rather died than failed. Failing is not in the SF psyche.

After passing the in-house course we were sent to one of the country's hard-pressed civilian hospitals to work as trauma medics. This arrangement was only possible because of the fantastic relationships that had been built up over many years by the RAMC doctors and medical staff who manned our medical centre in Hereford. We would provide the doctors and nurses from these hospitals with what we called educational or familiarisation days. They would spend a full day, or sometimes two, at the Regiment's Hereford base, during which time we would take them on the ranges and teach them to abseil on the eighty-foot regimental climbing wall. Then we would take them up 200 feet in a chopper and have them abseil from that.

On occasion they would also take part in a siege training exercise run by the Special Projects team. Here they would play the role of a hostage at our mock embassy, or in the 'killing house' – a purpose-made building that provided our live firing CQB (close-quarter battle) environment. The stun grenades and bullets were always real, and the lights were always off.

These arrangements were a simple trade-off. We would provide the doctors and medical staff with a day or two filled with excitement and adventure. In return they would provide our medics with the months of experience they so desperately needed. The type of experience that would mean we could operate at our very best when away on operations. It was really just another 'hearts and minds' exercise.

Finally with part one, the theory portion of the course, finished, on the Sunday night I was sent down to Cardiff to begin my three-month hospital attachment. The hospital was a large rambling Victorian building located close to the city centre. I considered myself very lucky to be sent here. Some of the guys on my course were sent to much quieter hospitals, whereas this one was very much a full-on environment.

I arrived in the Accident and Emergency department at seven o'clock that first evening and introduced myself to the consultant. He then took me into a booth with a junior doctor and stuck a number of X-rays up on the screen, before saying, 'This man is complaining of chest pains and is finding it difficult to breathe. What's wrong with him?'

Even though he'd spent four years at university getting his degree and another two at medical school, the young doctor could only see this as a 'him or me' situation. But I'd learned years ago that it didn't pay to jump straight in. In a near panic the youngster quickly started to come up with an endless string of suggestions, everything from indigestion to a full-blown heart attack.

The consultant looked at me. 'What do you think?'

I had spent the time the junior doctor had been running off at the mouth closely studying the X-ray, and could see exactly what was wrong. But, of course, there was still a chance I was wrong. I took a deep breath and said, 'His windpipe has shifted over to the left. I think he has a pneumothorax. He's either received a direct blow to the throat or experienced a very heavy fall. As a result his lung is probably starting to collapse, which is making it hard for him to breathe and is possibly also the cause of the chest pains.'

The consultant smiled. 'Well done, spot on. What about this one? Can you tell me roughly how old the person in this X-ray is?'

The X-ray was of the knee and lower leg. I stood and looked at it. I'd sat enough exams and spent long enough looking through a microscope to know that when you were asked a question of this nature the answer would have to be some-where on the X-ray, and there it was. 'I would say the subject was probably under twelve.'

'Why under twelve?'

'Well, that shaded piece between the shaft and head of the fibula consists of flat, crescent-shaped cartilage. It allows both sections of the bone to grow independently, at their own rate, but it's only present until the subject reaches around twelve years old. After that it begins to ossify and become solid bone.'

He smiled once more. 'Spot on again. Are you ready to start work now?'

'Sure. Where do you want me?'

I was given a white coat and put to work. I was still working at six o'clock the following morning. Such was my thirst for knowledge and practical experience that I would regularly start work at six in the morning and would still be there at two the following morning. I would then go back to my room, grab a shower and a few hours' sleep and be back in casualty for eight o'clock.

During the three months I was at the hospital I would be part of a very hard-working trauma team. Being positioned just off the M4 motorway we would regularly be called upon to deal with serious multi-car pile-ups and other road traffic accidents, as well as mining injuries because the hospital was also the main trauma centre for the mining valleys of Wales. Injuries like the traumatic amputation of fingers, arms and legs and major crush damage.

On a Friday and Saturday night we would also have to deal with numerous bottle, knife and gunshot wounds: the results of fights between local drunks in the city centre and fallouts between foreign seamen in the city's busy docks.

Apart from being fortunate enough to work in such a busy hospital, I was also very lucky that the team in charge – the senior surgeons and consultants (these were the days before the bean counters had got their feet under the table) – were very aware of the type of experience I required and how valuable it would be to me later, when on military operations.

They were very willing to let me get stuck in and mucky. I would spend hours in the minor surgeries theatre removing the debris from, and suturing, wounds while covered in blood. AIDS wasn't a problem in those days, and I don't think it had even been discovered. The facial maxillary surgeon, who had to be called down to A&E if there were any children or women's faces that needed to be sutured, watched me stitch an old lady's leg one night. She had tripped getting onto a bus a few days earlier and smashed her shin on the platform, leaving a gaping, eight-inch gash. She didn't want to be a burden to anybody, so had just wrapped it up the best she could and soldiered on.

As a result the wound was still wide open and you could actually see the shiny shin bone. Because of the delay before treatment, the edges of the wound had started to heal, which made it impossible to suture the two sides of the wound together as they would no longer knit.

Also, as you get older your skin gets thinner, and she was so old that hers now resembled clingfilm, which made it very susceptible to tearing if you were too rough with it. After deadening the area, I spent over an hour cutting back the edges of the wound so that both sides would have a chance to knit. I then began pulling together the insides of the wound with very fine dissolvable stitches, before eventually closing it completely.

Once I'd finished, the surgeon looked at the wound and then said to the sister who was assisting me, 'I'm putting his name in the maxilla book. There's no need to call me if he's down here.'

I also spent a lot of time in theatre. The consultant anaesthetist – we'll call him Tom – was ex-military and although he hadn't seen any combat himself, he was still very much aware of the pressures I would face in the future. As a result I would watch with interest as he intubated patients. This is where you pass a thick tube down an unconscious patient's throat so that they can be fed oxygen during an operation. It was the only way of keeping a casualty's airway open after serious facial injuries, such as gunshot wounds and bomb blast. You also have to be very careful when performing this procedure as, if you push the tube too far, you will end up inflating the patient's stomach instead of their lungs.

Like most of the military, Tom had a very dry and black sense of humour. I can still hear him the first time I tried intubation. 'You've got sixty seconds to get it sorted, then I'm taking over before she dies.'

On one occasion he took the laryngoscope off me and said, 'You won't have one of these in the jungle, so let's see if you can intubate him with this,' as he handed me a dessert spoon.

I must have carried out well over a hundred intubations during my time at Cardiff.

Three weeks later – it was a Saturday night and as usual I was working in casualty – we had a guy brought in with multiple stab wounds. His wife had caught him playing away games with one of her friends and, in retaliation, she had stabbed him in the side of the neck, severing his jugular. She had then stabbed him in his upper chest and abdomen, before plunging the bread knife deep into his left thigh for good measure.

By the time he got to us he was losing a lot of blood. In fact at one stage we had two nurses squeezing in two bags of O Positive blood at a time. In situations like this, when there is no time to cross-match blood, you can always use 'O Pos'. You can only give group A to A, group B to B, and group AB to AB, but you can give O Pos to anybody.

His heart had also stopped by this stage and I was pumping his chest in an effort to keep what little blood he still had in his system circulating around his body. Along with the massive blood loss, his other problem was that his left lung had collapsed and he was now finding it hard to breathe on his own.

In this situation you immediately call for the anaesthetist as the patient will need to be intubated before being put on oxygen, either from a bottle or from the mains supply piped into A&E. The sister put out the call for the duty anaesthetist. Tom was on duty that night, but was already busy in theatre. Two minutes later the phone rang. There was a short exchange of words. Then she brought the phone over to me and said, 'It's Mr ——. He wants to speak to you.'

She put the phone to my mouth. 'Yes, boss?'

'Do you think you can intubate him and keep him alive for about twenty minutes, until I can get down there?'

'I'll do what I can, boss.'

'That's all we can ask. I'll be down as quick as I can. Put the sister back on the phone.'

'He wants to talk to you again.'

To cut a long story short, I intubated him and we kept his heart going while he took another twenty-odd units of blood. But we did keep him alive and eventually he made it into surgery shortly after one in the morning.

Tom asked me if I wanted to observe as I'd done all the hard work. I jumped at the chance. After cracking open his chest (cutting through all of his ribs with what looked like a pair of bolt-cutters) in order to get at his major arteries. We didn't get him closed up and into Intensive Care (as it was then) until after six that morning, by which time I had been on duty for over twenty-four hours.

I learned a whole raft of things while at the hospital. I learned how to deliver babies, a skill that would come in very useful a number of weeks later, as I delivered my first baby at two in the morning on the M6.

I also learned how to suture kids without hurting them, something that most doctors seem to have failed to pick up on. I learned that, if you put a few drops of the local anaesthetic lignocaine into the wound to deaden it first, then inject it into the surrounding flesh through the wound itself and let it take effect before beginning the procedure, they don't feel a thing. There's no point in giving a local anaesthetic if you're going to hurt them by stabbing them countless times while you're administering the drug. You might just as well stitch them up without it.

This would be great for future 'hearts and minds' operations, as no parent likes to see their child in pain. It also came in useful when stitching my son up at home. He never ever went to hospital. He would come home bleeding from some childhood wound and just call me as he made his way upstairs to the bathroom, while I got my kit and stitched him up.

But probably the most important skill I gained was how to perform nerve blocks. This is where you deaden all the nerves around a particular part of the body. A femoral block deadens the whole leg from the hip down. A radial block deadens the whole of the lower arm and hand. Both these techniques would come in very useful in the coming years.

The first time I performed a femoral block was with Tom in theatre. At the time it was common practice to use a femoral block on elderly patients who were having pins removed following hip surgery. A radial block was used when amputating fingers (a much more common procedure than most of us think). In both cases using a block meant that you no longer had to put the patient under using a general anaesthetic. You only had to sedate them and then deaden the relevant body part in order to ensure a pain-free procedure.

Tom had shown me how to find the femoral nerve by dissecting a line that runs between the iliac crest (top of the pelvis) and the groin. I used to draw lines on patients' bodies with a felt-tip pen. You would then use a syringe to inject the anaesthetic in several places in the same area and follow the drawn lines in order to ensure you hit and deadened all the nerves. I often wondered what they thought the first time they looked in the mirror after their operation and saw all these coloured lines around their crotch.

Tom had already sedated the patient, and I had completed my masterpiece and administered the femoral block. We then wheeled the patient into theatre. She was drowsy, but still responsive. The surgeon then said, 'Are we all set, ladies and gentlemen?'

Everybody spoke up, confirming we were all ready to go. As the surgeon lifted the scalpel and approached the woman's upper thigh, Tom leant over to me and calmly said, 'If she screams, you fucked up big style.'

She didn't make a sound, and I would go on to perform a number of these procedures before leaving the hospital. The knowledge and procedures I learned there would become invaluable in future years when working in the field. If one of the guys was shot in the arm or leg, you didn't want to fill him full of morphine. With such a small patrol you needed each man to be at his very best regardless of his physical condition. The last thing you needed was for one of them to be away with the fairies while still holding a loaded M16. If you have the ability to deaden the pain, or even take it away altogether, while leaving him still able to make rational decisions and continue fighting, it's a definite bonus.

But, without doubt, the most valuable thing I learned was that the human body can take an enormous amount of punishment and there is no point in pussyfooting around with it like it's made of fine glass. You just have to get stuck in and grab it by the scruff of the neck.

However, being a patrol medic places a huge amount of extra responsibility on your shoulders. For starters, you are responsible for the upkeep of your patrol's basic health needs and maintaining their fighting efficiency, sometimes in what can only be described as some of the most unhygienic places on the planet. Like the filthy Belizean jungle. You are also responsible for keeping them alive when wounded. This level of responsibility will place an enormous and sometimes almost unbearable burden of stress on most of us.

Each man in the patrol will look to you to save the life of a wounded comrade and some of them will get really pissed if you fail. When you're under pressure to save a badly injured man, most will see you as some sort of magician. This means that if you failed, it wasn't because he was too badly injured – damaged beyond repair – but because you are not working hard enough. This is another symptom of that legendary Special Forces culture, because 'although we die, we never fail'.

On occasion, when under pressure, I have even stitched my own hands and other parts of my body, much to the disgust of the other lads, who couldn't understand how I could do it to myself. But, as far as I'm concerned, if I can do a better job of stitching myself than they can, it's a no-brainer.

On the other hand, there is also an immense amount of self-satisfaction to be had from saving the life of another human being, especially when they are a close friend or colleague. It's then that all the hard work and responsibility that goes with such a position seems more than worthwhile. However, there were also times when I wished this responsibility had fallen on somebody else's shoulders.

Special Forces soldiers in the main are realists. We are more than aware of what the job involves and are happy to accept all the risks that go with it. With today's advances in medicine, and especially the development of prosthetic limbs, truly wonderful things can be done. But back in the seventies and eighties such things just weren't possible. We had guys who had lost the bottom of an arm and would be fitted with what was then a high-tech hook, one which would allow them to remain in a training role and part of the Regiment, but if you lost both of your legs or suffered a severe back injury you would probably spend the rest of your life in a wheelchair.

The face of battlefield medicine has, of course, changed dramatically over the past twenty to thirty years. Even as far back as the Falklands War, the San Carlos Bay FST's (forward surgical team) claim to fame was that 'every man who came in alive, went out alive': a huge accolade given the sheer number of serious battlefield injuries they were having to deal with.

One of the major contributory factors for this massive improvement in survival rates is the development of the battlefield helicopter. In the past most critically injured soldiers would be lucky to survive long enough to reach the operating theatre. Whereas today, thanks to the versatility of the helicopter, most receive surgery in less than an hour and as a result many more men are likely to survive the serious injuries they sustain on the battlefield, with a large percentage making a full recovery and returning to duty.

Thirty or forty years ago, and especially on Special Forces operations, it wasn't as straightforward as that. In most cases we would be fighting our secret wars far behind enemy lines or in remote locations, way beyond the normal operating range of our helicopters, or deep in the jungle, beneath a dense, 200-foot canopy, with no way of getting a chopper in. Although, on the odd occasion we have been known to use explosives to clear away enough trees to create an HLZ (helicopter landing zone) in order to get a seriously injured man out. But don't tell Greenpeace.

In such cases the level of responsibility and importance of what you're doing is increased dramatically, especially when working hard to keep a severely injured comrade alive while you wait for a casevac: evacuation of a casualty. This responsibility reaches even greater heights when one of the other guys leans over you and says, 'Don't work too hard, mate. He won't thank you for taking him home in that state. Although his wife and kids will initially thank you, he will never forgive you.' Sadly he was right. Although I managed to keep the injured man alive, albeit confined to a wheelchair, he never did forgive me, and although he didn't die until some years later, he never spoke to me again.

Strange Beings

Who are these strange beings?
trained warriors,
my comrades,
my brothers,
whose special calling turns my world upside down?

For saving a life,
whether it be friend or foe, matters so much more to
    them
than me taking one.

A feeling of guilt rushes over me
as I watch them working frantically to save a life,
a life which minutes before I had tried so hard to take.
Torn, I will share in their sorrow if they should fail
but feel anger should they succeed,
robbing me of my kill.

Whether saving my brothers in the heat of the fight,
or wandering the killing ground when the battle is done
in search of my enemy's life to save,
their task is endless.

They spend each day covered in blood,
and every night grieving

for those they couldn't save.

These are our 'Medics', half soldier half saint.

For the Love of a Good Woman

These days every man and woman in the British Army is a volunteer, and thank God for that. 'Pressed' soldiers just don't have the same commitment or enthusiasm for the role. But, in spite of all the technological advances that make modern warfare what it is today, being a professional soldier is never going to be an easy life. The decision to 'take the Queen's shilling' and join any of the three armed services is not one that should be made lightly. Although your chances of seeing action were remote back in the seventies and eighties – unless you were part of a Special Forces unit or deployed in Northern Ireland – it's not the same today. All those who join the army today are more or less guaranteed to see a lot more action than the line units did back then.

This will also affect any woman who's considering marrying a serviceman, especially a Special Forces soldier. If you're a young woman looking for what will generally be a caring, loving relationship from a man who's not scared of hard work, you won't go far wrong with a soldier, although I can't testify as to what it might be like for the man who marries a female soldier.

But, if you're looking for the type of relationship where your man gets every weekend off and comes home at the same time every night, or a man who will come home with a pay packet that will keep you in a manner you could only previously dream of, one which will allow you to pay the bills, feed the family and still leave you with enough money to build up a formidable collection of shoes and handbags to wear on those wild nights out, you should probably look elsewhere for your ideal man.

An army wife is a very special animal and, like soldiers, not all of those who volunteer will actually make the grade or go the distance. As soldiers we will regularly face bombs and bullets, and we will fight in what can only be termed some of the worst shitholes in the world. But it's our wives who will inevitably suffer the most. It's them that we will leave behind to spend their days and nights looking after our children, sometimes in sub-standard housing, with very little money and always alone, sometimes for months at a time.

As the wife of a Special Forces soldier it's likely you will also have to spend those long, lonely days and nights not even knowing where your man is, when he's coming home, or if he will be wounded or even alive when he does eventually return. If your man is lucky enough to be sent on an operation that is widely publicised, you might have a fairly good idea where he's going. Then, armed with this minuscule snippet of knowledge, you might even believe that you have a fair idea of what he may be doing. But nobody is going to take you into their confidence and openly share all the fine details with you.

When the Regiment was sent to the Falkland Islands in the spring of 1982, everybody knew where they were going, but only members of its HQ and a few of the high command, those who were actually in theatre at the time, knew what operations they were carrying out. Nobody knew that they were destroying countless enemy aircraft on a remote island, or gathering intelligence on East and West Falkland, some two to three weeks before the main body of the British invasion force landed at San Carlos Bay.

It was the same during the First and Second Gulf Wars. Members of the Regiment were actually across the border in Iraq, identifying targets for the bombers and naval Tomahawk crews, weeks before the main offensive actually kicked off.

As a result of the harsh lifestyle, the Regiment has the highest divorce rate in the three services. The only other unit that even comes close is the Royal Navy's Submarine Service. It's widely accepted – a type of unwritten rule – that if your wife stays with you during the Selection process (although she's not actually there) and then through those first traumatic twelve months which are so unlike anything else in the army, she will probably stay for the duration, the full term of your secondment to the Regiment. But nothing is guaranteed.

Back in the eighties, I remember, my wife told me about a conversation she'd had with one of the other wives that morning over coffee. She had been invited around to the house of a young German girl – let's call her Suzie. Suzie had arrived in Hereford a few months earlier with her husband, but things were not going well. As they sat there chatting the girl told my wife that she had had enough and had already seen a local solicitor about getting a divorce.

My wife was shocked. We had been married for over ten years, and although we had spent around half of that time apart, the thought of getting a divorce had never even crossed her mind. Well, I don't think it had.

She had then told Suzie that it wouldn't be that easy and that under English law it would probably take ages. The girl looked at her, smiled and then said, 'That's what I thought. The solicitor asked me how long we'd been married. When I told him it was only around eighteen months he didn't look very hopeful. He then asked me, "What's your husband done? What are your grounds for the divorce? Is it adultery, abuse, cruelty?" I told him it was none of those, that Terry had never laid a hand on me, or been with another woman. It's just that I couldn't cope with the not knowing where he was, or when he was coming home.

'He then smiled at me. "Is your husband in the Regiment?"

'"Yes. "

'"Well, that's a totally different matter. We can file for divorce under 'mental cruelty'. It will take about six months."

'So I told him to go ahead.'

In those days little was also known about the cause, symptoms and treatment of Post Traumatic Stress Disorder. It was something that was never talked about. You learned to keep it to yourself. Admitting that your work was affecting your mental health was a sure-fire way of getting yourself RTU'd, returned to unit – the last thing any of us wanted. In most cases being RTU'd would not mean the end of your career as far as your original regiment was concerned. Given the fact that you had made it through Selection, and gained an enormous amount of experience during your time with the Regiment, you would still be a much-treasured asset in the normal army. But we knew that our inner feelings of failure – the very feelings that had driven us to try for and pass Selection in the first place – would rip us apart.

As a result, the mood swings, angry outbursts and long silences that followed our return home from a deployment were simply put down by our wives to us being moody, grumpy sods.

Most Special Forces units are very close-knit, and that applies to our wives as well. Any wife who will listen to another while she has a good moan and gets things off her chest, without passing judgement or broadcasting it to the world, will be inundated with invitations to morning coffee. This can be extremely tiring, and can at times have an adverse effect on her own relationship. But it can also help her realise that she is not alone, and that others are suffering just as much as she is.

My wife has always been a good listener, and on another occasion she was told by another girl, 'I don't think he loves me any more.'

'Why do you think that? Do you think he's seeing another woman?'

'Well, no, but you know he's just come back from six months overseas?'

'Yes.'

'Well, we're now going through the traditional mood swings and long silences.'

'Yeah, but they're all like that when they first come back. Theo's the same. He'll just sit and stare at the television for hours without actually watching it.'

'I know, and I can handle that, but this time he hasn't touched me since he's been home. So, the other afternoon while he was at work, I moved the exercise bike from the garage into the front room. Then, after he'd had his dinner and was sitting in front of the TV, I went and got stripped off. I mean totally naked. Not a stitch on. I then came back into the front room, got on the bike and began peddling. He didn't even notice. He didn't bat an eyelid.'

I was shocked. She was a really good-looking woman and, although I didn't say anything to my wife at the time, I did think to myself, if she'd done it in front of me, there would have been no holding me back.

But, joking aside, they were a great couple who worked well together, and although they managed to work through it for a while longer, in the end it just got too much for her and she eventually left. I still see him now and again, when he's back from his stint working on the 'Circuit' as a 'security consultant' or as a bodyguard for top company executives or other VIPs. But he will spend days trashed out of his brains, just waiting to go back out. Don't get me wrong: he's still a very formidable soldier. Even with a drink in him you wouldn't want to cross him. It's amazing how quickly someone like that can sober up. You also couldn't wish for a better man to watch your back when the shit starts flying. But when you take him out of the danger zone and put him back among the normal people, his life will inevitably turn to rat's shit.

The love of a good woman is very important to any soldier, but especially to a Special Forces soldier. They are essential during our service years, when their providing a stable environment for us and our children. And, even though we're seldom there, they also provide a safe haven and a friendly face for us to come home to.

Although we rarely treat them as the princesses they truly are, most of us would really struggle to do what we do without their unconditional love and support.

I once heard a colonel refer to soldiers' wives as '120lb of excess baggage'. Needless to say, he wasn't in the job long. But, in the big scheme of things, you can't help but wonder just how many of these very courageous and devoted women feel that that's exactly what they are.

Living in the Cross Hairs

As soldiers we make our living in what is at times an extremely hazardous environment. Training is designed to remove or reduce some of the danger associated with battle by making the various procedures and actions second nature. But training itself poses a risk to all those taking part.

Although it's not widely publicised, a number of soldiers are killed or injured each year while taking part in training exercises in the UK or overseas. Some of these deaths and injuries will be down to simple everyday causes such as road accidents. However, others will be the result of parachuting accidents, live firing incidents on the ranges, being hit by deadfalls (large dead trees or branches that will fall without warning, crushing those beneath them) or being swept away by flash floods during jungle training.

Accidents will always happen in military life. It should also be remembered that, if not gainfully employed, most soldiers will prat about. Given their ingenuity, if you then put a 55-ton tank, a lorry stuck in the mud, a loaded rifle, or a thunderflash into the close proximity of fragile human flesh, you have a ghastly accident just looking for somewhere to happen.

But, to a Special Forces soldier, training presents an even greater risk to life and limb as our training wings do their best to make each exercise more realistic than the previous one.

Our Mountain troops train on some of the most dangerous peaks in the world and so the threat of death or serious injury is always there. In fact it's just over the next ridge. In the eighties we lost three very experienced climbers in a single incident when they were all swept to their deaths while training high in the Alps.

Our Air Troops are regularly involved in HALO descents. HALO is exactly what it says on the tin. Those taking part will leave the aircraft (C130 Hercules) at 25,000 feet, around five miles, high. At this altitude the air is very thin and contains very little oxygen. Each man is fitted with his own independent oxygen supply in order to ensure he doesn't black out during the two minutes he will spend in free fall, while travelling at close to 120 mph.

They will then deploy their canopies at between 2500 and 3000 feet. Pull your chute too soon and you're up there for what seems like hours, while at the same time running the risk of compromising the whole operation and putting your mates' lives at risk. All HALO rigs are fitted with a barometric device which will cause your chute to deploy automatically at a predetermined height if it's not deployed because of human error.

However, just because these jumps are free-fall, they can in no way be classed as sport parachuting. And they're definitely not 'clean fatigue' either. No, each man will have a Bergen containing his personal equipment, weighing anything up to 200lb, suspended between his legs, and his personal weapon strapped down the side of his body. Also, these jumps take place in the dead of night. It doesn't matter how experienced an operator you are, when training is being conducted in such hazardous environments, accidents are bound to happen and sometimes good men are either crippled for life or die.

Practically all room or CQB scenarios are conducted in a live firing environment. Even when hostage-recovery scenarios are practised in the 'killing house', the hostages, like the stun grenades, are all real. The rounds are live and the lights are off.

You would think that living the whole of your working life in such a high-risk environment would be enough for any man, and for most of us it is. But it doesn't end there. Even when you're in civilian clothes, trying to enjoy a quiet pint and relax at the end of a long, hard day, you will still be in somebody's cross hairs. Most of us try our hardest to live our lives as what the Regiment terms 'grey men', those that nobody ever notices. That can be hard sometimes. When you're walking around Hereford in the middle of January, heavily tanned and built like a brick shithouse, you do tend to stand out a bit.

What isn't widely known is that as a Special Forces soldier, if you are caught fighting, drunk and disorderly in public, or convicted of any criminal offence whatsoever, you're gone: Returned to Unit. Although you will only be cashiered from the army in the most serious of circumstances, you will be returned to your mother unit, the one you first joined from civvie street.

At this point your career as a Special Forces soldier is basically over. Even if your actions can be put down to pure self-defence, you're still at risk of being 'binned', RTU'd. The Regiment has always shied away from any sort of press, either good or bad, and will quickly distance itself from any individual who brings the spotlight to bear on it.

As a result, although we have been known to fight among ourselves behind closed doors, most of us will avoid trouble with 'civvies' at all costs, even to the point of apologising for something that was not our fault, simply to avoid confrontation. We've all worked far too hard to get where we are and don't want to risk everything just for the sake of sorting out some arsehole with a smart mouth.

However, just because you're Special Forces, it doesn't mean you know everything and, for most of us, life is one huge learning curve. We live in an environment where we never stop learning or training. As a result we spend a lot of time attending specialist courses provided either in house or by other regiments or corps or in some cases by civilian agencies.

We also spend a great deal of our time passing on our hard-earned experience to other military personnel. One example is teaching combat survival skills to those who may find themselves isolated in a hostile combat environment, such as pilots who are at risk of being shot down behind enemy lines and forced to live off the land while they try to evade capture.

But, once the lessons are over for the day and preparations for the next day's periods have been completed, it's normally time to head 'down town' for a well-earned pint.

One of my roles was helping to run the first phase of a selection course for entry into a small but extremely specialised unit. The initial part of the course, known as 'Camp One', lasted for three weeks and took place at a military training area in the Midlands. The aim of the course was to filter out those men and women of all ranks, and from all the three services, who would not make it onto phase two. Phase two lasted around another six months and took place at a purpose-built complex close to Hereford.

Around 120 would start each course, all volunteers who aspired to become part of a very select and specialised group of operators. The failure rate for the complete course was equal to, if not greater than, SAS Selection. Of these 120 maybe fewer than thirty would make it to phase two. From these possibly only six would pass the course and finally make it onto operations.

For those who managed to complete and pass the course, the only thing they could be sure of was that they would live the next three years of their lives working undercover in what was then one of the most dangerous environments in the world. One foot wrong, one slip of the tongue, and it was all over. The end result would be brutal torture, followed eventually by a very painful death, and their bodies might never be found.

We used this particular training area purely for reasons of security. There was no point in disclosing the location of the unit's headquarters to a large number of individuals who were never going to make the grade. However, like most military training areas, it was always overbooked and therefore in constant use by any number of regular and territorial units.

On this particular occasion we were sharing the training area with a company of Grenadier Guards (commonly known as 'Woodentops' because of the way they march everywhere – you have to be of an age to remember the children's TV programme of that name), although they were billeted in a totally different part of the camp. Nevertheless, we would occasionally run across them during our daily routine out on the training area, and the whispering and pointing would begin.

Phase one of selection consisted of long hours of tough physical and mental exercise. The students would be worked hard all day. Then, after very little sleep, they would be woken and asked to complete a series of very complex mental tasks lasting anything up to three or four hours while under exam conditions.

After setting the candidates their next task, one which would take them until well after two in the morning to complete, a few of us not needed to supervise the current exercise decided to go down to the local pub for a pint. We were a mixed group of men and women. The women were all former operators who were now on their R&R (rest and recuperation) phase before going back on operations.

At the pub we ordered our drinks and then positioned ourselves in a corner of the bar. We spent the next half-hour discussing the day's events and the performance of various students in hushed voices, basically just keeping ourselves to ourselves. It was about nine forty-five when, surprise, surprise, it was my turn to get them in. I took everybody's order and made my way up to the bar. I told the barmaid what I needed and then leant against the bar as I waited patiently for our drinks to appear.

After a few minutes a tall guy appeared at my shoulder. He had to be a Grenadier; they don't make normal soldiers that tall. I turned and nodded to him. 'You OK, mate?'

'I ain't your mate.'

'OK. Sorry, no problem.'

He must have mistaken my apologetic attitude as a sign of weakness and leaned in closer before saying, 'We know who you lot are, and we don't think you're that hard. In fact I think I might just take you outside and give you a fucking good hiding.'

He was that close that I toyed with the idea of just dropping the head on him, but then thought better of it. Fighting in public was one thing, but a senior rank giving a Tom a bloody good hiding in a crowded bar, regardless of the provocation, was something totally different.

So I just turned and looked at him. I then leant in even closer so that I wouldn't be overheard and, with our heads very nearly touching, I quietly said, 'Listen, I can see you're a big lad and you can probably handle yourself. But, before you start something you may not be able to finish, you need to consider this. We could go outside and you might even manage to give me a good hiding. But it's a really big "might". However, for the sake of argument, let's just say you do manage it. The big question is, can you live with the aftermath?'

He looked puzzled. 'What do you mean, aftermath? What aftermath?'

I smiled. 'Well, let's just say on this occasion you're really lucky and you leave me lying on the floor. Are you prepared to spend the rest of your life looking over your shoulder? Because every time you go to open your front door, start your car, pick your wife up from work or your kids from school, you're gonna wonder if I've been.'

I let what I'd just said sink in for a moment, then followed it up with, 'Now the only thing that will be certain in your life from this point on is that one day I will have. If you can live with that, then be my guest and let's go outside. However, if you and your family can't live like that, then fuck off and leave me alone.'

He thought about what I'd said for a minute or two. Then, with a rather nervous smile on his face, he said, 'Can I buy you a pint, mate?'

'No thanks, and I'm not your fucking mate.'

It was at this point that the barmaid reappeared. I paid her. I picked up my drinks and returned to the table. As I put them down Sammy looked at me and said, 'What did the Wooden-top want?'

I just smiled. 'Oh nothing, we were just talking about his wife and kids.'

Sammy smiled. 'They never fucking learn, do they?'

PART VI:
AT THE POINTY END OF THE SPEAR

Combat

Getting into combat is what soldiering is all about. Let's be honest, it's why most young men join the army in the first place, as misguided an idea as it may be. Well, that and the pulling power of the uniform.

These days' young men are enticed from a very early age by blockbuster movies and video games. The ones where the hero wins every battle, then goes on to get the girl and collect the medals.

But being thrown into combat will be a devastating experience. Watching men die violently for the first time is not something I would wish on any young man. Yes, many who have not served will say, 'It will make a man out of you, son,' but what do they know? In reality combat will destroy far more men than it makes. It will leave many dead or crippled for life, some with wounds you can see, but far more with wounds which you cannot.

You spend the initial months of your army career learning your trade, how to execute the most basic of military skills, like learning how to march. Even this basic skill, which many feel is for the sole purpose of showing off to the public, entertaining the masses, in fact has practical origins. Drill, as it's known and in the form in which we know it today, was devised by the Romans and polished in Napoleonic times as the most efficient way of moving large numbers of men around in the heat of battle.

Weapon handling and basic field craft teach the individual recruit confidence in his own abilities, as well as those of his leaders and comrades. A soldier's life from the minute he enters the brotherhood is spent either training for combat or actually being involved in it. These days the interval between a soldier completing his basic training and being delivered into combat for the very first time can be very short indeed.

Combat can at times be extremely complex and has several phases. The first of these is pre-operational training, where each soldier's skills are honed for a specific task. Then there is the delivery phase, whether it's by landing craft (not very often these days), motor vehicle, or helicopter or parachute in the case of the Airborne. Once we're in situ, actually have our boots on the ground, is when the other more dangerous phases of combat kick in.

Such as the advance to contact. This is where your stick, troop or platoon will move forward, normally on foot, looking to engage the enemy, and you actually go looking for trouble. Then there's the ambush, where, working on reliable intelligence, you lie in wait for the enemy.

However, whether you're advancing to contact or lying in wait, both scenarios will inevitably result in a fire-fight. This is the deadliest phase of all. It's where men, some of them your friends, will be wounded and some may even die. The final phase is the recovery. This is where, your task completed, you and any casualties you may have are then withdrawn from the combat area and returned to safety.

I attended one briefing during Officers' Week. This is where the officer candidates attempting to pass Selection are given complex military problems and tasks to study. They are then expected to devise a comprehensive and workable operational plan, including a detailed breakdown of all the logistical and manpower requirements needed to achieve a successful outcome. They will then be required to present this plan and all the supporting information to an audience made up of 22 SAS personnel of all ranks, everybody from troopers to squadron leaders. In an effort to increase the pressure, the physical activity of these young officers is also increased while their sleep patterns are totally disrupted.

On this occasion the young officer in question presented a very detailed and comprehensive operational plan, at the end of which he asked if there were any questions. One man raised his arm.

'I notice you haven't included a recovery phase as part of your plan. Is there any particular reason why you have omitted this very important element?'

Brimming with confidence, the young officer answered, 'I see this as a *no* return operation.'

The room fell silent. Then a very experienced officer pointed out to him that at the time it took around two years, and a cost of well over £1 million, to train just one soldier for the Regiment. Taking this into account, was he now proposing to throw away a whole squadron's worth of very experienced military talent, at a cost of well over £70 million, on what was, as he put it, a 'no return' operation? He didn't pass.

Special Delivery

Surrounded by my friends
but still I am alone.
The chatter and laughter that once was commonplace
has dissipated,
to be replaced with an absolute silence
broken only by the clatter of the old Dakota's engines.

Looking down on the world as it silently rushes by
I can do little but wonder at its raw beauty,
then feel sorrow
at the pain and suffering far below,
and the thought of what may be to come.

Maybe they won't need us today?
I live in hope.
But if they do,
it is I who must take that first step into hell
and pray that I reach the ground
before the fatal round finds me
whilst I hang helpless in the air.

I comfort myself
by thanking God that I only have to jump
and not fight my way off a landing craft
through water thick with blood and bodies
in a desperate bid to reach the false safety of some
    foreign beach.

Prepare for action; stand in the door; red on;

bugger, it's turned to a bag of shit
and now it's my turn
to jump and do my bit

Green on – GO.

Fear

Fear is a funny thing and it manifests itself in many different ways. To a child it may be a fear of the dark, heights, spiders, the water or even clowns. To a man it may be the loss of his job, or the breakdown of his marriage and the loss of the love and respect of his wife and kids. To many of us it is simply the fear of getting old and eventually dying.

But to a soldier it's not the dark. In fact to a Special Forces soldier darkness is our friend; it's when we do our best work. It's not the fear of dying either. That's an occupational hazard and one we face every day. No, a soldier fears failure. It could be failing a simple course, or not making the grade on selection. However, his biggest fear is that he will let the side down when it really matters, under fire, on the battlefield.

Most of us manage to fight through our fear of going into combat, the fear of being injured or killed. Most of us have to consider ourselves immortal just to carry out the orders we receive under fire. And, during this time, some of us will display remarkable courage and fortitude in the face of horrific circumstances.

For an officer or NCO there is also the added pressure of holding it all together for every man under your command. Your men will have complete faith in your ability to plan and execute an operation, or take control and win through an unplanned contact. There is nothing more sobering than being under heavy fire and have a young soldier turn to you and say, 'You will get us out of here, won't you, colour?'

It's questions like this one which turn ordinary men into reluctant heroes. Unlike the fear of water or heights, which, once conquered, the mind can then be retrained to overcome in the future, the fear of failing under fire, in combat, never leaves us and must be relived and re-conquered before every mission.

What If?

What if I fail
to meet the expectations of my leaders
to cope with my fear,
crumble at the bloodshed
or succumb to the horror of what is to come?

I can't fail
to complete the task I've been set
to take the war to the enemy
to carry out my duty
to support my brothers
or help them win the day.

I didn't fail
to move forward
to stand my ground
to take life
or defend my position without faltering in any way.

It's only now,
now that I've proved myself in battle,
now that I've seen my friends suffer and die,
that I've earned the right to be called a warrior.

God help me.

First Kill

Next in a long line of warriors
going back some two hundred years,
but this will be the first time I have felt the heat of battle
   on my face.
Moving slowly forward into contact
my one hope
my first
will be a long-distance kill.

I trust my corporal
but still my guts twist with fear.
As the distance between the two sides closes
I know that far from being fought at long distance
this
my first
will be up close and personal,
fixed bayonets
hand to hand.

Nervously I select my target from those before me,
I can see the weapon in his hands,
the colour of his eyes,
I can even hear him pant.
I pull the trigger
once
twice
and a red mist bursts from his chest
his legs give way and he begins to fall
and I brush him aside like an empty suit hanging lifeless
   in the air.

Like a robot I am already searching for my next target.
locked on I fire again
and as I eat up the ground between us my nerves turn to fire,
my blood is replaced with pure adrenalin
and as my bayonet overcomes the resistance of his shirt
    and skin,
sinks deep into his chest,
I find myself repeating,

'I am Airborne,
I am my nation's best.'

Finally it ends
and in the early morning mist the killing ground falls silent.
Standing alone and drained,
combats torn by close calls and covered in blood,
I survey the fruits of countless months of training.
I have my first,
my second,
even a third kill,
but realise nothing has really changed.

Have I made a difference in this battle?
Yes
but not the war.
I have merely robbed the world of yet another father,
husband, brother, son,
and like a hammer blow to the head
the reality of my actions hits home.

Tomorrow there will be another battle
and whether I win or lose

the killing will go on.

The Big Match

I have chosen the ground well,
the ground where the match will be played today.
It couldn't be better.
It's flat,
the grass is short,
it's deep and wide
with a ditch,
tall trees and thick bushes all along one side.

My team is hand-picked,
they're the very best I've got.
Each one is a local lad,
a chosen man,
seasoned players;
those I know will not flinch when tackled
or hesitate when the time comes to take the shot.

They have their positions
and go about the business of making ready,
for this game will be hard,
the type of game where reputations will be won or lost.
But we are fit,
well motivated,
drilled and experienced.

Hello Three Two Alpha, Three Two Delta.
Contact!

Shit, the visiting team has arrived.
I catch my breath,

my heart quickens,
my time is here,
my moment of truth.
I raise two fingers,
'Stand by, stand by.'

A chosen man,
no more than a boy, looks to me for reassurance,
reassurance that he will survive,
that we will win the day.
I wink,
it's all I have to offer him,
but it's enough and he smiles.

Unknowingly they approach the ground,
the ground I have chosen for their final game.

They must all be on the field before it kicks off.

If I have done my job well
not one of them will leave this place alive,

for this is my killing ground,

my ambush.

Forlorn Hope

The majority of our politicians, the world's media and Hollywood filmmakers normally portray Special Forces soldiers as some sort of unfeeling, unrelenting assassins. The sort of individuals who should be kept in a glass case with a label that says 'break glass on outbreak of war'.

But, in the case of British Special Forces, nothing could be further from the truth. When it's required, we are more than capable of killing clinically and without mercy. However, a lot of our time is also spent helping to improve the lives of those who help us, the local population in operational areas, while at the same time putting ourselves in harm's way to protect others. Such as taking the place of ordinary people who have been identified as potential terrorist targets, and providing 'close protection' for high-risk politicians.

The British Army has always led the world when it comes to providing first-class military training programmes for foreign troops. I was part of one such military training team in East Africa and our task was to bring two indigenous warring factions together. They had been fighting each other and the whites for nearly ten years when we got there. Both factions wanted the same thing: the whites out and their own particular version of self-rule to prevail. Things don't change that much, do they?

There were eight white Brits trying to mould 700 fully armed ex-terrorists into a single viable military entity. English was the only language common to both factions, but they both insisted on speaking their own tribal dialect. As this was a rapid-response deployment, we hadn't had enough time to learn either of the languages. The only solution was to have two regular black army corporals, one from each tribe, who would act as an interpreter, while we Brits ran the numerous training classes in English. The end result could at times border on the farcical as neither dialect had any modern technical vocabulary.

As you can imagine, our small training team, living with two large ethnic groups who had been ripping lumps off each other for close to a decade, and situated over forty miles from the nearest town, was extremely vulnerable. We were also without any form of reliable armed support as our regular black soldiers also belonged to one of the two tribes involved, and would most probably side with their own people if push came to shove.

During the three months I was engaged in this role – I was actually in the country for the best part of seven months but was doing other things – we had many tense incidents and two full blown mutinies. The first of these was more of a domestic dispute that got out of hand when a local Rupert tried to combine the washing and cooking area of the two groups with near-catastrophic – although to me entirely foreseeable – consequences.

The second was a different matter altogether. It began with the killing and mutilation of six of the regular black troops. It then developed into an armed stand-off which now had to be talked down as there was no way the eight of us were ever going to win an all-out fire-fight with 700 armed men.

I drew the short straw. As they say, rank has its privileges. The objective was to go and talk to the leaders of both groups and try to reach a solution that wouldn't end in even more bloodshed.

As I began to walk the 300 yards down the dirt track towards the large tented area with my two black regular army corporals

– neither of whom was very happy with their current predicament – I have to admit that many things ran through my mind, but in particular the Indian Mutiny and Rorke's Drift, neither of which ended well for the whites involved.

To say I was slightly nervous just didn't cover it, and the black humour began to creep in: things like, 'Why worry, you still die?' and 'There's only 700 of them'.

In an attempt to ease the tension, I decided to share these thoughts with my two black corporals. Now, if these had been regular British troops, these comments might have even got a laugh, but I was totally unprepared for their reaction. No, they didn't run. But first one and then the other took me by the hand and held on tight, like two young children going to school for the very first time.

As we walked that last fifty yards I was the only white face in a sea of black and the symbol of everything they hated in this world. I decided I just had to front it out, as to show any sign of weakness would mean the three of us would be the first of many to die.

How did it end? I'm still here . . .

What's Mine Is Yours

As I said earlier, sharing is something that should come naturally to a soldier, sometimes in ways you just don't expect. We had started a four-day patrol earlier that morning and I had now decided to call it a day just before dark. It got dark very quickly here. Dusk and dawn in Africa aren't anything like they are in Europe. There is no slow, pretty build-up to the arrival of the morning light and evening darkness. Although the sun is huge at both these times, and stunningly beautiful, you can watch it rise above and sink below the horizon, changing dark to light and vice versa in a little more than fifteen minutes.

My corporal, Thomas, was a six-foot-two black soldier from one of the indigenous tribes. He was an immensely powerful man who had been unusually quiet all day. We had cooked our rations and as we began to eat he finally spoke. 'Boss, are you married?'

'Yeah, why do you ask?'

'Where is your wife?'

'She's at home in Europe.'

'How far away?'

'It's about 6000 miles.'

'How far is that?'

This could be a hard one, I thought. I quickly did the maths in my head and translated the distance into something he might understand. 'Do you know how far it is from our barracks to where we are now?'

'Yes, boss, about one hundred miles.'

'Great, well, it's about thirty times from our barracks to here and back.' He fell silent as he tried to picture the journey in his head. After a while he said, 'That is a long, long way, boss.'

Twenty minutes later we'd finished our meal, which didn't take very long at all – army rations are never a banquet – and we were now cleaning our weapons and sorting out our kit for the long night ahead. Thomas had spent the previous twenty minutes in deep thought and near silence, when suddenly he spoke again. 'Boss, while you are here, in my country, you can share my wife.'

Well, to say I was shocked would be a massive understatement, and although I was deeply touched by his kindness, this was one place I didn't want to be. Apart from the fact that I wasn't really into legalised adultery, without wishing to be unkind I must say that most of the black African women I'd met were rather on the large side. They also had some very dubious hygiene habits by Western standards. As a result I needed to come up with an exit strategy and quickly. However, how could I get myself out of this very sticky situation without hurting his feelings or insulting him?

'That's a very kind offer, Thomas, but we don't do things like that where I come from.'

'She is very pretty, boss.'

'I'm sure she is, Thomas, and I really do appreciate your kindness, but really, I couldn't.'

Leaving aside the fact that I don't do blind dates, our two versions of 'pretty' were probably planets apart. So I declined Thomas's offer one more time in the hope that he would just let it go.

It was about a month later that we finally got some well-deserved leave. On the Thursday afternoon I was doing some paperwork while the rest of the platoon were busy tidying what was affectionately referred to as 'the cage'. This was a ramshackle collection of metal shelving formed into a hollow square. In the middle of this there was a selection of tables and chairs in various colours, liberated from a number of different locations that had been left unattended. The whole area had then been surrounded by a chain-link fence that stretched from floor to ceiling and separated our cage from those on either side.

At the front of the cage there was a lockable gate which kept out the uninvited. There were about half a dozen of these cages (one for each platoon) situated around the inside perimeter of the company hangar. It was where each platoon stored their operational gear, and also where the young Toms would take refuge when hiding from the head shed. As a result of the constant coming and going it would very quickly resemble a major disaster area, so we tried to sort it out at least once a week.

I stopped what I was doing and turned to Thomas. 'We've got a long weekend, Thomas. Are you going home?'

The massive African looked up and shook his head, 'No, boss. My village is a long way, so I'll stay here in my room.' I suddenly felt sorry for the big man.

The population of the country was made up of different tribes. Thomas' tribe were a warrior race, taller and more muscular than the others, and it was these people who now made up the vast majority of the army's native black forces.

'How far is it, Thomas?'

'Three, maybe four, hours, on the bus, but then I will have to walk for another two hours through the bush.'

I had nothing planned so I scrounged a Land Rover from the HQ Company MT (motor transport) lines and said I would take him. He was over the moon and spent the rest of that day telling me about his wife and how beautiful his village was. First thing the next morning we loaded our gear into the Land Rover and set off on the long drive north.

The strange thing was, that unlike Europe, where one town tends to merge into the next, leaving only small areas of unspoilt countryside in between, when you left a town, or even a city, here, the buildings, street light and pavements would just end. It was like someone had sliced through them with a knife. There were also very few vehicles on the road outside of the towns, and as a result we spent over three hours driving almost alone through a very beautiful and wild countryside.

Eventually we turned off the empty tarmac road and began to make our way along a narrow dirt road. The rough track looked like it wasn't used very regularly – well, not by vehicles anyway. In places the overhanging branches of the bushes and trees that lined the track would do their best to invade the cab of the Land Rover through the open windows. I had just been smacked in the face by yet another branch when I turned and asked, 'How much further is it, Thomas?'

'About another five miles, boss.'

As we continued on our way down the track I suddenly had a terrible thought. What would I do if the subject of sharing came up again? My act of kindness was suddenly turning out to be a really bad idea and I was beginning to panic.

Eventually the narrow track opened out into a small clearing and we were presented with a group of around half a dozen red mud huts. They were circular and much larger than I had imagined and had roofs of dried blond straw. It was the type of scene that every European schoolboy associated with stories of Tarzan and Africa in times gone by.

But it wasn't the type of building you expected to find a modern-day people living in. However, these weren't a modern-day people. Yes, they were living in modern times, but they were still living the same way their ancestors had for the past 1000 years.

We had only been stopped for a matter of minutes but were already drawing a small crowd, especially the kids. We unloaded our gear and Thomas ushered me towards one of the huts. He looked like he had just grown another foot taller and his face carried a broad smile. I'd never seen a man with so little look so proud.

As we approached the hut, its rough wooden door opened and a vision of beauty appeared. She must have been close to six foot tall, with the figure of a goddess. Her flawless ebony skin shone brightly in the afternoon sun. She had eyes that were so large and dark you got the impression they were bottomless pools. The type you could've fallen into and never be seen again. Her beauty was blinding, drawing every breath from my body. I was speechless.

Although she was obviously very surprised to see Thomas (there are no phones or post in the bush) I think she was even more surprised to see him with a white guest in tow, but she maintained her composure and stretched out a slender hand in friendship.

'My name is Sophia. I'm Thomas's wife and I'm very pleased to meet you.'

As I took her hand my mind was racing. 'Hi. I'm Theo,' and under my breath, 'I'm the silly bastard that didn't want to sleep with you.'

The offer was never made again. Bugger.

PART VII: CONTACT

Breaking All the Rules

I had been sent as part of a military training team. My primary task was to help train the local forces. The situation on the ground was deteriorating rapidly, and the colonel of the local regiment I was helping to train said he had a personal favour to ask me.

'What do you have in mind, sir?'

I was certainly interested but had no idea of what he had in mind. The thought of running an office, filling out ration rolls or counting boots in a quartermaster's store, held no appeal. No, if that was the case, I would just get hold of my boss and have myself reassigned.

'How would you like to take temporary charge of one of our troops, as a senior NCO troop leader?'

'Where's their current troop leader?'

'He was killed in a contact two weeks ago.'

'You do realise that this is strictly against my orders, sir?'

'Well, if you don't tell anybody, then I promise I won't.'

That could have been an interesting conversation, hearing him trying to explain to my masters how I had been wounded or killed in a fire-fight that I wasn't supposed to be anywhere near. He offered me a coffee and we sat and discussed what the role involved, what he wanted, and what I had to offer.

Later that morning I was introduced to my new troop. Taking the place of an officer killed in action was always going to be a daunting prospect, and especially for an SNCO. Looking around the room I couldn't help but notice that, apart from a few of them, most were in their early twenties, fit, well muscled and tanned, with mops of blond hair. I thought to myself, most of them could make a bloody fortune in Europe as male models or rent boys.

The look on my face must have said it all.

'Don't let their fresh young faces fool you, colour. Each one of them has passed Selection and is an experienced bush fighter with the heart of a lion.'

I smiled to myself. 'I'll reserve judgement on that and let you know later.'

I carried on looking around the room. In the corner I spotted a face I knew. The last time I had seen him he had been a Tom in the Parachute Regiment. He had filled out a bit now and had two stripes on his arm.

'Hello, Corporal Wheeler.'

His face lit up. 'Hello, colour. I didn't think you would recognise me.'

I had taken him through P Company some four years earlier.

'Once seen never forgotten. You've done well for yourself. What are you doing here?'

'You know how it is, colour. You get bored, go in search of adventure, then all of a sudden you're in the wrong place at the wrong time. I'll tell you about it over a pint.'

'OK.'

The colonel introduced me to my new charges and then in true Rupert fashion left me to get on with it.

'Right, lads. You know who I am and I'm sure if you ask him nicely Corporal Wheeler will fill in the nasty bits and any blank spaces later. But for now let's find out about you.'

Starting with Wheeler I went clockwise round the room and asked each man to tell me their name and rank, what their role was within the troop, and a little bit about themselves. They were a pretty mixed bunch, coming from a wide range of backgrounds, though most were the sons of farmers.

With the introductions over I sent them off for lunch and

told Corporal Wheeler to give them something constructive to do for the rest of the afternoon. Something that would take them a couple of hours. He was then to meet me with the other two corporals at 1400 hours on the field by the Traina-sium. I spent my lunchtime sorting out my bunk in the sergeants' mess and getting some new uniform, boots and webbing, as our DPM (disruptive pattern material, or camou-flage) and webbing was of a completely different pattern from theirs. The last thing I wanted to do was stand out, making myself a target. With five minutes to spare I made my way from the sergeants' mess to the field alongside the Trainasium, arriving at 1400 hours sharp: bad timekeeping is one of my pet hates.

The Trainasium was a cross between P Company's Aerial Confidence Course at the Para Depot in Aldershot, the Royal Marines' Aerial Rope Course at Lympstone in Devon, and a standard army assault course. It consisted of a series of high obstacles constructed from scaffold, rope swings and thirty-foot-high narrow walkways, all without safety rails. Put a foot wrong as you ran along them at speed and you were in free fall to the nearest hospital. There was also a large selection of high brick walls and water obstacles. It was all designed to test a man's fear of heights and confidence, while at the same time assessing his ability to take orders under pressure. There's no time for hesitation when you're standing in the door of a C130 or, in these guys' case, a Dakota DC3, with thirty guys behind you who are just desperate to get out.

The three corporals were waiting for me, catching rays in the afternoon sun. I sat myself down on the grass facing them. They all looked pretty relaxed considering they had been informed only a couple of hours earlier that they were to be led by someone they had only just met.

'Right, lads. Before we start let's sort out some ground rules. Firstly, I'll never ask you to do anything I wouldn't do myself.

Secondly, I will defend you against the Devil himself regardless of what you've done, although we *will* square things up afterwards, Para style [by which I meant we would end up around the back of the gym trading punches, and although they were allowed to fight back I never lost]. Corporal Wheeler will tell you how that works. Thirdly, when we're away from the head shed I will call every man in the troop by his first name. However, I expect everybody to play the game and respect rank. In other words, I expect you to call the troopers by their first name, but I expect them to call you "corporal". I'll answer to "colour", or "boss", and nothing else. The first man to call me "Theo" will wake up surrounded by a crowd. Lastly, if you let me or the troop down in the field, or try to screw me or any of your mates over with the head shed, I will personally dig a hole and bury you alive. Do we understand each other?'

They all nodded and agreed and I noticed a smile on Corporal Wheeler's face.

'You got something to say, Pete?'

'No, boss. Just glad you're here.'

I opened my pack and pulled out four bottles of locally made Coke. Same colour, same-shaped bottle, but it definitely wasn't Coke – well, not as we know it – and I gave one to each man. We sat and sorted out some minor admin points and I familiarised myself with some regimental etiquette while we drank. I asked them if they had any questions and Pete, who now seemed to be the spokesman, shook his head. 'Not at the moment, boss.'

'Well, I need to know when there is a question or a problem, and before it turns into a crisis. So I expect each one of you to come to me straight away, regardless of what it is. Nobody's going to rip your head off just for asking. OK, there's no point in me trying to reinvent the wheel, so I need to know how you guys operate: patrol format, field craft and IA [immediate action] drills. But first I want you to get hold of your stops [their version of a British Special Forces patrol] and bring them up to speed with everything we've discussed this afternoon. First thing after breakfast tomorrow we'll spend the morning doing dry runs of all the operational drills. I'll watch at first. Then, when I'm happy I know what's going on, I'll get involved. If I think there's anywhere I can make improvements, we'll discuss it as a troop. Then, if it's appropriate, we'll feed it in. Danny . . . ?'

He looked a little shocked to be called by his first name.

'Will you book a range for after lunch tomorrow? The next week or so will be hard work for everybody, especially me, so strap in. Pete, what are you doing tonight?'

'Nothing, boss.'

'OK, can you meet me in the office after dinner, say 1930 hours? Bring one of every weapon the troop uses and we'll play Lego.'

Tom and Danny looked bemused.

'I need to make myself familiar with everything we use. I need to be able to strip and reassemble each weapon blindfold. The last thing you guys need is for me to get a stoppage during a contact and not be able to clear it.'

Over the next week we slowly gelled into a team, a single body of men. They had pretty much perfected the art of bush warfare. Well, they had been at it for years now. I remember watching them clear an area of thick bush during one training exercise and thinking to myself that a lot of regular British troops would really struggle operating in these conditions, as we had been brought up on European Cold War strategies of urban warfare and in particular those used in Northern Ireland. I fed in a couple of new drills and made additions to a few others, which, once I had explained the reasoning behind them, were accepted without too much fuss.

I pushed them all hard during the following weeks and for such a young group there wasn't a lot of whingeing. These youngsters were totally committed to what they were doing, but most soldiers will initially resist change. It's part of their generic make-up, and is especially apparent when change is instigated by an outsider. But we did everything together: ran, trained in the gym, worked on the Trainasium, and performed live firing exercises and chopper drills until we could do them in our sleep.

It wasn't long after that I informed the colonel we were operationally sound and ready to earn our pay. Within a week we would be operating from a Fire Force base in the South, facing a highly experienced and well-armed enemy.

We Could All Be Dead by Then

We had been out for over three hours now.

Our helicopters had taken off just after daybreak from a Fire Force base deep in the bush. A Fire Force base is a purpose-built collection of huts situated within a compound, surrounded by a defensive wall of concertina wire (coils of barbed wire) sandbag bunkers and a ditch. This one was over eighty miles from the nearest town. Its primary purpose was as a forward operating base, a way of getting us closer to where we were needed.

We were now searching for an enemy unit that overnight had attacked an isolated farm about ten miles to the east. Luckily the family had managed to fight off their attackers. It wouldn't be until later that I would discover at first hand what would have happened if they had failed.

We had spotted about fifteen lightly armed 'gooks' (the local name for insurgents) about eighteen miles from the farm heading east and back towards the border and safety. They were resting up in a deserted village – a small settlement of red mud huts with straw roofs – when the K-Kar spotted them, marked the target and called us in.

The K-Kar was a Belgian-made Alouette III helicopter carrying the detachment commander, or 'Three Niner' as he was known. Its role was to locate the enemy, mark the target, and then hover high above the contact area, directing the troops on the ground. If necessary, it would also provide covering fire from its door-mounted 20mm cannon.

The ground troops were delivered in what were known as G-Cars: Hueys (Bell UH-1s) or Alouettes, each carrying between four and eight men in a group known as a 'stop' (so called because it was their role to perform blocking actions on the enemy). In this case each stop consisted of four men: a section leader who was a corporal or lance corporal, two riflemen and a machine-gunner. The idea was to drop the stops as close as possible to the target area. They would then advance to contact on foot. This system was well tested and extremely effective.

My stop and one other had been dropped to the south and east of the village, in an effort to cut off their escape route back to the border. We were to work our way in towards the village, while a further two stops remained airborne to pick up 'the slack', any that managed to escape to the north and west. This was not something the enemy would do willingly as it would mean them moving even further away from their safe haven over the border.

Why not just surround them?

Great in theory, but when the lead starts flying, those rounds that don't hit their intended target will stand a good chance of going straight through the area and hitting your guys coming in from the other side, which is nearly as stupid as setting up an ambush on both sides of a track, but I've seen that happen before.

The Huey didn't actually touch down – well, if it did it was only for a split second – and as soon as my boots hit the ground it was already on its way back up. It had reached a height of about ten feet when its nose dipped, the tail lifted and it started to power away. Each member of the stop had dropped onto one knee in an effort to escape the rotor wash and the debris being kicked up by its powerful blades. All of a sudden it was gone, leaving us behind in a near-silent world.

The format was simple but effective: work as a single unit, hold your position in the line, and anything that appeared in front of you was the enemy. The enemy had only two options: surrender immediately, or die.

As I lifted my head I shouted, '*Heads up.*'

And then, like a robot high on speed, I started to systematically search the ground to my front for any potential targets. I didn't have long to wait: within seconds I saw a muzzle flash about thirty metres to my front. The gook was well hidden among the shadows and partly concealed by the trees and the thick undergrowth. If it hadn't been for the tell-tale muzzle flash from that first round I may never have known he was there. Missing me with his first shot would now cost him dearly.

'*Contact, front and centre.*'

As the words left my mouth, I lowered my profile, my finger squeezed the trigger and as the first of two rounds sped down the barrel of my rifle, I started to move forward. My quick response had spooked him, and he had already raised his profile in preparation to withdraw. But he was too slow and another two rounds were already on their way. As he reached his full height, but before he had time to turn, the first round had found its mark and smashed into his chest, lifting him off his feet and pushing him backward through the air before his body finally fell to the ground. I didn't need to check if he was dead. This wasn't the first time I'd killed, and you can tell instinctively that they're dead by the way their body falls. But all the same, as I moved on past him I dropped down onto one knee and with my left hand searched his neck for a pulse. Nothing.

I looked down at him. He didn't look very old, maybe early twenties. He'd obviously spent a while in the bush as his jet-black skin had lost most of its shine, indicating that he hadn't washed in a while. I could also see that he was bruised around the eyes and some of his teeth were broken. Discipline in these insurgent units was extremely harsh and seldom fair. He'd obviously stepped out of line at some stage and been severely punished for it, but I felt very little pity.

Life meant nothing to these people, who butchered and horrifically mutilated men, women and children, both black and white, in what they called their struggle for freedom. Although such atrocities were common practice here, the world wouldn't be introduced to such horrors until years later when the media would report on the genocide being committed in Rwanda and Sierra Leone. Regardless of my feelings, the man's face was now etched on my brain, along with the rest whose lives I'd cut short, and it was one of the many that in time would come back to haunt my dreams.

As we continued to push on through the thick bush, the gooks fought a determined running battle, but with little success. Although the action involved two four-man stops you were basically fighting in twos and threes. You could hear what was going on around you but because of the thick bush you could see very little on either side of your own position. At the end of the thirty-minute contact, although one of our guys had been wounded when he took a round through the thigh, we had managed to kill nine of the raiding party on our very first sweep, two of whom were mine. However, the other six or so had managed to split up and slip away through the dense undergrowth. The race was now on to catch them before they reached the border. With any luck we would get this all wrapped up and be back in our base by nightfall. And then, with the remaining gooks either captured or killed, we could look forward to a relatively quiet night.

This was our first contact since I'd taken command of the troop and although I was initially unsure of how the guys, especially the youngsters, would perform under fire, once we were on the ground their training kicked in and everybody knew exactly what needed to be done.

The rest of the troop – i.e. the other two stops – were now on the ground at our location, just to the east of the village, and were bagging bodies while the K-Kar flew low over the area, providing cover. We were a fair distance from base now and because of the time we'd initially spent searching for the enemy, the choppers were running short of fuel. So I decided that we would load the bodies onto one chopper, and I would join Pete's stop and carry on the follow-up while the rest of the troop went back to base under the command of Corporal Tom Cummings. The choppers would then refuel, the lads would replenish their ammo stocks and then return to a pre-arranged RV and continue the operation.

I added one more man to Pete's stop. This meant it would be bigger than a regular stop, six instead of the normal four, and in fact it was also a bit top-heavy rank wise, but it would give me a chance to see two of my corporals perform under operational conditions.

Corporal Pete Wheeler, the guy I had taken through P Company some years earlier, was the stop leader. He was about five-ten, wiry, with a mop of curly black hair. He had told me earlier over a drink that after leaving the Paras he had joined the mercenaries of 'Colonel Callan' (aka Costas Georgiou) for their little adventure in Angola in 1977. A lot of the guys from the Parachute Brigade had done the same. Fed up with a growing number of tours in Northern Ireland where their hands were tied, reduced to nothing more than over-trained policemen, they had gone in search of a war to fight, one where they could get to grips with the enemy and do the job they had been trained for.

Sadly, somebody had put an idiot in charge: Callan. Well, what else would you call someone who tries to rob a post office in Northern Ireland only a few hundred yards from his barracks, and then uses a forty-nine-seater army bus as a get-away vehicle?

The operation in Angola had been a total disaster from start to finish. When it had inevitably turned to rat's shit, Pete and a few others had 'taken the gap' (a Rhodesian expression for escaping from a desperate situation) and headed across a huge swathe of Africa on foot, and after being refused entry by a number of countries on the way, they eventually ended up here, where they were allowed to stay, as long as they agreed to join the army.

The extra man I added to Pete's stop was Lance Corporal Danny Brookes, who was a typical Jock, as broad as he was tall, red-haired and pale-skinned. He looked like he'd only been in the country for a few days, but in reality he had already been here for nearly three years. Like Pete, Danny was also an outcast from the regular army when he arrived. He had spent the previous six years with the French Foreign Legion's Paras, completing a number of active service tours in Chad and a few other places. The thought of this broad Glaswegian trying to speak French (a necessity in the Legion) always brought a smile to my face. The thought of the French trying to understand him would make me roar with laughter.

Three troopers completed the stop. John was an ex-US Marine who had completed two tours in Vietnam. A typical West Coast Yank, blond and body beautiful, if you ever wanted him in a hurry you only had to go as far as the weight room in the gym. A good soldier, who never knew when enough was enough when it came to drink-induced stupidity. As long as you could keep him sober he would never let you down. I thought if he had been able to stay off the sauce he would have been a corporal, maybe even a sergeant, years earlier.

Although these three were foreigners, and while Pete had made some bad choices when he got mixed up with Callan in Angola, and Danny was on the run from the Glasgow police when he joined the Legion, you couldn't call them 'mercs', mercenaries. Yes, they were here doing what they did best, soldiering, and yes, they were fighting somebody else's war, but they certainly weren't doing it for the money, as 'soldiers of fortune'. They were on regular army pay, eating the same food and living in the same conditions as those who were born here, and I was glad to have them with me. And when it came to their turn, what was left of them would be buried in the same box and in the same patch of ground as everyone else. It was a hard way to earn your own six-by-three plot.

Ian was the son of a farmer. The result of a good education and hard manual work, he was typical of the breed: fair-haired, fit, strong and fiercely defensive of his race, his country and the war they were now fighting.

Dave was an unremarkable-looking but likeable lad, about six foot tall with cropped fair hair and a moustache that just wouldn't grow. The type of lad that, when you first saw him, would always beg the question, 'Does his mum know he's out here on his own?' His father was a banker and he was the product of a good public school, which ensured he always took a lot of stick from the others. But in spite of his background and his youth he was a seasoned fighter who had already been wounded.

The K-Kar landed in the clearing, and it and the other three choppers, their rotors still spinning, looked like four giant insects that had just settled on their latest meal.

While Pete set about collecting the spare ammunition from the rest of the troop who were returning to the Fire Force base with Tom, I made my way over to the K-Kar and the OC (officer commanding). Between us we worked out a potential follow-up route, and selected an RV point where they would meet us after the choppers had refuelled.

As I rejoined Pete and the others he handed me four fresh twenty-round magazines for my Belgian FN (the Fabrique Nationale version of the British SLR, except we had the short-ened-barrel version, which was more manageable when moving about in choppers and easier to parachute with, our two primary means of deployment). I slipped the 'mags', each weighing about the same as half a house brick, into my chest webbing, making six in all. Pete then divided up the extra belts of link (200 rounds each) for the MAG which was to be carried by Danny. The MAG was the local version of the British GPMG (general-purpose machine gun), a formidable weapon in the right hands, and far superior to the insurgents' Chinese-made RPD: a GPMG of a similar pattern to the Kalashnikov AK-47.

I briefed the guys and made sure they all knew exactly where we were going and what our mission was. John, who was an experienced tracker, offered to take point for the first stint. As we moved off, the stops who were returning to base were loading the last few body bags into a cargo net that was slung beneath one of the Hueys. After about 400 metres we entered a thick wooded section.

We had been going for about fifteen minutes when our four choppers screamed low overhead as they began their journey back to base. The roar of their engines scared the game out of its cover, while their rotors cast menacing shadows through the canopy. In less than a minute they were gone and our world took on an eerie silence. We were now on our own.

It was about thirty minutes later when we finally broke cover and the sky changed from a pale green to brilliant blue. Africa was one of the most beautiful places I had ever seen.

On the whole I was happy with the troop: they were well motivated, experienced and receptive to new ideas. John was about fifty yards clear of the wooded area when he stopped and dropped onto one knee. The rest of the stop spread out and crouched down in the long grass, minimising their silhouette and their target size. John called me forward by placing his left hand on top of his head.

'What's up, John?'

'There are two sets of tracks here, boss. Some are about an hour old but others are a few days old.'

'How many are we talking about?'

'Well, the recent ones belong to maybe five or six walking in single file, possibly the ones we're after. The older ones, well, that's a much bigger group, maybe twenty, thirty-plus.'

'Could it be the same group: the larger set of tracks from those heading for the farm, the smaller one from those coming back after the contact this morning?'

'No. You see the grass, the way it's all laying the same way, away from us, that shows us both groups are heading in the same direction. The grass on the wider track is the larger group. You see the way it's beginning to recover, stand back up. In the smaller, narrower track it's still laying flat, meaning it was done more recently. This is one group following another.'

'OK, if the tracks split, let's follow the smaller, fresher track. Well done, mate.'

I went back to my position about midway through the stop, took up a crouched position and began to update the others, who now resembled meerkats, listening, but constantly surveying their designated arcs, ensuring we had 360-degree cover.

About forty minutes later we started skirting around a large gomo, a lump of grey rock shaped like a half-buried billiard ball with hardly any vegetation on it, roughly 1000 metres across at the base and about 100 metres high. The lack of vegetation and the steepness of the sides meant there was little cover for anybody who was thinking of using it as a vantage point, but all the same we took up defensive positions and had a long look before moving round its south side.

As we skirted the bottom of the gomo and started to move away from it, into open ground again, John lifted up his left foot, tapped it twice and pointed at the rocky outcrop just to the front of the gomo. If we got bumped and needed to take desperate measures, this would be our fallback position. We would fight our way back to this point, regroup and then disappear. As each man passed the same point he would mimic John's movements: lift his left boot, tap it twice and point at the rocks, ensuring that the man behind him knew this was the latest fallback position.

The tracks John was following were leading us towards a thick area of bush about 500 metres away. The wooded area was too wide for us to go around without losing a lot of time and maybe even losing touch with the enemy altogether as we would be forced to spend valuable time relocating their tracks. We were about 200 metres across the open ground when John sank low on his haunches and raised his left hand, signalling us to stop. Everybody crouched down. Then, using two fingers, he pointed first at his eyes and then to his front, indicating that we were to look to where he was pointing. There, on the edge of the wooded area, was a gook, his AK resting against a tree while he had a piss.

'This could be the most expensive piss you ever take.'

The gook was still relieving himself when he looked up and straight at John. He still had his cock in his hand and you could see he was torn between putting it away or leaving it hanging and grabbing his other weapon. As he started to move towards his AK John let rip with two rounds in quick succession, which hit him in the left side of his chest just under the left arm and dropped him like a stone. Impressive shooting at that distance and especially with a side-on target.

Within seconds the vegetation at the edge of the wood seemed to come alive, filling up with a long line of black faces. My heart rate quickened and the adrenaline started to rush through my veins as it dawned on me that the six we were expecting to find had now grown into a much larger group. We were heavily outnumbered. If you ever needed a demonstration of why a black man should still wear cam cream, then this was it: their shiny black faces stood out among the green vegetation like a row of Belisha beacons.

There must have been thirty or more. They seemed to be everywhere.

Like a well-oiled machine, the whole stop reacted, and keeping their position in the line, they moved to either the left or right side of John, forming an extended line running parallel to the edge of the wooded area to our front, which gave each man a clear field of fire. Each had lowered his profile and turned slightly side on, reducing his target area, making him harder to hit. Then they all let rip. Although there was little to cheer about at the moment, what had really impressed me was that none of them, not even the two youngsters, had surrendered to their fear and hit the ground. The problem with hitting the ground is that you then have to stop firing to get back up. We had worked hard on this drill during the beat-up period – an intensive training programme of physical activity and military skills designed specifically for use in an upcoming operation – and now it was second nature.

Although the gooks returned fire almost immediately – their muzzle flashes were now making the shaded edge of the wood look like something resembling the Blackpool lights – we had the advantage at the moment as our FNs were a lot more accurate at this range. However, that wouldn't last long. Danny poured half a belt of link from the MAG in short bursts along the wood line, which was no mean feat. Although the MAG had been designed as a mobile infantry weapon, it was heavy and was normally fired from the ground while supported by a bipod. Firing it from the hip with accuracy, even with the help of a sling, took a great deal of strength.

But as Danny was built like a brick shithouse he was probably the best equipped for the job. Yet, even taking into account the impressive firepower of the MAG, we still had a massive fight on our hands. A fight we would have to win at the first attempt if we were to stand any chance of getting home alive. There would be no second chances here.

I had John, Pete and Dave in front of me, and Ian and Danny behind me. We had practised the fight-back IA drill until we were blue in the face; we were now about to find out if all that hard work had actually sunk in.

'John, Pete, prepare to move. *Move!*'

Without any hesitation, and with little regard for the rounds buzzing around them, the two stopped firing, turned and ran back through the four of us, zigzagging as they went, while we continued to fire to either side of them. They then took up position at the rear before opening up again. The next thing I heard was Pete's voice.

'Prepare to move. *Move!*'

Dave and I turned at the same time and started our run back through the hail of bullets being laid down by the others before taking up our positions at the rear. I then heard Ian shout, '*Fresh magazine.*'

I waited for him to change mags, and as he resumed firing, I shouted, 'Prepare to move. *Move!*'

Ian and Danny had just run past me when, above the din, I heard Danny shout, '*Man down!*'

I knew instinctively that it was Ian, the farmer's son, but without any hesitation Danny took up his position at the rear of the stop and started laying down fire with the mag, then shouted, '*Prepare to move. Move!*'

As Pete went past me I shouted, 'Pete, check Ian!'

A few seconds later I heard the dreaded words, 'Too late, boss. He's dead.'

My heart sank.

'OK. Leave him. Push on.'

Pete took up his position in the formation with John. It was now my turn again, but this time it wouldn't be straightforward.

'*Prepare to move. Move!*'

As I turned I spotted Ian's body lying face down about

thirty metres behind, and to the left of me. I ran over to him and put two fingers against the left side of his neck. Nothing, not even a glimmer. In my heart I already knew the answer. I could see a round had hit him in the back of the neck, so I started to remove his pack. I know, heartless, but he was carrying the radio and we were going to need it if we were to stand any chance of getting out of this alive. We also needed any ammunition he was carrying, so I rolled him over. His green eyes were wide open, but lifeless. He looked like a small boy. The front of his throat was missing, the round having gone straight through his neck and exited just below his chin, leaving a hole the size of a fist. As I closed his eyes I thought, you should be playing rugby and chasing girls, son – not out here fighting a fucking war.

I wanted desperately to pick him up and take him with me, but there was no time. As I removed the spare magazines from his chest webbing I felt a round slap into the side of my Bergen, a second cut a three-inch slash through my trousers, grazing and burning my leg as it went. I picked up Ian's weapon, slung it around my neck and set off again.

We carried on like this, leapfrogging each other over the last 120 metres back to the fallback position designated by John earlier, before finding any substantial cover. Finally we had time to draw breath and sort ourselves out.

Up until now we had managed to keep the gooks pinned down in the woods. The contact had been going for about six minutes. However, they were now getting braver and were beginning to move into the open grassland about 400 metres ahead of us.

'Everybody OK?'

Pete shouted up first. 'I need a new set of combat trousers, boss. These are ripped to shit, but nothing more than a few scratches.'

'Anybody else hit?'

I got three resounding no's. I threw Ian's bloodied pack over to Dave, who initially just sat and looked at it.

'Dave, see if you can get that radio going, while I work out our position.'

I had calculated our exact position earlier, when we had stopped on the other side of the gomo, so knew with some certainty where we were.

'Danny, get yourself set up somewhere where you have some decent cover but a good field of fire. We're going to be depending on you.'

'No pressure then, boss?'

'Pete, get me a rough head count on the number of gooks.'

Dave handed me the headset for the radio.

'Hello, Three Niner, this is Three Two Alpha, contact wait out.'

I checked the grid again.

'Pete, how we doing with that head count?'

'I reckon about thirty-plus gooks, and oh goody, it looks like they've got a mortar team.'

'Shit, this just gets better and better. We start off chasing six lightly armed gooks, now we're facing over thirty of them, and a mortar team. Let's hope they haven't got any armour hiding in the bush.'

Although this was a flippant comment, a piece of black humour, and I knew there was very little chance of this being the case, I quickly cut short this train of thought. There was no point in tempting providence and making things even worse. I quickly turned my attention to the job in hand.

'Hello, Three Niner, Three Two Alpha. Contact at grid two seven niner, three four seven. We have been engaged by thirty-plus, I repeat thirty-plus, insurgents with heavy support weapons. I have one dead and require immediate backup. Over.'

'Three Niner. Wait out.'

Dave had been watching me for a minute or so. He had a worried look on his face.

'Colour, are you sure? I mean, are you sure Ian's dead?'

'I'm afraid so, son. You know there's no way I'd have left him out there had he not been. Now get that FN going.'

The radio burst into life. 'Three Two Alpha. This is Three Niner. Our ETA at your location, forty-five minutes.'

'Three Two Alpha. Roger out. Bollocks, we could all be dead by then.'

The gooks had obviously spent the previous ten minutes getting themselves sorted out before making their next move. I now knew that this wasn't a bunch of lightly armed locals. I could see from their dress and the uniformity of their weapons and equipment, combined with their high level of field craft, that these were well-drilled, heavily armed professionals. At the time the world's super powers were using the whole of Africa as a sort of proving ground for their weapons and equipment. A sort of living, breathing R&D environment. Given their direction of travel this group were probably from the faction that was being supported by the Chinese. In another part of the country we would have probably been facing troops supported by the Soviet Union. It was widely known that both these countries were providing extensive training programs at specially built facilities for a large number of emerging African nations back in their own countries, as well as financing their efforts here in Africa. As I looked around our position, with its large boulders which were now providing us with cover, it struck me that it was only about six to eight feet deep and about twelve feet across.

'Some prison cells are bigger than this. Let's hope it doesn't end up as our tomb. Right guys, listen up, we have to hold this lot off for up to forty-five minutes. It's about 500 metres from here to the wood line. If we can hold them back behind the 200-metre line for as long as possible we may stand a chance.

The first thing we have to do is stop them bringing that mortar into play. What's the ammo situation?'

Pete, who hadn't taken his eyes off the approaching gooks, and, despite the distance, was calmly selecting his targets with some success, shouted, 'Five mags, and what's left of this one. So a hundred and some change. Plus a belt of link for the MAG.'

It wasn't common practice for each man in the stop to carry an extra belt (200 rounds) of ammunition for the MAG, but I had introduced it during the beat-up training. Although it increased the weight carried by each man by about 20lb, it makes perfect sense when you think the MAG accounts for around 40 per cent of a stop's firepower.

'I've just started on my second belt, so have another two left.'

Danny was an ammunition freak. Even though the MAG weighed over twice as much as an FN, he still insisted on carrying more link than anyone else.

You couldn't hear yourself think with the noise of the MAG and four FNs bouncing around the rocks that surrounded our small position, and were providing our defensive wall.

'John?'

'Four full and some change, boss, plus my share of the link.'

'Dave?'

There was no answer from the youngster. I turned to look at him. He had stopped firing and was propped up against a boulder, just staring at his weapon. I punched him hard in the left shoulder.

'*Dave* – how much ammo do you have left?'

'Er, five full mags.'

'What about the link?'

I knew what the answer would be, but I needed to bring him back down to earth.

'Er, yeah, and a belt of link, boss.'

The shock of losing his best mate had kicked in.

'Listen, son, you have to switch on. We need you to be at your very best. We're all depending on you.'

He looked at me and smiled but I could see the fear in his eyes.

'You will get us out of here, won't you, Colour?'

'Of course I will, and we'll all go down Samantha's when we get back and get absolutely trashed. But right now I need you to get angry, really angry and start killing gooks.'

With that he lifted his FN to his shoulder, rolled around the boulder and began to fight back. I did the maths in my head and estimated we had around twenty-four full mags of FN between us, about 480 rounds, plus another 1400 link for the MAG, which included what I'd recovered from Ian's body and two mags of 'nine-mil' for my pistol, which I carried in a shoulder holster under my left arm.

'Listen up, lads. I reckon we can hold out ammo wise as long as we make every single shot count. Danny, you have to stop them bringing that mortar into play.'

Under normal conditions, and even though we were outnumbered by at least six to one, we still had the edge when it came to firepower. Although our FNs and the MAG used the same-calibre ammunition as the gooks' AK-47s – 7.62mm – ours was '7.62 Long', which had a slightly longer cartridge and held a little more powder than their '7.62 Short'. It may not sound much, but it gave our weapons greater punching power and improved our accuracy over a greater distance. However, that mortar was a different kettle of fish altogether.

In our current position that was what was known as a battlefield winner. If they did manage to get it operational they had two options. They could use a 'creeping barrage': drop one round as close as they could to our position as a 'sighter', adjust the elevation, drop another one, adjust again, and so on until they eventually dropped one right on top of us.

Alternatively they could just 'bracket' us, meaning, in very simple terms, use a series of three rounds, one round as close as possible to the front, one behind and then one in the middle. But, regardless of which method they used, they only had to drop just one round into the confines of our cramped position, and with the blast and shrapnel being contained by the surrounding rocks, it would have the same effect as dropping a grenade into a bucket of frogs, and we would all die. We had to stop that mortar becoming operational at all costs.

'Has anyone seen any RPGs?'

There was a resounding 'no' from each man.

'Well, that's a plus if nothing else. The bastards probably used them somewhere else.'

The gooks loved their rocket-propelled grenades but couldn't carry a lot of ammo for them. It was too heavy and cumbersome, so once it had been exhausted they would normally discard the launcher if the going got too hard. However, unlike the mortar which needed to be worked in, in order to find the exact range, the RPG was a 'point and shoot' weapon, which meant it could be used in much the same way as a rifle, and with more immediate accuracy than a mortar. Again the last thing we needed was RPG rounds crashing in on us while we were trapped in here. The blast on its own would cause devastating injuries, not to mention the fragmentation effect.

But for now we needed to concentrate on the job in hand, firing from in between the rocks instead of over the top, so making the best use of the cover. We were taking a lot of fire, although, because of the distance involved, most of the incoming rounds were lacking accuracy and hitting the boulders in front of us, the ones we were using for cover. Of course, as the gooks got closer their weapons were becoming more accurate and they would soon begin to find the gaps in our defences. Those rounds that were getting through the rocks were hitting the hill behind us.

This created another problem, ricochets: rounds that were

hitting the gomo and bouncing back among us. Basically at times we were taking fire from two sides. The confines of our position were also so tight that we were continually being hit by the hot spent cartridges as they were ejected from each other's weapons. And the noise of the incoming fire, combined with that from our own weapons, was so loud we had to shout at each other.

The gooks were now making steady progress across the open ground, and were now only about 250 metres away. They weren't rushing the job. They were performing well-rehearsed infantry section drills, moving in twos and threes, leapfrogging each other as they moved closer and closer, with those who were stationary providing covering fire for those on the move: not dissimilar to the drills we had performed when we had reversed out of the initial contact. But, instead of just crouching as we had, they were being forced by our accuracy to go all the way down onto their stomachs, into the prone position.

When the enemy does that the trick is to hold your nerve, pick one, watch him go to ground and then wait, without ever taking your eye or your sight off the spot where you saw him last. Then, as he begins to get up, squeeze the trigger, and another one's dead. I had just sent two to meet their ancestors when a movement on the left caught my attention. It was three gooks working their way around to our flank.

'Danny. Reference the large rock. Three hundred metres, eleven o'clock.'

'Seen.'

'Come right fifty metres, into the long grass – that's our mortar team. That's your priority: you need to stop them bringing that thing into play!'

'Roger that.'

Danny immediately brought the MAG around to target the designated area and opened up using short bursts. If he could keep them on their stomachs there was no way they could bring the mortar into action.

John had just shouted 'Fresh mag' and was in the process of changing it when a round slipped through a gap in the rocks and smashed into his right shoulder, spinning him around and slamming his back into the boulder he was leaning against. He was now clutching his shoulder and swearing like a drunk, trying to focus his anger on the bastard who had shot him and away from the pain which was now causing his right leg to jump uncontrollably.

'*Pete!*'

'I've got him, boss.'

With Pete now tending to a wounded John it was up to me, Danny and Dave to keep the fight going. Danny still had the mortar team pinned to the ground, leaving me and Dave to deal with the rest. Although we were basically holding our own they were making slow but steady progress across the open ground, getting closer and closer with every passing minute.

'OK, Dave, if they break seventy metres, we'll bring the grenades into play, but not before.'

I know John Wayne can throw one a lot further than that but, believe me, when you're pinned down behind rocks, having real bullets fired at you, seventy metres is a hell of a long way to throw a grenade!

'What I wouldn't give right now for just one M16 with a grenade launcher.'

Pete had now sorted John out. Although the round had entered just to the left of the right shoulder joint, smashing the bones and making his right arm virtually useless, it had missed all the main arteries and the lungs. Pete had plugged the hole with a piece of gauze ripped from the pad on a field dressing. He had then pushed it deep into the hole with his index finger in an effort to stop the bleeding, then packed the rest of the wound, making John shout and swear even more. Over the top of it he applied another field dressing.

However, now unable to hold a rifle, John was basically out

of the game. Even so I needed to keep him focused, keep the adrenaline flowing, delay him going into shock.

'John, do you feel strong enough to act as number two on the MAG and spot for Danny?'

My question was answered with an immediate but very shaky, 'No problem, boss.'

Using his left arm and his legs John managed to drag himself over to where Danny was positioned. Together they started to home in closer and closer to the mortar team.

It had now been almost thirty minutes since I had spoken to Three Niner, so at best we still had to hold on for another fifteen minutes. Dave had recovered his focus and was now doing his part to keep the gooks behind the 150-metre line. We had probably reduced their number by around fifty per cent but it didn't seem to have affected their rate of fire, which was becoming ever more accurate the closer they got. The only thing working in our favour was that our kill rate had knocked their confidence and their field craft had gone to shit. They had temporarily abandoned their push forward and taken up static positions behind small rocks and in the long grass. They were now picking at us while they waited for the mortar team to open up.

'Danny, how we doing with that mortar team?'

'I've got them pinned down, boss, but I don't actually think I can get at them. They seem to be in some sort of shallow hollow. The good news is I don't think they can set up and operate without exposing themselves.'

With Ian dead, John wounded, and the ammo starting to run out, the shit was getting deeper by the minute. Worse still, it was now only a matter of time before that mortar team found a way to get themselves operational. Our best chance now was to get the rest of them, the mortar's supporting infantry, close enough to use our grenades effectively and reduce their numbers to a point where those that were left, and especially that mortar team, lost interest and bugged out.

As I got back to the business of dishing out pain I glanced around our position at the boys. Apart from Dave's little wobble, they had all played an absolute blinder. The fightback had been textbook perfect and we were now holding our own against far superior odds. I wasn't prepared to let them die now. A few minutes later I knew what I had to do.

'Right lads, listen up, I have a plan. It probably won't get us out of here immediately but it should ease our situation and buy us some extra time while we wait for backup. We need to pull them in close enough to use the grenades.'

I glanced over my shoulder. Dave's mouth was wide open in disbelief.

'You're going to let them get even closer?'

'Yeah, we aren't making any progress now they've gone to ground. We need to get them closer so that we can use the grenades, giving us a better chance of hitting more of them in one go. Grenades are like a bar of chocolate, Dave: throw one into a crowd and everybody gets a bit.'

The response from the other three was more predictable. They had all seen a lot more action than Dave and had been in positions like this in the past. They knew we had to even the numbers if we were going to stand any chance of survival.

Danny, who hadn't flinched at the statement, and without taking his eyes off the job in hand, simply said, 'Go for it, boss.'

John just nodded. The poor guy had lost a lot of blood and couldn't care less as long as we got out of here. Pete, who had been working away steadily, never flinching, looked over at me. 'Sounds like a plan to me, boss, and to be quite honest, I would rather die in here than fall into their hands alive. Let's go for it.'

'OK, here's the plan. Danny, you keep working away at the mortar team: we need to keep them out of action. They're far enough to the left of main field for the brave ones in the main group to think they're safe from your fire. Pete, Dave and me will lower our rate of fire down to the odd shot. With any luck they'll think we're running out of ammo [which wasn't a total lie] and then start to move forward again. As they break the seventy-metre point we'll let them have one grenade apiece and follow it up with ten rounds of rapid fire. If they break the fifty-metre line we'll repeat the exercise. Everybody clear?'

One by one they all answered with a 'roger'. Even John managed an enthusiastic 'Roger that, boss.'

Pete, Dave and I removed the grenades from our webbing and laid them on the ground in front of us. We then slowly lowered our rate of fire. At one point we stopped firing altogether and the gooks took the bait. As they started to gingerly rise and move towards us, Pete and Dave looked over at me. I picked up one of my grenades and holding the handle tight pulled the pin. I then motioned to the others to do the same. I didn't know if this was a good idea or not, but the plan seemed to be working. Suddenly about ten of them overcame their fear and decided to rush us. Once they were on their feet, and realising that there was nobody shooting at them, they began to run towards our position screaming like banshees, firing from the hip. I raised two fingers.

'Stand by.'

As they reached the designated point just in front of us, Pete and Dave copied me as I opened my fingers and let the safety handle spring free. I counted to two and screamed, '*Now!*'

As though we were all connected by rods we delivered our first salvo of three grenades within a split second of each other.

As the grenades hit the ground among the oncoming gooks they exploded almost in unison, the white plumes of 'phos' shooting high into the air and overlapping each other, shower-ing an eighty-metre-wide stretch with deadly white phosphorus. The screams of men being hit by shrapnel and burned alive were horrendous. Like robots, we then poured ten rounds of rapid fire into the lingering grey smoke. Suddenly there was nothing. No incoming fire. In fact there was nothing at all apart from the relentless sound of Danny on the MAG. With any luck the combination of grenades and bullets had got most of them and it seemed for just a minute we might all actually get out of here alive.

It was just then that all hell broke loose and a barrage of bullets began hitting the rocks all around us.

The pain in John's shoulder, combined with the massive blood loss, had made it impossible for him to spot for Danny any longer, and he was now propped up against a large boulder. Suddenly he shouted, '*Boss!*'

As I turned to look at him I saw a gook coming up over the rocks behind Danny. As he gained his footing and reached his full height he lifted his weapon to fire, and the years of CQB training kicked in. I wasn't going to be able to swing my FN round and take aim without either being too late or running the risk of hitting one of the others. I dropped it and drew my pistol from my shoulder holster. There was no time to take aim, so as my right arm straightened, the palm of my left hand cupped the bottom of the pistol grip, providing me with a stable platform. Instinctively I double-tapped him in the chest. I saw both rounds hit him left of centre, high in the chest, and he froze momentarily where he stood. I was toying with giving him another two when he started to fall backwards and behind the rocks.

This wasn't part of the plan and now doubt started to creep in. Maybe I'd got this wrong. Maybe they were too close and we were about to be overrun. We all held our breath.

I kept my pistol trained on the spot where the gook had just been standing, waiting for the onslaught. But there was nothing: nobody else appeared. He had obviously escaped the fallout from the phos grenades and our follow-up rounds, then found himself with nowhere else to go but forward, in what I call 'hero territory'. Unable to turn and run or stand still, you just have to push forward. It's how heroes are made, medals are won and far too many graves are filled.

'Right, it's a one-off. Back to work. I reckon we have about another five to hold out until the choppers get here.'

The words had just left my mouth when John shouted again, '*Chopper, boss.*'

I looked over my left shoulder, up the side of the gomo, and caught sight of the K-Kar inbound, about 1000 metres out, with three G-Cars coming up behind.

Danny was still banging away on the MAG and, with the knowledge that backup was close by, Pete and Dave had resumed firing at any gooks who had escaped the grenades. The sight of the choppers had spooked the three-man mortar team and they were already starting to withdraw. However, Danny had seen his chance as they began to move away and had brought down two of them. I grabbed hold of a smoke grenade, checked the wind direction and threw it into the open ground just to the right of our position so as not to obscure our field of fire.

'Hello, Three Niner. Three Two Alpha. Do you see my smoke? Over.'

'Three Niner. I see red smoke. Over.'

'Three Two Alpha. Affirmative. Drop your stops on the north side of the large clearing to the east of the gomo and fight through. Over.'

'Three Niner. Willco. Out.'

As requested, three stops were dropped in an extended line about 200 metres to our left, and began to quickly move forward. At the same time the K-Kar dropped to about 150 feet and took control of the operation, providing extra covering fire from its 20mm cannon. A few minutes later Danny had to stop firing for fear of hitting the incoming troops as they got closer to his arc.

But Pete, Dave and I were still shooting at anything we could see, most of it with its back to us as the gooks retreated across the open ground and back towards the cover of the wooded area. Confident that the danger had passed, I moved over to John, who was now drifting in and out of consciousness.

'Don't worry, mate, the doc will be here soon.'

I don't think he heard me. Backup finally reached us and moved through our position about ten minutes later, with the medics hot on their heels. The action over, Danny, Pete and Dave were now propped against the rocks totally exhausted but smiling. The floor of our position was covered in a shiny golden carpet of over a thousand brass cartridge cases, which were now moving underfoot as you walked across them. There were so many packed into such a small area that it was like walking on ball bearings.

I made my way over and patted each one of the guys on the shoulder. Dave, who was now shaking uncontrollably, just looked at me; his mouth was moving but nothing would come out. I just winked at him, ruffled his hair, and eventually he smiled. By this time the medics were now working frantically, trying to get lines into John's rapidly collapsing veins in an effort to replace the blood loss and save his life.

The field to the front of our position was strewn with the bodies of the dead, the air full of the moans of the wounded. Thankfully only one of them was mine.

I stood up, and with weapon in hand, I started to climb between the boulders that surrounded our temporary tomb, and on towards the killing ground. Smoke was still rising from those caught by the grenades, and I could smell the flesh as it continued to burn on their dead bodies. As I reached the top of the boulders and jumped to the ground Pete called out to me, '*Where you going, boss?*'

I never even looked back.

'I'm going to get our boy.'

Box or Bag?

It's a proven fact
all soldiers are slightly mad.
It goes with the territory, I suppose,
but the big question is,
are you a frog or snake?
And do you live in a box or a bag?

'Have you seen what that young Rupert's got in his
      pack?
Books of all things
and more spare clothes than my bird.
There's no room for his scoff
or his share of the ammo.'

'But you know what he's like,
he's as mad as a box of frogs.
I'll have a word.'

This sort of madness is considered to be
slightly eccentric
irrational
silly
thick
even stupid,

but in a funny sort of way.

Then there is the other sort of mad,
the scary type,
the type that lives in a bag.

'Did you see the Colour during the contact today?
I don't know how the rounds missed him,
it was as though he didn't care.'

'Yeah, ever since Paws was killed last week,
he's been as mad as a bag of snakes.'

This sort of madness is born out of anger,
its father
an unrelenting search for revenge,
its mother
a burning hunger to get even.

It feeds voraciously on one's sense of
loss
guilt
frustration
and will always out
regardless of the cost or danger.

But unlike the frog that lives in a box and has many
    flaws

the snake that lives in a bag has only one;

it walks a fine line,
the line that separates the homicidal maniac from the
    hero.

Frogs, beware!

PART VIII: DARK TIMES

God Doesn't Know Me

The Regimental Plot Hereford.

Most people will find it hard to understand how religion and soldiering can ever coexist. In many people's eyes, especially the do-gooders, the peace activists and the born-again crowd, soldiers break the most important commandment of all, 'Thou shalt not kill', with impunity. However, for a soldier it's different. Most of us truly believe that what we are doing is not only right, but necessary in order to make our country and the wider world a better and safer place to live.

Soldiers are often seen as heathens, especially when we're drunk or fighting among ourselves. It's also true that many of us will dodge attending a church parade in any way we can, and that it will normally take a homicidal sergeant major armed with an electric cattle prod just to get us close to the church door.

In my view this reluctance of so many of us to demonstrate our faith to others may simply be a symptom of
military programming. As young recruits it's continually
drummed into us that we are the very best our nation has to
offer and that we are capable of overcoming any obstacle
that is placed in our path. So the thought of praying to, or
asking for help from, someone or something spiritual, something that we can neither see nor touch, may be viewed by
others, and especially our mates, as slightly soppy or a sign
of weakness.

Even so, when faced with an event or action that may cost
them their life, some soldiers will naturally seek solace by
asking God for his help. I've sat next to men in an aircraft and,
just before they are about to jump, you will hear them mutter-
ing under their breath, as they try to broker a deal with God.
I've heard them promise that they will curb their drinking
habits while at the same time offering to attend church every
Sunday if he will only let them survive the fall.

Personally, I could never understand this particular line of
approach. I was always led to believe that if you wanted something you had to work for it, so asking for help from God
without having paid your dues through prayer was always
going to be a bit of a non-starter for me.

However, my reluctance to attend church or talk to God
was the result of something different. Right from those early
days during my childhood I can still hear my mum and her
mum, my nan, harping on about God like good Catholics do.
It was the early fifties, and in those days the poorer classes
seemed to put a lot more store by what they could expect
from God. You would continually hear about how powerful
and good he was to us poor mortals. How lucky we were to
have him and how everything could have been so much worse
if he didn't exist. Although I sometimes wondered just how
much worse it could get.

I also remember what it was like sitting on the cold stone floor of the old church in East Lane Market when attending Sunday school. I would spend the whole afternoon listening intently as the preacher spouted on about how God forgave everybody. I used to sit there thinking that I would be OK, as the preacher said that He even forgave the thieves and murderers.

Just a year later, as I lay alone in that cupboard at the Maudsley, I wondered to myself why God hadn't come for me. I hadn't been that bad. I mean what's stealing a few spoilt oranges and apples from the floor of the market, staying out late or back-chatting your mum, compared with proper stealing from people's houses and murder. Anyway, whatever I'd done in the past, it was nothing compared with what people were doing to me now.

Then I thought that maybe He just didn't know I was there, but then I remembered that the preacher at Sunday school had said that God could see everything, so He must be able to see me, even though I was hiding in a cupboard.

The logic of a six-year-old is a truly wonderful thing: it's totally linear and simple. My logic told me that if the preacher was telling the truth, and I had no reason to think he wasn't, and God could see everything, then there were only two possible answers. Either God didn't know me or, even worse, he didn't want to know me.

This was a devastating conclusion for a six-year-old boy to come to. However, regardless of how stupid this theory may seem to you now, or others at the time, it would be continually strengthened over the years as I grew older and was forced to deal with the mountain of crap that the world would regularly throw at me.

As a result I would do everything I could to avoid going to church services and morning assembly at school. In fact you could say that in my younger days God, and the serious business of keeping out of His way, helped me to hone my deception and evasion skills: all useful attributes for any soldier and especially a Special Forces soldier.

As I got older God's lack of interest in me was reinforced on a daily basis. It wasn't as though I was an atheist, nor that I didn't believe in a higher being: it was just that I thought that for some reason I was off his radar. Even when I was living rough on the streets and Dave took me to the Sally Bash (Salvation Army) kitchen close to Waterloo Station to get a meal, we would get our food and then be expected to say grace before we could begin to eat. It was as if we were supposed to be grateful to God for the life we were leading, and of course the bowl of soup. However, instead of saying grace I would quietly hum along to some Motown song, like 'Walk Away Renee' by the Four Tops, until the preacher had finished and we could get on with the business of warming our bellies.

This attitude of ignoring or avoiding God persisted into my early military career. Here again I would volunteer for extra guard duty or cookhouse fatigues (pan washing) in order to avoid having to attend a church parade. Talk about cutting your nose off to spite God's face. I don't have anything against anyone who believes in God. In fact I envy those whose faith is so strong that they passionately believe that this spiritual being has the ability to actually improve their life, even when it's rapidly turning to shit.

I've often heard it said that you will never find an atheist hiding in the bottom of a foxhole, but I have seen loads of them standing on the edge looking in at the broken bodies of their friends. I suppose if you think about it, it's true: no man ever needed God as much as the one crouching in the bottom of a foxhole as the bullets fly past overhead and shells are exploding all around him. Over the years I've spent a lot of time searching the battlefield for God without any luck, although at times I would be surrounded by the fruits of the Devil's work.

However, that said, I also greatly admire anyone who has dedicated their life to His service. My attitude may seem somewhat of a contradiction to most, and raise the question, 'How can you on the one hand dismiss God as being uncaring, and then on the other admire those that worship or serve him?' But it's not their faith or commitment to God that I admire: it's their enormous strength and belief in a greater good.

During my time at P Company I met a captain, a padre, whom we'll call JC. Whatever they are called in civvie street, whether it's 'vicar', 'father', 'priest', or one of the many other names for clergymen of the various religious orders, to the ordinary soldier at that time they were all padres. The policy concerning a padre who wished to join the Airborne Brigade was simple. If you wanted to minister to airborne soldiers you had to be one yourself.

That meant that you first had to earn the right to wear the coveted crimson beret. You did this by first passing P Company. The only exception to this rule was HRH Prince Charles. During a visit to the Depot, following his appointment as Colonel in Chief of the Parachute Regiment, I asked him, 'How did you manage to get that beret without first doing P Company?'

The RSM (regimental sergeant major) gave me ten 'extras' – additional twenty-four-hour duties, in my case as an orderly sergeant – just for asking the question. Apparently it was too much of a security risk for the Prince of Wales to participate in P Company. I personally think it was so that he didn't have to be exposed to us, the P Company staff.

However, padres were in short supply in the Airborne Brigade at that time as most of them thought it was not necessary for a man of God to put himself to the test in such a way. So they didn't tend to volunteer. As a result, on the first day of JC's P Company course the CSM (company sergeant major) pulled me to one side and told me, 'Sergeant Knell, it's your job to get the God-botherer through to the end of the course in one piece and also make sure he passes.'

'Why me, sir?'

'Because you won't show him any favouritism. And it won't bother you to shout, swear and scream at a man of the cloth, or encourage him [give him the odd dig in the head] if he needs it. I can hardly do it. I'm a God-fearing Irish Catholic.'

He was also a drunken Irish Catholic who would fight with anything that moved when the mood took him, but that's another story.

About an hour later the whole course of hopefuls, 120 men and officers, was formed up in the quadrangle outside the cookhouse. Each man was wearing what is known as a cap comforter – the Second World War Commando woollen head-dress – instead of his beret, and without a cap badge. They were all dressed in OG trousers and jacket, with their individual course number painted in large white figures on both their right leg and left sleeve. This was so that we could tell them apart. Like your army number, your P Company number is something you'll never forget. When I did P Company I was number 49.

As we stood there waiting for the chief instructor, I walked to the front of the parade. 'Right, which one of you maggots' – I've always had a way with words – 'is the padre?'

A slightly balding, overweight man in his early thirties sheepishly raised his hand as if he didn't really want to be seen.

This is going to be harder than I thought, I said to myself.

I walked over to him and as I approached I could see his face drop. Then, standing in front of him, I leant forward and whispered in his ear, 'Do you really want to do this, sir? It's easy to leave, you know.'

'Yes, staff. I really want to be here.'

'Well, sir. As you believe in God, I take it you also believe in the Devil?'

'Yes, I do, staff.'

'Good. Because he's only keeping my job warm until I can get down there. And, for the next four weeks I'm going to be at your shoulder, like your worst nightmare. And at the end of those four weeks you will pass. Do we understand each other, sir?'

His heart sank and you could actually see the air leave his body. He then very quietly said, 'Yes, staff.'

To say he struggled through the whole course would be a massive understatement. But I have to hand it to him: he never gave up. Nor did he ever refuse to attempt any task he was given. In fact I don't think the thought of calling it a day and giving up ever crossed his mind, even though he was subjected to a daily barrage of words he had never heard before, along with the odd dose of good old Airborne 'encouragement'. He would always manage to reach the end of every tab or run we started.

Most mornings would start with a ninety-minute 'beasting session' in the regimental gym. During this time the students would be force-fed a continuous menu of shuttle runs, press-ups, sit-ups, squat thrusts and rope climbing. The session was brutal and non-stop. No instruction was given and there was no form of progression: it was just ninety minutes of do or die and, with the gym floor patrolled by a pack of hungry, rabid staff, there was no place to hide.

At the start of one of these sessions I was sent upstairs to clear the stragglers out of the changing room. The students would hide there in the hope that they could join the session after it had already started in some hopeless attempt to spare themselves just a few minutes of pain. With the main changing room empty I made my way into the toilets. As I started pushing open the stall doors I shouted, 'OK. Let's have you. Anybody still in here?'

'Only me, staff.'

It was the padre.

'What are you doing, sir? Come on, let's have you downstairs with the rest of the muppets.'

The door of the end stall opened and the padre emerged with his rugby shirt (officers wore rugby shirts when doing PT so that we could tell them apart from the other ranks) in his hand. He had taken a tumble during the previous day's tab as he was coming down Flagstaff Hill. As a result of his fall his upper body and arms were now a mass of gravel rash and bruises. I felt quite sorry for him. This guy was totally out of his depth. 'You OK, boss?'

He forced a smile before saying, 'Yes, thank you, staff. However, as I now have a body that resembles Joseph's coat of many colours, I have come to the conclusion that God's not going to get me through this. If I'm going to pass, it's something I'll have to do on my own.'

I whispered under my breath, 'I could have told you that,' but thought better of it – most soldiers have an enormous amount of respect for men of the cloth, whatever their calling – and instead just said, 'Good for you, sir. Now we've got that sorted out, get your arse downstairs and fall in with all the rest.'

'Yes, staff.'

As I watched him hobble off down the stairs and followed him into the main hall I called out, 'If you're looking for sympathy, sir, it's in the dictionary. Between "shit" and "syphilis". You won't find any here.'

This may seem rather harsh, especially when men are doing what they consider to be their best while in pain and suffering, but some will begin to feel sorry for themselves and look to someone else for sympathy. Someone who will tell them everything will be OK and it will be over soon. But in reality, and especially for an airborne soldier, it's seldom going to be all right and rarely will it be over soon, so you have to rely on your own resilience to get you through.

After four weeks of pain and misery, a lot of it dispensed by my own fair hands, JC passed P Company and was then on his way to the Parachute Training School at RAF Abingdon, where, after another four weeks, he earned his wings.

At the end of that October my son was born and although I personally had no time for religion my wife did. When the time eventually came to have the little lad christened, like any man I just did what my wife told me. But no 'God-bothering crap hat' was going to christen my son, so JC seemed to be the obvious choice to perform the ceremony. By the time the actual day arrived, JC had been in the Brigade for just over six months and had already started to develop that legendary Airborne sense of humour – in fact he had become a bit of a natural.

That Sunday morning the garrison church was packed with a congregation consisting of my wife's family along with most of the P Company staff and their wives. Once we were sure everybody was there JC started the service.

Everything was going swimmingly. We'd had the hymns and prayers and eventually we got round to the part where he anoints the baby's head with holy water. As he stood there with my son cradled in his arms over the font, he looked up and, with a dead straight face, said, 'If I had any compassion at all for the human race, I would drown this child now, just in case he turns out like his father.'

This comment totally split the congregation. One half, mainly my wife's parents and the rest of the civvies, stood there open-mouthed with horror. The Airborne contingent just roared with laughter.

JC was a total character, and was well liked and accepted by all ranks of the Brigade regardless of their religious beliefs.

I left the Airborne about eighteen months after the christening and moved onto other, sneakier, things. The next time I saw JC he was on the Falklands, standing at the head of a large open pit which contained the many bodies of those members of 2 Para (2nd Battalion the Parachute Regiment) who had been killed during the Battle for Goose Green. He had the look of a broken man, someone who had had his long-standing religious beliefs shaken to their core. I can only imagine how presiding over such an event would affect one's convictions, no matter how strong they were. Having to deal with such an event would test your resolve to its limits and, under such circumstances, some of us will find it hard to actually accept that there is a higher being.

Although it's a little easier these days, I still find it very hard to accept the death of my friends, especially those who have 'taken the gap'. (It seems logical to use this phrase for something as final as the desperate act of committing suicide.) I've also forgotten the number of times I've heard young soldiers say, 'If He's all-powerful, how can He let this happen?'

Seeing and being part of the carnage on the battlefield is bad enough. That's a soldier-to-soldier thing, an occupational hazard that we all accept, regardless of how much it hurts. However, it makes you sick to your stomach when the victims are innocent men, women and kids; those who have been killed or mutilated by some warlord in order to make a point, or to deliver a message to the local population.

In reality we couldn't do what we do, or live with the resulting horror, without a deep-rooted belief that what we are doing is both necessary and right. And believe me, before going into battle each and every one of us, no matter how hard we think we are, will search our soul and have a heart-to-heart with our God, whoever He may be.

Some Help Here, Please!

Hello, God, it's me again.
I know I only call when I'm really in the shit
but at least you know you're needed
and I'm not faking it.
I've heard men call your name
when they're about to jump;
they promise to never drink again,
to go to church every Sunday,

if you'll only let them survive the fall
and live to see just one more day.

But with me you know it's different,
I only call when it's something really big.

Well, God, today is one of those days.

I know you're busy elsewhere
with other
more deserving lives to save
but you must have heard that bloody great bang
and seen the white plumes of our Phos grenades.

To say we're outnumbered would be a bit of a joke,
the fire-fight's in full swing now,
the air full of buzzing bullets
and thick with acrid smoke.

I have two dead
and of the four that are left

two of us are carrying fresh wounds,
so as you can see,
we're in well over our heads.

I've spoken to Zero;
he says they're on their way
but it could be some time,
so it would be really good to get a second opinion
as to whether I'll live to fight another day.

Anyway, God,
needs must,
things to do and lives to take.

Thanks very much for listening
but I suspect the next time we talk

it could well be
face to face.

The Guilt That Comes with Loss

To a soldier the death of a close friend or colleague in battle is probably the one event where he is forced to confront his own mortality face to face. There is no time to consider such things in the heat of battle. As I said earlier, most soldiers have to consider themselves immortal just to stay alive. If we didn't, we could never carry out the orders we receive under fire and battles would never be won. But when the fight is over, whether you're standing over the mass grave of your fallen brothers at Goose Green, or alongside the coffin of a fallen comrade in the peace and quiet of the regimental church, for those of us who remain, there is nowhere left to hide.

Of course the loss of a valued team member and brother in the field will have a totally devastating effect on all those who knew him. But for the members of his troop and his close friends, the loss and its effects are immediate. This time can be rough on even the strongest of individuals. Every death is accompanied by an enormous feeling of guilt in those of us who are left behind. This is the guilt that comes from having been there, but surviving. What the trick-cyclists refer to as 'survivor's guilt'.

Each and every man who was involved will spend days, even years, repeatedly asking himself, 'Why did I survive when you didn't?' There was always the feeling that maybe I could have done more, even prevented it from happening in some way. Maybe even the loss of my own life would have been preferable to the guilt I felt at such times. Although your nights may be filled with nightmares of the event itself, there will be occasions when something will happen, a trigger that reminds you of the friend and the friendship that you've lost. It's at this point your day will once again be turned upside down and be filled with a terrible guilt.

I have carried such guilt around for many years and I suspect it will never leave me. It doesn't matter how long you spend around death, or how many friends you lose. On the contrary, the impact of each new event will be even greater than the one before, and those feelings of guilt will just grow stronger.

Guilt hits you even when you weren't there. I was 5000 miles away when my best friend was killed in an ambush, but I still felt totally ashamed of myself for not being there with him, for letting him down, leaving him to die alone when he needed me the most.

This enormous burden of guilt and sense of loss is multiplied tenfold when the soldier has a wife, and especially if he has kids. Sometimes the guilt of survival is so great you cannot even bring yourself to talk to them, as you feel so ashamed that you've survived while they have been robbed of someone they so desperately needed. At times like this most of us throw ourselves into our work, preparing for the next operation. Get absolutely trashed for days on end, or go on long runs just to try and forget, even if it's just for a few minutes.

But for some of us this burden of guilt will become too great to bear, and eventually this enormous sense of loss will come to dominate our daily lives. Since the end of the Falklands War far more soldiers have committed suicide as a result of what they experienced than were killed during the actual fighting. The war cemetery at Port Stanley holds the remains of those that fell in battle, but the children of the islanders have now dedicated a new area alongside it called the 'Suicides' Graveyard'. Each new death is commemorated by the planting of a tree with the name below. And while that first graveyard remains at a constant number, the 'other' graveyard is growing steadily as the conflict continues to kill its victims.

Over the years the sense of loss slowly softens and we lean towards the happier times we spent with these men. I used to wander the Brecon Beacons for days on end, alone, just following the routes we once walked together. But no matter how far I walked, the guilt would always be there, and still is.

I Just Wanna Talk

Sitting here alone on my cot
surrounded by my friends
in a silence that is deafening
apart from the one voice that's no longer here
but now booms out around the room

Few are willing to make eye contact
but those that do quickly turn away,
unwilling to share their feelings,
feelings that are trapped behind their pleading eyes,
eyes dancing with questions,
searching for answers,
answers to questions that none of us are willing to ask.

We've been back over an hour now
but still we are unwilling to surrender our weapons;
instead we cuddle them
like small boys with our favourite teddy bear.
It's the only comfort we have left,
providing the false safety we so desperately desire.

Eventually the silence is broken;
he's the oldest and wisest amongst us.
Such a heavy burden for one who's still only twenty-
    three.
'Let's get these weapons cleaned,
grab some scoff
and some shut-eye.'

But me
I would rather sit here and talk,
speak his name out loud,
search for those elusive answers,
shed some of this guilt,

because it coulda, woulda, shoulda been me.

Loss

Like tired ghosts we appear
one by one from the darkness of night.
The moon slides behind a cloud hiding our arrival
while the trees carry our grief
helped by the earth
which now cradles the empty shell that once was my friend.

Quietly we cry,
not like children who've lost a favourite toy,
but as men
here to bury a brother,
a warrior
and my best friend,
who in the eyes of his mother
will always be just a boy.

Your courage,
humour and compassion
even in the face of great adversity
are the stuff of regimental legend.
That infectious laughter,
like your generosity and love,
along with my guilt of having survived,
will walk with me always.

The service must be short, my friend,
much shorter than you deserve
for we still have things to do.
But as you lie here alone in this simple grave
with the frost gnawing on your bones
just remember
I promised I'd not forget you.
I will return and take you home.

When all has been said and done
those of us who remain will disappear
like the morning mist at the dawn of a summer's day,
to spend it laid up
in hiding
waiting
until once more the darkness becomes our friend.

When I'm asked
why do you grieve so?

my mind will return here
to your freshly dug grave

and I'll answer quietly

because with the loss of every friend my world grows a
little dimmer

and I've spent far too long in the dark already.

Remembering

It is a strange thing that anti-war protesters and some other well-intentioned but misguided individuals often refer to soldiers as warmongers. Ironic really, as in reality nobody is more conscious of the effects of war than soldiers, for it is they who will witness the horror, suffer the loss of their friends and may be called upon to make the ultimate sacrifice.

As a Special Forces soldier you make all efforts to avoid the need for all-out battle, working rather on stealth and through 'hearts and minds'. But there will always come a time when these two options are no longer viable and fighting becomes unavoidable. It's then that the good and bad on both sides will die.

I remember attending the funeral of a close friend who had been taken in the prime of life. A highly decorated sergeant major stood up and walked to the front of the church, and with a lump in his throat and a tear in his eye, began to talk about a man we had all known for many years. At the end of the eulogy he told a short story:

'St Peter stood at the gates of heaven, when in the distance he saw a man approaching. As the man got closer he noticed he was carrying a large, heavy pack and was dressed in ripped and blood-stained combats. The man stopped in front of St Peter and put down his pack. St Peter then asked him, "How long have you served, my son?"

'"Fifteen years with Special Forces, sir," came the soldier's reply.

'St Peter picked up the soldier's pack, put his hand on his shoulder and said, "Come on in, son. You've done your time in hell."'

Such times are very sad, but I always thought the saddest thing of all about a military funeral is that all the bull, cere-mony and tradition – the flag-draped coffin, the belt and beret placed on top, the firing party, the playing of 'The Last Post' and the fly-past – are not seen by the person who is being honoured. I often wondered if this was the Establishment's way of hiding its own guilt. Its attempt at saying sorry for first asking him to go that extra mile, then failing him in his hour of need.

The Garden

Walking down the quiet footpath,
the one that runs alongside St Martin's,
I look across at the garden.
The rows of white headstones have been scrubbed,
making the names stand out proud,
reminding passers by
of the young warrior that lies below.

'I see the RSM's wife's been again.'
She does a great job:
each man's bed has been tidied
and has fresh flowers to brighten his long and lonely
    day.

As I take my seat on the wooden bench
the memories of those that lie before me come flooding
    back.

'Morning fellas, how we doing today?
I know it's been a while since we last had a chat
but I've had some stuff to deal with,
you know how it is,
always in the shit,
it's just the depth that varies,

anyway I'm here now and I have news for some of you.

Ginge,
D Squadron is off to the Sand Pit again,
the advance party goes tomorrow,
they're replacing A Squadron, who will be glad to get
    back,
they've had a good tour,
it's been hard,
a few casualties
but thank God nobody else died.

H died last week.
After all the battles he's fought and won,
who would've thought the big C would get him?
He's been out for a few years now
so he won't be joining you here
but I'll go and wave him off,
give him your best.

Steve, I saw JD last week.
He's still scrapping,
running a CP team out of the Green Zone in Baghdad
he says it's OK,
his team are all ex boys*

---

* Members of 22 SAS.

so he's as safe as you can be in a place like that.
BS is also there,
as is TV who caught another bullet last week;
he's like a bloody magnet
when it comes to a full metal jacket.

Pete, I saw your boy today,

he's doing well,
turned into a fine young man,
you wouldn't recognise him now,
well, why would you,
the last time you saw him he was only three.

He joins the Airborne next month.

Zara's done a fine job
and she still looks great.

Like this place
some things never change.

The Lost Brigade

A lot of recognition is given to those who died serving their country during the Great War, the Second World War and, more recently, in Iraq and Afghanistan. And quite rightly so. These men and women put their lives on the line for us and many of them paid a horrific price. Thousands have died and many thousands more have been crippled or scarred for life in the service of their country, and all deserve such recognition.

But what of the others, those who fought in Korea, Brunei, Aden, Northern Ireland and the Falklands? Do they not deserve the same recognition? At the time of writing, more than 400 British servicemen and servicewomen have lost their lives in Afghanistan during the eleven-year war.

But what of the 1000 who were lost in Korea? Or the 400 that died in just three months during the Falklands War? Most of them were killed in vicious, close-quarter battle, hand-to-hand combat. In total some 5000 men, a whole brigade's worth of British soldiers, died in the service of their country between the end of the Second World War and the start of the First Gulf War in 1990, but they are very rarely mentioned.

Then there are the countless men and women of the Royal Ulster Constabulary, which is now known as the Police Service of Northern Ireland, and the men and women of the Ulster Defence Regiment. These extremely brave men and women have put their lives, and the lives of their families, on the line every day for over forty years and many have paid an unthinkable price.

And then there are the secret wars, those fought by our various Special Forces units. During the seventies those killed and injured fighting a vicious war on the Arabian Peninsula, a war which the British public were for the most totally unaware of, were flown back to the UK and buried in secret, their fate and feats unknown. Were their suffering and sacrifice any less valuable or heroic than those of soldiers dying today?

Every year, no matter where I am at the time, I attend the local Remembrance Day service. I have only missed a few services in over forty years. Not because I couldn't be bothered to turn up, but because I had no option. On those few rare occasions I would be on duty somewhere else in the world, but whether I was there or not I would always remember.

However, these days, now that I have left the army, there is nothing that would keep me from attending these very poignant services, even though I know that remembering the close friends, those whom I've lost and are no longer here, will bring back the guilt and end up wrecking my whole day.

Standing there among the other soldiers, those gathered to remember their lost friends, I look across the rows of medals hung from unfamiliar ribbons. The ones from what I call 'the forgotten wars', medals quietly awarded to unsung heroes.

Old Comrades

These autumn days, bright with sunshine,
still struggle to lift my heavy heart.
So I'll take myself off
buy a takeaway coffee
and sit for a while,
alone with my friends
on a bench by the park.

Later as I watch the children playing
and hear their infectious laughter
I am reminded why;
why my friends and I fought so hard
and why so many had to die.

But today it's that day again,
the eleventh day of the eleventh month.
It's always a trial,
it's the day that I and others will remember them,
those that were lost,
those of us lucky to survive
and those whose minds were so broken
they just wished that they had died.

It's been many years since I thought I had lost my last
   friend
but every year there are fewer here,
some will be sick
some will just want, no, will need, to forget
while others will have fought and lost their last battle,
leaving those of us that are left to soldier on alone.

Wrapped up against the cold,
surrounded by the youth of the day in their smart
   uniforms,
standing silently in front of a naked cenotaph,
one that's soon to be adorned with a thousand blood-
   red blooms,
I see the look on their young faces
as they whisper

'Look at that sad old guy
talking to himself.'

But I pray they never know the horrors of war,
the suffering,
the guilt of having survived
when so many others had to die.
Otherwise
what's it all been for?

And just because they can't see my friends

it doesn't mean they're not all here.

The Aftermath

But, once all the training and battles are over, and the sound of gunfire and bombs has all but faded in our ears, most of us will be left to face the long nights and its darkness alone. As soldiers we all carry scars. It's an occupational hazard. Some of these scars will bring a smile to our faces as we remember that night, the one where we were too drunk to stand but still thought it would be a good idea to try to break the regimental assault course record while pissed and in the dark.

Then there are the other scars, those that will fill us with a strange sort of pride. The scars that will mark our rite of passage, the ones that were earned on some distant battlefield. The same scars that over time will become so hard for us to look at, or talk about, even with our loved ones, without having to relive the trauma and pain.

However, the most damaging scars will be those that can't be seen by others. Those scars that only become visible to us when we're alone in a troubled sleep or the darkness of night. These unseen, invisible scars can have a devastating effect on both us and our families. It's why we suffer the mood swings, the flashbacks, the recurring nightmares and the enormous anger felt by so many of us even years after the event. The feelings that as soldiers we learn to hide so well both before and after the battle, and will then refuse to discuss with anybody, especially our loved ones, in order to avoid having to relive the horror all over again.

I've heard people say, 'Pull yourself together, it's over now, you have to move on.' These people have no idea what it's like to be imprisoned in a deep sleep, a sleep you can't wake up from no matter how hard you try. Reliving every sound, smell and taste as you walk through a nightmare which you know will only ever end one way. Finally waking, moody, angry and totally drained. Or even worse, not wanting to go to bed and sleep, because you know what will come if you do.

As Special Forces soldiers we were actively discouraged from talking about our feelings and the effects that combat had on our mental health. At the time, even talking to a doctor could be perceived as some sort of personal weakness, a flaw in our make-up. One which might even result in us being RTU'd – so you learned to keep quiet, bottle it up and crack on.

When Darkness Comes

When darkness comes
again I'll climb aboard the Huey,
its rotors spinning wildly as it skims across the tree tops
pushing the morning mist before it,
the endless chatter of radio traffic ringing in my ears.

When darkness comes
again the old farmhouse will come into view,
its white-washed walls standing proud amongst the
    jacaranda,
in vivid contrast to their stunning mauve bloom,
the only sign of civilisation on this vast and ancient
    landscape.

When darkness comes
again the signs of war become apparent,
the bullet-scarred walls,

an empty hole, scorched black at the edges with broken
　glass,
the only clue to the window that once was there.

When darkness comes
again the family dogs will lie motionless at the foot of
　the porch steps,
and as I step over them I can already smell it,
the smell and taste of iron
that accompany the stench of blood and death,

Please God, not the kids as well.

When darkness comes
again I will reach for the handle,
and the bullet-riddled door will swing gently away from
　me on the breeze.
So I catch it and push it wide
and the full horror of that day
will be laid before me once again.

When darkness comes
again old man Vanderbilt,
his face battered and bruised
with a single hole in his forehead,
will be lying dead on the kitchen floor.
His wife,
naked with her throat cut, will be slumped in the corner,
but still I must push on.

When darkness comes
again I will find the three girls half dressed and dead,
their many wounds no longer oozing the brown sticky
　goo

which once was their life force,
but now just sticks my boots to the floor.

When darkness comes
again I will search for the baby boy
but will have no luck,

maybe they managed to hide him.

In the kitchen,
again I will see the large pot boiling on the stove.

PLEASE GOD, NO!
When darkness comes
again I will lift that lid.

It is said that you can only awaken once from a dream
but if that's true,

then why do I wake from this same nightmare every
   single night?

The Genie

A young soldier
home on leave
had been out with his mates for a drink.
Walking home alone he starts to kick an old tin can left
   on the street.
After three or four kicks there's a puff of smoke
and a rather cross-looking genie appears.

OK, listen up,
there's no more of this three wishes shit,

you only get one, so make it good.
The soldier thinks for a while then says
'Well, I've always wanted to visit America but I hate
    flying.
Could you build me a bridge so that I can drive
    instead?'

The genie looks at him and shakes his head.
'Do you know how much concrete, steel and work that
    would involve,
even for a master of magic like me?
No, it's impossible,
it just can't be done.
Make another wish.'

The soldier thinks again,
and after a while he looks at the genie and says
'During my time in the army I have seen things that no
    one should ever see.
Do you think you could take away the flashbacks,
the feelings of loss,
guilt
and the endless nightmares?'

The genie smiled,
and with a solitary tear rolling down his cheek,
looked at the soldier and shook his head,

'Where do you want this bridge, son?'

Letters I Should Have Written

During my time in the military there are a lot of things I should have either said or done. There are also many things I wish I had never said or done. But one of my biggest regrets is the letters I didn't write. Letters to the people I cared about the most. I think that when the chips are down and you're finding it hard to cope with things that are sometimes too raw or painful to talk about, even with those who love and care for you, a simple letter will go a long way to ease the confusion and isolation they must be feeling.

My wife has been my best friend (some sarcastic bastards would say my only friend) for over forty years. In fact they're probably right. She is the only real friend I've ever had, which is a sad indictment for a man of my age. But over the years, with all the shit I've put her through, the numerous disappearing acts, those that were without warning and at the drop of a hat, returning months later – once in a wheelchair – she has never once doubted my love or walked away from me. She has always been there for me.

On reflection, I could have made her life so much easier just by writing her a simple letter. A letter that would have told her what I was going through. It would have avoided all those difficult questions, the ones which I either couldn't answer (for security reasons) or didn't want to answer in an effort to avoid the pain. A simple letter that would have told her that none of this was her fault. That my bad moods and just wanting to be left alone were not the result of something she or my little boy had done. And that, although I was continually pushing them both away, I needed them more than ever during those troubled times.

I'm not talking about the type of letter we all write when we're away. The ones that don't tell the truth. The ones that say everything is OK and they shouldn't worry. No, I'm talking about when you're back at home and in one of those dark places. It's then that you should write your letter and leave it somewhere it can be easily found. It may even help you to shed some of the guilt of knowing how difficult you've made their lives.

PART IX: LIFE AFTER DEATH

Moving On

Possibly the biggest challenge facing any career soldier is when he actually leaves the service. Even for a happily married man like me. The loss that is felt when suddenly you are alone, no longer part of the regimental family, is enormous. These feelings are then multiplied as most of us will be forced to move away from our current regimental locations, leave our friends and go back to the area where we lived before we joined the army. By the time I left the army both my parents and my wife's parents were no longer with us, so we had no roots or anywhere to return to.

My dad was still bumbling around the planet somewhere in Australia, but I didn't know where he was, and to be quite honest, after years without any form of contact, I didn't really care. So we stayed where we were in Hereford and, although I saw my mates regularly, shared a coffee or a pint with them and talked about the old times, I was no longer a part of their unit or privy to the operations currently in play. And quite rightly so. Although there was now a little distance between us, we had lived together for so long that I knew exactly where the line was, and that if I wanted to keep my friends I would never put them in a position where they would be forced to choose between me and the security of the Regiment. As I've already said, if you needed to know someone would tell you.

Although I never realised it, their support, invisible as it had seemed at the time, was always there, but now it was gone.

It's said that the four most stressful events during an adult's life are losing your job, moving house, going through a divorce, and the death of a loved one. It's hard enough having to deal with just one of these events, but try to imagine what it would feel like to be forced to deal with two of them at the same time. While also losing daily contact with all of your closest friends.

Somebody once asked me how it felt to leave the army after twenty-two years, and did I miss it? The only way I could put it was to liken it to a premiership footballer, someone who was still at the top of his game being told he was now too old to play, past his sell-by date and therefore no longer wanted.

The day I left the army I was looking forward to a well-earned rest and a brand-new start. I was tired – not the sort of tired you get when you've had a hard day at the office – no, I mean the mentally and physically exhausted type of tired. The type of tired that covers you after the battle, when the adrenaline finally stops coursing through your veins and your will to go on, no matter how strong it is, can no longer override your body's need for rest.

As an officer or senior NCO in the army you spend every waking minute under scrutiny. Regardless of where you are, whether you're away on operations, back in camp, at a mess dinner or a squadron social with your wife. Everything you say or do will be seen by someone, and your actions will either make or break your career. It's also not just you that's being constantly assessed. When I was a young lance corporal in the cavalry I was told by a sergeant major, 'It won't be long before we see you in the sergeants' mess, Knell, as long as you can keep your nose clean.'

I demonstrated my humility (well, nobody likes a cocky bastard) by informing him that there were other corporals in the regiment who were much more senior than me and had more time under their belt. He agreed, but then said, 'Yes, but their wives will let them down. They just won't fit into mess society.'

It was at this point that I seriously considered sending my wife on a gunnery course in an effort to advance my career.

However, when I drove out of those gates at Hereford for the very last time it was supposed to be the start of a brand-new adventure. A new life filled with excitement. But it was also tinged with a little bit of fear, as neither I nor my wife had had to function in the civilian world for well over twenty years.

I had reached the rank of warrant officer (sergeant major, for the uninitiated) but had turned down being commissioned as an officer because I just couldn't see me sitting behind a desk for the next fifteen years, reduced to nothing more than a well-respected bean counter, as opposed to a fighting soldier. The powers that be, the civilian pencil necks from Whitehall, using the colonel's wife for backup, had even cornered my wife one morning and asked her if there was any way she could talk me into taking a commission. This was a huge decision, for by refusing a commission I was turning my back on fifteen extra years of security, a regular wage and a greatly improved pension on leaving the army at the age of fifty-five. But, after twenty-two years together, she knew me better than anybody else, and as a result I now had to leave the army.

We had bought our first home some six months earlier, a house which now had to be completely renovated, furnished and turned into our new home: there goes the bulk of my pay-off. Then there was the other hurdle to overcome. I was still only forty and had to find some sort of gainful employment, but, like most ex-soldiers, I was totally unprepared for what lay ahead of me.

The second thing that hits you really hard is when you learn that the skills you spent so long learning and perfecting, the skills that kept you and your team alive, are not needed by civilian employers. As one guy was told at the Hereford job centre, 'There isn't a lot of call for someone who can deal death from 25,000 feet.' Which, loosely interpreted, means, 'Can you drive a bus?'

The day I handed in my ID card, the day I left the army, as far as they were concerned, I ceased to exist.

This situation can be totally overwhelming for some men. Once that feeling of uselessness and isolation sets in, most of us will search through our memories for the good times, the times that made us happy and feel worthy of respect. Unfortunately, in most cases, it will manifest itself by dragging up the really bad times as well.

Suddenly I found myself in a world where I was totally alone. I was no longer a personality within my peer group. In fact I no longer had a peer group. I was now a total oddball: a trained killer living among the normal people. I also no longer had that invisible support provided by my mates, the only people in the world who truly understood me. Well, apart from my wife, that is, but there was so much she never knew. I was also without the structured existence that my time in the military had provided for so much of my life. In fact the last time I felt this alone was the day I left boarding school some twenty-four years earlier.

For the past twenty-two years all I'd had to do was turn up for work. I didn't really have to think about paying rent or fuel and light as these were taken out of my pay before I even got it. This, of course, is contrary to the civilian fairytale that servicemen and servicewomen live rent free and receive loads of added extras.

But, even after all the bills were paid, we would always be able to find enough money for food. However, now I had to learn the basic skills of juggling my very limited financial resources and making them stretch. Something my civilian counterparts had learned to do from the day they first left home. I had given more than two decades of unflinching service to my country and 'the Colours', but was now totally alone.

My wife and I had married when we were both just eighteen. She had stood by me on that day, as she had done for the past twenty-two years. She had never stopped me from doing what needed to be done, or nagged me about spending so much time away from home. She had never once doubted or turned her back on me. But how would I now repay this enormous debt of love and devotion?

Sound Advice?

As I told you earlier, at sixteen, and in between leaving boarding school and joining the army, I had spent around nine months living rough on the streets of south-east London. That was before going to live with my nan and granddad. At the time they were the only ones prepared to take me in. I was extremely lucky that they came along when they did. Those nine months that I had spent on the streets had turned me practically feral.

My nan and granddad were obviously much older than most of the adults I had come into contact with during my short life. They also had what I like to call the old values. The same values that had held communities together during the tough times of the thirties, through the Second World War and the postwar depression. Things like supporting each other and lending a helping hand when the chips were down. Trust and honesty. I know, those last two are hard to swallow, especially from a cockney. But it was true.

However, all joking aside, these two wonderful individuals taught me how to behave properly in an adult world. Even now I can hear my granddad sharing his words of wisdom, and one of the things he told me then was about to come in very useful.

When I first started going out with girls I would ask his advice. Not about the more intimate side of the 'boy-girl' thing. No, I thought I had got all the information I needed on that front. (How wrong can one man be.) And his little gem 'On no account are you ever to use your gran's bed' was extremely valuable advice as my nan was a formidable woman when riled.

But what I was really looking for was advice on building a relationship. At that time I was seventeen years old, but I'd never really had a real relationship, not even with my family, in fact not with anybody. My latest experience, living rough on the streets, had meant that I didn't trust anybody. Instead I had learned, and had become willing to do, whatever it took in order to survive, anything to get me through just one more day.

However, this wonderful old man was about to share another piece of simple, but very valuable information. A piece of advice that would help me to keep my marriage intact through the very difficult times ahead. I can still see him now, sitting on the edge of his old armchair, ankles crossed, with his elbows resting on its arms, leant forward and talking in whispers so that my nan wouldn't hear. 'Never ever lie to a woman, son, because if you do, one day it will come back and bite you in the arse. They're strange creatures. They're not like us, boy: they never ever forget. Better not to tell them anything than lie to them.'

Sadly, what I didn't know at the time was that this once powerful man with a legendary sense of humour was already dying. The day I joined the army would be the last time I would ever see him.

My wife and I had spent our first six months in civvie street renovating and furnishing our home and she had done a fantastic job. I was lucky that she loves decorating and although I helped out where I could, I'd never been one for DIY, although I do make a really mean brew, so I had my uses. The whole house had a warm and welcoming atmosphere. Each room was tastefully furnished and colour co-ordinated, making it the type of place that every soldier dreamed about retiring to. However, as a result of the enormous expense of sorting it all out, money was now running short and this was 1992 and Britain was only just starting to come out of recession.

Work was still proving difficult to find, not because I didn't have the necessary intelligence or was unwilling to learn a new set of skills. No, it was because I hadn't attended one of those very expensive two-week management courses in somewhere like Surrey, and been given a magic piece of paper that said I was now God's gift to British industry. It was as though all my past training and hands-on experience was now totally worthless.

I remember attending one interview – I think it was for an administrative post with the local council (not my first choice but beggars can't be choosers) – and being asked by a balding pencil neck in a pinstriped suit and horn-rimmed glasses, 'Do you have any leadership qualifications? Can you command respect?' The minute that word 'qualification' raised its ugly head I could see where this was going. 'Well, I've been leading and managing men for over twenty years. I've never had any trouble convincing them that standing their ground and risking life and limb in order to get the job done was a good idea, when it was required.'

'No, we mean do you have any diplomas from a recognised management school?'

I didn't get the job. Some pillock straight out of university got it, probably on the strength of the time he'd spent as captain of the university hockey team. However, I did notice that they re-advertised the post a number of months later.

As time progressed things steadily got worse, much worse. So, following my granddad's advice, I hid the truth from my wife about just how deep the shit actually was. I never lied to her. I couldn't do that so, like granddad said, 'I never told her anything.' It was my role to protect her and that's what I was going to do, regardless of the personal cost to me.

We had talked about me going out on 'the Circuit'. The war in Algeria was in full swing at the time and the major oil companies – the likes of Mobil (before it was Exxon Mobil), ELF, BP and Halliburton, the oil exploration company – were all looking for highly trained and experienced ex-Special Forces soldiers to provide security for their desert rigs. There's good money to be earned fighting new battles with old friends in foreign lands as a security consultant (a new posh PC term for an old-fashioned mercenary). But my wife wasn't too keen, and I could understand that.

She had spent years bringing up our son and living on her own, wondering if I was ever going to come home. But after all the shit I had put her through I just couldn't bring myself to tell her how bad it really was, and how much I needed that job.

It Would Be So Easy

So I never told her about the year I spent fending off the bailiffs who wanted to take our furniture because of Council Tax arrears. Although, I must say, I got quite good at bluffing my way, coming up with last-minute solutions to impossible fucking problems. Well, let's face it I'd had lots of practice over the previous twenty-two years, as well as learning to hide from bailiffs as a child.

Most collection agencies (a new posh term for an old-fashioned bailiff) tended to use a very select sector of society to represent them as they went about the daily task of collecting what was owed. Most of these individuals can only be described as morons, those that had failed every one of their exams at school; those that had spent years either as bullies or being bullied in the playground, and as a result were now incapable of earning their money in any other way apart from intimidating others. Not that my predicament was their fault. In fact it was nobody's fault but mine. But when they turned up at my front door they quickly became my problem.

They would always turn up on your doorstep in pairs. Some might think that this was done to ensure that they could adequately defend themselves if their call suddenly went wrong and turned confrontational. Personally, I think this form of approach was always intended to be used as a form of intimidation. The other possible reason for always having two of them is that, by combining their brain power, they might even manage to come up with some form of coherent conversation.

The process was remarkably simple. They would knock on

my door. I would open it. They would ask me my name, and once they were sure they had the right person, they would tell me who they were and why they were so intent on ruining what was already a really shit day.

They would then go to great lengths to explain my situation, something which I was already aware of. Shit, I was living it. Both sides would then participate in a sort of game where we would discuss and agree a suitable payment plan, which normally included a high percentage of interest to cover their greatly inflated costs. I would then agree to enter into this magical payment plan, one which both sides knew I wouldn't be able to keep to. Not because I didn't want to, but because I didn't have enough money to do so.

However, I would try to stick to the plan as best I could. But I always knew that, sooner or later, there would come a day when it just wasn't possible to come up with any more money and I would be forced to devise an alternative plan.

I had now been fighting this type of rearguard type of action for about eight months. It was just after ten-thirty in the morning, my wife was out shopping and I was in the house on my own when the front door bell rang. Even before I answered the door a sixth sense told me it was going to be bad news and I was right.

I opened the door and there, standing on the doorstep, were two gorillas dressed in ill-fitting, cheap suits. I had spent years making sure that I was always presentable. Even in the field I would somehow find the time to slap a coat of fresh polish on my boots, to keep the water out if nothing else. But, standing there looking at these two idiots, I found myself asking the question, 'Did you two muppets get dressed in the dark this morning?'

One of them finally spoke. 'Mr Knell?'

'Yeah.'

Then together they spent the next fifteen minutes telling me what I already knew. That was probably the most galling thing of all. The fact that they assumed I was so thick that I had no idea what was really going on in my life. So I just stood there and listened while they tried to lord it over me with their very limited vocabulary. Up until that point I didn't know it was possible to have a conversation that consisted purely of one- and two-syllable words but, as amusing as it was, I wasn't really interested. Yes, my physical presence was stood there on my doorstep, but my mind was now functioning in some kind of parallel universe.

As a result I soon found myself running a tried-and-tested CQB scenario in my head. One I had used a number of times to get myself out of trouble in the past. One of those where it would be so much easier just to kill them both right now. It wouldn't take much, starting with the leaner of the two, working on the assumption that being lighter he would be able to move a little faster than the chubby guy, which was why I needed to disable him first.

It would be so easy to deliver a barrage of strategically placed blows to the throat, solar plexus and groin. In just a few seconds it would all be over, done and dusted. However, moving the two corpses and then burying them in the garden, especially the fat bastard, could prove to be more of a problem.

I was so fed up and so near to actually doing it that it terrifies me to think about how close I came to killing them both.

I also never told my wife about the number of times we were threatened with eviction. How I'd first had to negotiate with the bank in order to stop them repossessing our house. And then later, when we'd finally given the house up and moved into rented accommodation, the number of times I'd had to placate our landlord in order to keep a roof over our heads.

And I never told her about the number of personal treasures, the things that were irreplaceable to me, like the limited-edition regimental picture 'Stand By' which was only available to members of the Regiment, but sought after by military collectors around the world, along with the other things, that I had to sell in order to put food on the table. Although when she started to notice that my things were beginning to disappear I would simply say, 'Oh, I got bored with looking at them and fancied a change. They're in a box in the garage.'

I would always try to have a smile on my face, but at times it was very hard. And although she knew we were struggling, I always tried for as long as I could to shield her from just how bad it really was, never letting her know that, with each passing day, life was becoming ever harder to deal with.

Dark Days and Endless Nights

It's generally accepted that in the majority of cases post-traumatic stress disorder will take anything up to fourteen years or more after the event to raise its ugly head. But something that isn't generally known is that, as a sufferer, when your everyday stress levels become elevated, the effects of combat-related PTSD are greatly increased.

Our personal circumstances, and in particular our financial situation, had become steadily worse over the previous months and, as a result, my personal stress levels were now totally off the scale. As I struggled to find a solution to our mounting debt problems, my days were becoming a melting pot of guilt, anger, remorse and feelings of personal failure. I was also fast approaching the point where I would do anything I could just to be alone. This wasn't because I no longer loved my wife: nothing could have been further from the truth. But in fact I just couldn't believe that she was still with me.

The smallest thing, a sound, say the unexpected roar of a low low-flying fighter aircraft, would send me back ten years and halfway around the world in the blink of an eye. At the time we lived in a designated RAF low-flying area, about twenty miles north of Hereford, so this type of event was a frequent daily occurrence. At one stage it got so bad that I would continually search the sky for aircraft as I walked my dog, just so that I wouldn't be caught unawares.

Even an everyday smell, something as simple as a tyre being burned on a bonfire, would trigger a flashback, plunging my world into a tailspin and bringing on bouts of depression.

Once the depression had begun to set in, then each night would also become just another horrific journey of personal survival as in my mind I walked among the sights, sounds, smells and horrors of some long-forgotten engagement. One where the same people would die, one that would only ever end one way, the same way it did the first time I fought it.

However, this type of event is not confined to the times when we are alone or in a troubled sleep. Even a simple thing like going to a café or restaurant with your wife and family can have the ability to make you feel uneasy. This isn't down to a lack of confidence, for as a warrant officer I would regularly have to stand up and talk to audiences of well over a hundred total strangers. It's also not the fear of walking into a crowded room and being surrounded by people we don't know. No, it has more to do with a feeling of being trapped, and not being able to defend ourselves and our loved ones should something happen.

Over the years my wife has learned to identify the various environments and events that can push the wrong buttons. She struggled in the early years and, in truth, I suppose we both did. I had no idea why on my return from a trip away I would purposely avoid crowds and shy away from large social gatherings, even those that involved my friends.

Even now if we go out for lunch or a coffee she will try and pick a place where we can sit outside. If the weather doesn't allow for that she will pick a seat near a window or close to an exit, allowing me to sit with my back to the wall with a clear view of the door and the street outside. I thought for a long time that it was just our little secret, one that nobody else had ever noticed. That was up until a few weeks before this book was finished and we went out to lunch with my brother-in-law.

My wife and her brother had gone to find us a table while I ordered the food, and as usual my wife had done her thing and found us a table not only next to a window but also close to a door. I ordered our food and by the time I got to the table they were both seated. I had a seat with my back to the wall, facing the door and the window. Later that afternoon, after my brother-in-law had left us, my wife turned to me and said, 'While you were up ordering the food at lunchtime and Albert and I were sorting out the table, he turned to me and said, "You better let Theo sit there, he won't feel comfortable sitting with his back to the window."'

Reflections

It's just before the dawn;
they say it's the darkest hour
and as I wander down these lonely streets
past houses with their curtains drawn,
I envy those warm and content inside
with their trimmed hedges and manicured lawns.

The town centre,
once a dark and empty place,
slowly struggles back to life.
It's where insomniacs and the tormented mingle
    unnoticed
amongst those just finishing
or starting their day.

At the end of the precinct stands a Starbucks,
its yellow lights flickering
like a welcoming beacon amongst the dark and empty stores.
Once inside I grab at my coffee
like a junkie with a long-needed fix I'll head for a
    corner,
any corner,

as long as I can get my back to the wall
and still see the door.

Across the aisle sits a stranger
hunched over a large black coffee,
elbows on table,
head bowed,
pulling quietly at his unkempt hair,
he has those same smoky eyes
and that 1000-metre stare.

There's nothing on earth that can open up old wounds

like a mirror.

At 3 a.m.

I'm bloodied but still alive.
Death stood at my shoulder again tonight
but went away disappointed.
Others weren't so lucky
and now lay faceless at my feet
dressed in black rubber
zipped to the top.

My naked body,
ice cold
but running with sweat,
eyes wide open
but drowning in tears,
lies motionless beside you
as I try to gather my senses,
clear my mind of the carnage that's gone before.

Turning
I watch you sleeping,
reaching out
I touch your velvet skin
try to slow my racing heart,
try to match your gentle breathing.
I whisper I'm sorry,
sorry for another angry day
and another restless night,
but in spite of all this
I love you desperately.

but you don't hear me,
nobody does,
and in the absolute darkness
at 3 a.m.
nobody ever will.

The Demon Drink

Many soldiers will return from war haunted by their battle-field experiences. Moody, jumpy and unable to settle down, they drink too much, use drugs and are given to fits of rage and despair. Most will feel utterly alone and unable to connect with the people who love them.

But, as I've already explained, in most cases it can take fourteen years or more for the symptoms and effects of PTSD to appear. I personally think that this lengthy period of incubation is only possible because during the early years we are faced with this type of traumatic event on a regular basis. That the continuous exposure to such events merely has the effect of lessening or deadening the impact of the trauma and making us temporarily immune to such experiences.

At the same time, we are also preoccupied with the immediate task of staying alive and achieving our objectives, while living in the structured and supportive environment which is the modern British Army. The condition then grows stronger when we no longer have this level of support or the underlying distractions. When our mind is no longer preoccupied with such events and is left free to roam.

However, when they are on their own, looking a potential disaster in the face and feeling unable to share the burden with someone they either trust or love, some men and women will naturally turn to drink in order to find some form of escape. But drink was never really going to be an option for me. I'm a social drinker. I will drink with my mates as part of a celebration or commiseration or at a dinner. I have also been known to get absolutely trashed on the odd occasion, but never, ever alone. I can go for a whole year without a single drink if a suitable opportunity doesn't present itself. I know only too well the risks associated with drinking alone, unlike some of my closest friends, who, when alone and in a dark place, instinctively turn to the bottle.

We're not talking about the secret drinker. Those individuals who are able to hide their affliction by taking a little but often throughout the day and into the evening. Or the ones who seem unaffected by their addiction, the ones nobody notices as they go about their daily tasks. No, these are warriors, those who have made the Regiment and the British Army what it is today. Those who are now working out on the 'Circuit', still operating in some of the most hostile places on earth, and constantly under fire.

But, when away from the bullets, bombs and battles, they will be so alone they will turn to the bottle and get totally trashed for days on end. There is also no attempt to hide their condition as they wait, even long, to go back to where they will be valued and respected, earning their living with their hard-earned skills, living on their nerves and among like-minded individuals. Sober again, well, at least for the next three months.

However, it's at times like these that some of us will become totally dependent on alcohol and, in the worst cases, once it has lost its ability to do its job we may even turn to drugs in an effort to escape the accumulated pain, misery and feelings of loss which we have accumulated over the previous years.

Looking for an Exit Strategy

The one thing that's drummed into you throughout your army career, and especially when you attend the various junior and senior NCOs' tactics courses, is that before you take on the enemy you should 'always have an exit strategy'. Of course this isn't easy when the shit unexpectedly hits the fan, but you should always have a prearranged fallback position, whatever the unforeseen circumstances. This would give you just enough time to consolidate and defend yourselves while you come up with a creative way of getting you and your men out of harm's way.

My wife and I had now been out of the army for about eighteen months and things had got progressively worse. As a result, all the hard-won training and survival techniques were now beginning to kick in on their own and I could see the need for an effective exit strategy.

I had lost some good friends to suicide when they left the army. Good men, brave and decorated soldiers who, without gainful employment, the friendship of their mates, or the love of a good woman, had struggled with life on the outside and had taken the tragic step of ending it all.

These men were my friends, but it didn't matter how close you were to them, no matter how many times you met them and shared a coffee or a pint, they weren't the type to ask for help. Their subsequent actions weren't a desperate call for help either. When you live alone and decide to hang yourself, or fill your car with carbon monoxide in your garage and with all the doors locked, you're not looking for anyone to come in at the last minute and save you. Likewise, there is no changing your mind or expecting someone to talk you out of it, when you suddenly open the door and throw yourself out of a light aircraft at 12,000 feet without a parachute.

However, suicide isn't in my psyche. It was never going to be an option. But my wife never knew that at one time things were so bad I seriously considered joining this sad band of brothers. It was never a problem when we were both together. No. Together we could overcome anything. It was only when I was left on my own that I would entertain such dark thoughts. I wasn't a quitter, I was just tired of pushing string uphill, in the rain (it's a mental thing and you have to picture just how hard it would be to push string uphill and in the rain). I was an intelligent, well-trained, ethically sound and well-motivated individual who couldn't even get a job as a milkman. And, believe me, I tried.

On top of all this crap there were the nightmares. They had always been there. Ever since the early days following that first restaurant blast in Ulster, where, covered in blood, I had had to carry women and kids who were badly burned, most of them still alive but missing arms and legs, out of the rubble. Now, and because of my elevated stress levels, these night-mares were becoming more frequent, robbing me of the sleep and rest I so desperately needed, especially if I was going to get us both through this difficult period.

My wife had managed to secure a secretarial job in Here-ford, but, although her monthly wage was an absolute godsend and we couldn't have survived without it, her having a job while I didn't just added even more shit to my feelings of per-sonal failure. I used to take her into the city each morning and would then meet some of the guys for coffee and see if there was any work going. I would do anything I could to make a little money, retrieve a little self-respect.

However, on the days when there was nothing doing I would just drive home alone, and the dark thoughts would resurface again. On the road home, just after the village of Canon Pyon, the hedgerows on both sides of the road would suddenly disappear, giving an uninterrupted view of the Herefordshire countryside, and an unbroken view of the road ahead. At this point the road runs downhill in a virtually straight line for about a mile, before turning into a sharp right-hand curve followed by a sharp left.

At the bottom of the long straight, just before the right-hander, and set back on the left side of the road, stood a very large oak tree. Given its size it must have been there for a hundred years or more. This tree would be where I would embed my car and finish it, if it all became too much for me. I had found my exit strategy.

I drove down that stretch of road and past that tree, rehearsing the final minutes of my life, every day for over six months. I was still willing to fight on until the bitter end as I had done on so many previous occasions. But, just knowing I now had an exit strategy in place as I had so many times in the past, allowed me to put a mental tick in the box and then carry on the fight.

Performing this simple procedure now allowed me to concentrate all my efforts on the task of surviving. Thankfully, my will to survive, the love of my wife and my sheer bloody-mindedness to win the fight always overrode my need for flight, and to 'take the gap'.

Just Give My Head Peace

We soldiers are a proud and resilient breed. Even under the most extraordinary circumstances we'll take everything you can throw at us, get knocked down and then, broken and covered in blood, we'll stand up and shout back, 'Bring it on.'

So it's no wonder that when people try to help us to deal with our problems we will naturally resist. Even our loved one's efforts, which will be met initially with, 'Don't worry, babe. I'm all right. I'll get it sorted.' Over time this will escalate into, 'For fuck's sake, just give my head peace.' So you can just imagine what our reaction will be to the suggestion, 'Will you please try and get some professional help?'

It will also come as no surprise that most of us are also in total denial when it's suggested that we may be struggling to come to terms with events that have taken place in our past. As a nation we will ask our military to routinely do things that only the bravest few among us would ever dare to do. To see the things that none of us should ever see, to watch their friends, colleagues and innocent men, women and children die in the most horrific circumstances. We then ask them to live with the consequences of this for the rest of their lives.

As Special Forces soldiers, we are seen by our politicians, the general public and even our own generals as some kind of infallible, Teflon-coated individuals, who are totally unaffected by killing, death and our life experiences. This throwaway attitude is probably partly our own fault, as we work without complaint, while at the same time are reluctant to admit to anybody that the job is having any adverse effects on our bodies and our mental well-being. It takes a special kind of soldier to admit he has a problem and ask for help. It's not like attending an AA (Alcoholics Anonymous) meeting, where a large group of people will get together regularly and eventually one of them will stand up and say, 'My name is John Smith, and I'm an alcoholic.'

Soldiers won't do that. It's not in our make-up. We'd no more stand up in front of a group of fellow soldiers and say, 'I'm having problems coming to terms with the mental effects of the job,' than we would say, 'I'm scared shitless, count me out, you can face the next fire-fight without me.' I'd been out of the army for over fifteen years when I first started writing this book and was introduced to a very special woman who worked as a US-based PTSD counsellor. When I met her she had already spent many years working with the NYFD (New York Fire Department) and the NYPD (New York Police Department), as well as the US military in both Iraq and Afghanistan. As a result of her genuinely unique approach to the treatment of PTSD, and her ability to return men to full fitness and back into work – in the majority of cases, back on the front line – she had become known as the 'Cop Whisperer'. When I met her she was working with the Police Service of Northern Ireland, which had replaced the old Royal Ulster Constabulary.

The idea was to find out if, given her expertise and experience, she saw any therapeutic value in my writing for those suffering from PTSD. I met her for coffee one morning at the Carrickfergus Marina in Northern Ireland. Even though I'd been out of the army for many years, I hadn't lost the old skills, and as a result I was on my toes and very much aware of my surroundings and those around me. Granted the situation in Northern Ireland doesn't make the news on the mainland the way it used to, but the problem hasn't gone away. The paramilitaries are still shooting at, and placing bombs under the cars of, off-duty policemen and soldiers in their attempts to murder them, as well as blowing up banks and government offices. Killing someone like me would make a very nice trophy indeed.

Although I was convinced that her experience and input would be invaluable for the book, I was also a little apprehensive. I had met her type before. Most of them were little more than stuffed-shirt academics, carrying around massively inflated egos and full of their own importance. Individuals who had gained all their experience from reading books and attending lectures, but who had no practical experience of what their clients had been through, or how they were suffering now.

However, even from our limited time together (less than five minutes at that point), she seemed to be different. But I was still prepared to stand up, shake her hand and walk away. We sat down and she poured the coffee. Once the traditional pleasantries were over we started to talk about the manuscript and its contents. We'd been talking for about thirty minutes when she looked at me and very calmly said, 'I need to know how long it will take you to get back from where you are now.'

In just talking about the manuscript and my experiences, she had seen me drift back to the actual event we were discussing and, as a result, I was now reliving it all over again, feeling the pain, and experiencing that initial trauma of loss.

In answer to her question I quickly said, 'I'm back.'

But then I'm one of the lucky ones. As long as I'm awake I have the ability to put my demons back in their box very quickly, while others struggle to control their feelings for what can seem like an age.

At the end of our three-hour meeting she leant across the table and quietly said, 'You know you're suffering from PTSD, don't you?'

I shook my head and told her, 'I'd like a second opinion, please?'

'So you're still in denial then?'

But, moving on, she saw great value in the manuscript, not necessarily for the clients, but for their wives and loved ones. Those who had no idea what had caused the changes they had seen in their loved ones upon their return from operations. Even though she is now working back in the US we have become good friends and talk regularly, but never about my problems, the ones I don't have.

Yes, I consider myself one of the lucky ones. I'm someone who lives each day with one hand tightly around the throat of his demons while at the same time getting on with my daily life. I think my attitude and willingness to carry on the fight has a lot to do with my childhood and the fact that I learned to face my fears and deal with them alone from a very early age. I also have a wife whom I love very much and, armed with the patience of a saint, she has supported me throughout our forty-year relationship. During my time in the service she never once questioned what I was doing, or moaned about how much time I was spending away from home. Don't get me wrong, she's no pushover, but apart from being the only person in the world who sees me sleep, she is also probably the nicest person I know.

Even now, as I embark on what in reality is my third career change, she is still extremely enthusiastic and supportive. Without her I probably wouldn't be here today. I definitely wouldn't be writing this book.

But, for those of us who don't live in such a relationship, or have this level of support, those of us who are unable to find the new opportunities or a safe passage through this minefield of problems, the downward spiral can be steep and extremely rapid.

Many of us will suffer broken marriages, lose the respect and love of our kids, turn to drink and drugs and may even end up on the streets, homeless and totally alone. If this happens we will be forced to spend our remaining days searching for food, another drink and a safe place to sleep. Our nights will be spent fighting long-forgotten battles, running from endless nightmares, feelings of guilt and failure that we were unable to make it on our own.

Wounded Mind

The paths I tread tonight
hold more fear for me than any desert or jungle might.
It's fear and rage that drive me on,
alone and with nothing,
life is just an endless fight.

An endless search for food,
another drink,
a safer place to sleep.
All these things are foremost in my mind
and they push aside the fading memories
of the family I so cruelly left behind.

In a shop window I catch a glimpse of a man I once
    was,
the claret beret
Airborne wings and DZ flash,
like long lost friends they call me back.
But unwashed and unshaven
now it's backbone they say I lack.

A pitiful shadow of my former self,
I duck into a doorway to escape the cold and driving
    rain.
Tired and wet

I slide slowly down the wall
my body racked with pain.

Sat on the cold damp tiles
I see the fear and disgust on their faces as they hurry
 past.
Eager to avoid eye contact
they never look back
and I wonder just how long their fragile peace will last.

To escape my world I close my eyes
but they're there again,
cold and empty without smiles.
The faces of the dead,
men I have fought, drank and laughed with;
we marched a thousand miles.

They said it was normal,
just a passing phase,
the headaches,
depression,
all that hidden rage.
That's when it started,
the blackouts and flashbacks,
the nightmares that just went on for days.

Surrounded by my memories
in a place that's close to hell
I spent the early days hiding in the shadows,
around corners,
just to catch a glimpse of my wife and our baby girl.

She's all grown up now with a son of her own,
that makes me a granddad, I suppose,

but I'll never hold him,
collect him from school,
help him fly his kite
or watch him as he grows.

The soup kitchen has finally arrived
and with my precious food I squat in a doorway.
In my rucksack, a medal for valour won in the heat of
   the fight,
my baby's socks and a picture of her mum
exchanged for a short note the night I left their lives.

Too cold to sleep
I walk alone by the river.
I feel stronger when I'm moving.
'Prepare for action,
stand in the door,
red on
green on
GO.'
I launch myself into space.

'Thousand and one
thousand and two
thousand and three

check canopy
feet and knees together.'

But instead of the bone-jolting crash
the ground is soft
and I pass straight through,
into a cold wet darkness.

Maybe here,
at last,
I'll find my peace

amongst the other forgotten soldiers

who've died of their wounded minds.

Sitrep

The term 'sitrep' might be unfamiliar to some of you, but the military are experts at shortening things. Less time spent talking means more time doing. 'Sitrep' is army talk for 'situation report', and that's what I'm going to do now: provide you with a sitrep and bring you up to date. Well, up to the point where I put the pen down on this book before hopefully picking it up again for the next.

As you can see, I didn't actually need to use my exit strategy. I eventually managed to fight through the enormous mountain of unexpected shit that was waiting for me when I left the military. As I said at the beginning of this book, 'I in no way consider myself a victim, neither do I blame anyone else for the cards life has dealt me, or for the life I've led.' The same cards that meant I had to grow up fast, tough and street-wise. The army had turned me into a consummate professional, and taught me the value of honour and friendship. It had also taught me how to control my extremely short Latin fuse. Well, until it was time not to control it. My response to any threat is, as it has always been, swift and extremely violent, but in a controlled, cold type of way, some might even say clinical.

I'm also not blaming the army or any other agency for the difficulties I encountered upon leaving the army, as most of them were created by me. Although I do think that after spending twenty-two years working my bollocks off in the sterile environment which at that time was the modern British Army, it wouldn't have been too much to ask to get some form of meaningful preparation for life on the outside.

However, with the love and support of my wife, and the arrival of my grandson in 2002, I eventually managed to straighten myself out and get our lives back on track. As soldiers, most of us will make shit fathers. Not because we don't love or care about our children: it's just because we're never there. Someone once told me that our grandchildren were God's way of rewarding us for not killing our kids. Personally, I think our grandchildren are God's way of providing us with a way to make amends.

We're not rolling in money by any stretch of the imagination, but I have managed to clear our debts. I also no longer have morons knocking at the door each day and, in the end, nobody had to die. Nor did I have to spend a morning digging graves or laying a new patio either. It's taken a while but, in the end, and as always, it was well worth the effort.

I re-established contact with my little brother some five years after leaving the army, and we now have a great relationship. Although we currently live hundreds of miles apart, we speak on the phone at least once a week and try to get together at least once a year. However, I still think he has the odd moment when he doesn't quite know how to take me, or what he's got himself into. I don't see anything of my sister or my other brother, the son of the South African, but it doesn't seem to bother them, and it definitely doesn't bother me, so it's 'win-win' again. As for my mother, well, she and my father are now both dead, and to be honest, although it may sound a little hard, I didn't feel any sort of loss when they went.

I am still losing my friends on a regular basis. Some are lost fighting battles abroad on the Circuit while working as 'security advisers' – that is, mercs – but far more are being lost fighting battles at home. It's funny how as soldiers we only seem to become ill or succumb to our numerous injuries when the shit finally ends. We don't seem to have the time to get sick while we're working.

However, those deaths that hurt the most will be of those who finally succumb to their feelings of loneliness and abandonment and end their suffering by their own hand. I still have my dark days when something will trigger a memory and send my mind into a spiral, along with those endless nights I spend fighting long-ago battles with the ghosts of my friends.

But now, living in one of the most beautiful parts of the United Kingdom, with some of the friendliest people on the planet and in the fold of my wife's family, life is as good as it gets, and I have very little to complain about.

My new occupation keeps me on my toes and the adrenaline flowing. A few years ago I got myself retrained and qualified and I now work for myself in one of the most hostile and cutthroat environments in the civilian world. Like all old soldiers I still need the rush, and old habits die hard, but that's another story.

Volte Face

After you've read this book my one hope is that the next time you see a serviceman or servicewoman, or the old man sitting on the homeless shelter steps proudly displaying a chest full of medals, you will pause for a few moments and try to look beyond that confident, sometimes brash, some would even say arrogant, exterior, to the person that lies within. A person who has worked hard, seen things that none of us should ever see, and in some cases suffered horrific injuries. Someone who will continue to suffer, either physically or mentally, but mostly in silence, for the rest of their life, while at the same time still retaining hope and a strong belief in the greater good.

My hope for those warriors who pick up this book is that they will feel less alone when they read the words that capture something of their own joy, pain, fears, sorrows and stories of personal survival. I also hope that they can share this book with others, their family and friends, so that those they love and care for can at least develop the eyes to see and hearts to hear.

Take care.

Theo